Karaoke Fascism

The Ethnography of Political Violence

Cynthia Keppley Mahmood, Series Editor

A complete list of books in the series is available from the publisher.

Karaoke Fascism

Burma and the Politics of Fear

Monique Skidmore

PENN

University of Pennsylvania Press

Philadelphia

Copyright © 2004 University of Pennsylvania Press
Printed in the United States of America on acid-free paper

10 9 8 7 6 5 4 3 2 1

Published by
University of Pennsylvania Press
Philadelphia, Pennsylvania 19104-4011

Library of Congress Cataloging-in-Publication Data

Skidmore, Monique
   Karaoke fascism : Burma and the politics of fear / Monique Skidmore.
     p.   cm. (Ethnography of political violence)
   ISBN 0-8122-3811-7 (cloth : alk. paper). — ISBN 0-8122-1883-3 (pbk. : alk.
paper)
   Includes bibliographical references and index.
   1. Oppression (Psychology)—Political aspects—Burma.   2. Human rights—
Burma.   3. Subversive activities—Burma.   4. Government, Resistance to—Burma—
Psychological aspects.   5. Burma—Politics and government—1988–.   I. Title.   II.
Series.
DS530.65 .S59   2004
959.105—dc22   2004049477

Contents

Illustrations

Preface

December 15, 1996: Two-dozen student protesters, carrying shoulder bags, gather in a knot in the center of a major arterial road in Ahlone Township. They stop sixty meters away from a roadblock hastily erected by soldiers who are scrambling to get to the scene of each hit-and-run demonstration. Approximately eighty soldiers stand in front of twelve troop carriers with their automatic rifles aimed at the students. The soldiers cover the whole street and there are sometimes several rows of soldiers lined up in formation, holding circular wooden shields or bayonets. Their hats seem comical-khaki green plastic with a red star in the center-and yet these soldiers radiate menace and a lethal potentiality. Scarves are tied around the faces of the students, concealing all but their eyes. Some wear T-shirts with their heroes, General Aung San and his daughter Aung San Suu Kyi, emblazoned on the front. Others carry the fighting peacock insignia of Rangoon University and some wear the orange jacket common to the main opposition party, the National League for Democracy. Taxis and private cars with the license plates removed drive up to the students and thousands of bank notes are thrown out the windows at them before the cars race away. An unnatural and suspenseful silence descends upon the street. All traffic, commerce, and everyday conversation stops as the tense standoff begins.

I walk slowly down Ahlone Road until I am adjacent to the front line of demonstrators. Crouching behind the open door of an old Bedford truck, I listen with amazement as for the first time since the failed democracy uprising in 1988, Rangoon residents begin to speak to each other in public about what is occurring. "Aren't you afraid?" I whisper to a government engineer in his early forties standing beside the truck. Tears glisten in his eyes and he looks over his shoulder as he replies: "my whole generation has become familiar with fear and repression, and we're not really afraid of it anymore on a daily basis. There are government spies in the crowd. They have taken over every sector in Burma." A nineteen-year-old skinny student beside him wearing khaki army trousers whispers to me: "I'm scared, but I'm hopeful." Fear is evident in these snatches of conversation and in the body posture of the witnesses who partially turn their bodies away from the confrontation and seem to half crouch or draw in upon themselves. They gather in knots of two or three persons and keep their heads down. The character of the fear is that of anticipation, a barely repressed hope for change. I am startled by the thought that we are all within the range of the new Tatmadaw (*ta' ma do*) (armed forces) weapons.

The students begin to chant but then break off, a nervous shuffling occurs as they almost imperceptibly move together, leaving a gap between themselves and the onlookers at either side of the road. They advance a few steps until they are opposite a side road leading deeper into the township. The Tatmadaw men lower their shields and raise their weapons. The question, "are they just threatening the students?" races lightly across my thoughts, chased away by the nervous tension, the breathlessness of the moment. At that instant the students reach some silent consensus, perhaps from fear, or maybe pragmatism, and break off their advance, charging with a shout into the side streets, some behind me, and others seem to melt into the dark recesses of the tea shops lining the opposite side of the road. The troops clamber into their trucks and roar off in pursuit, but I am too busy breaking cover and scut-tling away with the rest of the onlookers, longyis (*lun: gjei*) flapping around their legs as they puff and wheeze along the sidewalks and disap-pear into the gloom of individual houses.[1]

The following day the troops are everywhere. Tanks are conspicuous in government institutions and bayoneted soldiers wearing flak jackets roam the streets and are positioned every fifty yards along major routes into the city. A month later the BBC announces that the Burmese mili-tary has sentenced twenty pro-democracy supporters to thirty years in jail for their role in the street unrest in December. The student demon-strations were evidence of what I had suspected for half of a year: that I was conducting fieldwork in a war zone, yet another of the everyday states of emergency that exist around the globe. I had arrived in Ran-goon to understand madness and to learn about medicine, but as I became attuned to the rhythm, the temporality, and the militarization of the city, it became clear to me that the emotional life and the everyday well-being of Burmese people could not be understood without taking into account the central affective element of urban life in contemporary Burma: fear. How does one research fear when doing so produces the very emotion in question, both in the researcher and the informant? This conundrum proved to be the most difficult personal, methodologi-cal, and ethical problem of my time in Burma.

To come to Burma, one of the few places where despotism still dominates, is to take both a physical and emotional journey, a critical ascent into fear and to become caught up, like most Burmese, in the daily management of fear. How do Burmese people survive under authoritarianism? How does one manage fear and live, years on end, with dis-ease and an unending sense of vulnerability? These are the central questions with which this book concerns itself.

Map 1. Burma (Myanmar). (Library of Congress)

Chapter 1
Rangoon: End of Strife

Rainwater leaks through the rooftop.

—Burmese proverb

A prostitute lies in the mud under a bridge, a knife pressed to her throat. A teenage boy, the son of an army colonel, squats beside a major arterial road plunging a used syringe full of almost pure heroin into his ankle. A young mother sucks betel paste off a banana leaf and presses her shriveled nipple into her emaciated baby's mouth while watching a Burmese romance in a video hut. These are images of Rangoon. Substitute the heroin for opium and a puppet show for the video hut, and these scenes could date any time from the latter part of the eighteenth century to the present. Throughout its history this port town has been the showpiece of whatever occupying army currently held lower Burma. Beneath and spreading out beyond the imprimatur of military and political dominance, Rangoon remains to this day a rigidly stratified society where hierarchical social relations slice through the topography of modern nationhood to reveal deep scars of social inequality.

Rangoon is a reluctant capital of "unified" Burma. Its name means "end of strife." It was founded by King Alaungpaya in 1755 and signified the end of Mon dominance of lower Burma and the ascendancy of the Buddhist kings of Upper Burma. This was a process begun at least as early as 1054 when Anawratha, king of Pagan, conquered the Mon kingdom of Thaton, now a dusty roadside town in Mon State between the Buddhist pilgrimage sites of Kyaiktyo and Thamanya. The demise of Thaton and the ascendancy of the Buddhist kings of Pagan eventually allowed Alaungpaya to ride triumphantly into Rangoon and thus "unify" the riverland plains and delta towns for the first time. Rangoon is now a city of over five million people that sprawls over the floodplains of southern Burma from its original location cradled on the northern bank of the turgid Rangoon river as it channels the Hlaing, Panhlaing, Pegu, Pazundaung, and Pagandaung rivers and streams and disgorges this great swollen flood of brown, silted water thirty kilometers farther south into the Gulf of Mottama.

Back in Alaungpaya's time, the town consisted of a wooden stockade surrounded by a moat and entered through one of five city gates. Social stratification was apparent at the outset. Rangoon housed elites with lesser-ranked persons living outside the defensive walls. Even in the eighteenth century there was a specified district for prostitutes, the precinct of Tackally. Rangoon's architecture and external façade deteriorated and in the late 1820s it was described by Michael Symes, the British Ambassador to the Court of Ava, as dusty streets filled with swine, houses resting above pestilent and stagnant waters with the official buildings falling into disrepair. On December 20, 1852, Sir Arthur Purves Phayre declared Rangoon annexed to the British Government located in Calcutta (Hall 1955: 651).

In the next two decades, British urban planners imposed a Victorian sense of order on the dusty tropical town. Foremost among these planners was a member of the Bengal Engineers, Captain Alexander Fraser, who was responsible for creating a city that could be a trading port for the British (McCrae 1990: 19). As Cangi (1997: 79–80) has remarked, "the laying out of colonial Rangoon was not an experiment in town planning but a well rehearsed process in which the symbol of the British Empire became neatly and irrevocably stamped on the map of Burma." Despite the colonial mansions, Victorian institutions, roads that intersected at right angles, and residential land plots of precisely 40 by 150 feet, Rangoon remained a town in which the elite class lived in splendor while the majority urban poor "lived in squalor in mean alleyways and narrow side-streets. Crime, grinding poverty, and recurrent ethnic riots characterized life for most citizens in Lower Burma" (Cangi 1997: 87).

Resistance to British rule was strongest among ethnic Burmans, and the Saya San revolt has become a key historical marker for such resistance. The incorporation of Burma into India ended in 1937. The invasion of Burma by Japanese imperial forces came at a time when there was organized and widespread resistance to British colonization (and communal rioting against Indian and Chinese mercantile interests). It was the Japanese who trained and enabled the formation of the Burma Independence Army by General Aung San, who had retreated to Japan in 1940. This army fought alongside the Japanese, switching sides at the last moment, to oust the fascists. The British administrators and their Indian troops escaped with few possessions; this exodus to the Indian border included anthropologists such as Edmund Leach, who left his field notes in the flurry to escape. An archeology of their undignified retreat can be charted today in the British and Ghurka war medals, writing implements, and other accouterments of Empire that lie under a thick layer of dust in cracked glass cabinets in the back streets of Mandalay. Almost a quarter of a million Japanese died in this attempt to control Burma and the brutality of their short rule is buried deeply in the collective psyche.

During that heady century of change and destruction, Rangoon residents agitated for independence under the leadership of their charismatic hero, General Aung San, and almost, it seemed, would actually achieve it. Aung San's party, the Anti-Fascist People's Freedom League (AFPFL), won 67 percent of the seats for Burma's first constituent assembly in 1947. Their victory was ended, however, when a bomb assassinated the general and his parliamentary cabinet on the eve of their assumption of power from the British in July 1947.

Burma then went to hell in a hand basket. The government of the day ruled only to the end of Rangoon's suburbs. It is beyond the scope of this book to explain the complex and often anarchic conditions that pertained in the rest of the country. Burma was the site for refuge and mobilization by remnants of the defeated Chinese Koumingtang Army, communist parties, anti-communist parties (funded by the U.S.), myriad minority independence parties, pocket armies, warlords, robber bands, and so on. Historians and political scientists who have studied this period (Callahan 1998, 2003; Smith 1999) point to the origins of current anti-democratic sentiment within the Burmese military as stemming largely from the chaos of these years. This period and the communist and anti-communist cold war machinations in the border areas of China and Thailand birthed five decades of suffering that has corresponded to the production and domestic and international consumption of the largest heroin crops in the world.

Mary Callahan (1998) shows how, despite these various actors (which she describes as "sinking schooners"), the Socialist party was winning the war in the 1950s to unify large sections of the country under its platform. It was not long, however, before a military coup led by General Ne Win ended the experiments with socialism and democracy begun during this decade. Although Ne Win called his party the "Burma Socialist Programme Party" (BSPP), it was a centralizing, nationalizing, and brutal military despot who ruled Burma from 1962 until 1988. These events of the twentieth century, a century of conquest and submission, colonization and fascism, socialism, democracy, and dictatorship, involved Burmese people continually seeking to remain neutral and free at a time when European empires crumbled as quasi-fascist states such as Japan brought war to Southeast Asia. Monks, students, intellectuals, and soldiers created democratic, communist, and socialist movements to resist Burma's incorporation into colonial and fascist empires, the cold war, and the emerging global capitalist market of late modernity.

In the new millennium, Rangoon bears the scars of its turbulent history and has once again been remade, this time bearing the imprint of its own army. The changes to the urban and peri-urban landscapes of Rangoon and Mandalay underpin many of the themes in this book. Mandalay, once the epicenter of the power of the Buddhist kings, now languishes as a "second city," having endured the ignominy of being colonized by the British and now, unofficially, by Chinese and Wa entrepreneurs, drug lords, and international middlemen. To the south by 695 kilometers, enduring all of these changes, is the Shwedagon Pagoda, originally 2.5 miles north of Rangoon. It squats in the suburb of Bahan, situated around the banks of Inya Lake. Such central townships are home to the Generals and to many members of the main opposition party, the National League for Democracy, most notably, Aung San Suu Kyi and U Tin Oo.[1]

In September 1988, when farmers and students, followed by almost every other sector of society, rose up in protest against the twenty-six-year dictatorship of General Ne Win, Aung San Suu Kyi became the most prominent symbol of pro-democratic opposition to both the violence that occurred in the suppression of the uprising and the formation of a new military council known as the State Law and Order Restoration Council (SLORC). Aung San Suu Kyi's father, General Aung San, was the founder of the Burmese army (the Tatmadaw), and the man credited with bringing independence to the nation. His daughter uses this enormous store of filial power to promote democracy. She was under house arrest for most of the period from 1988 until May 2002 and arrested and held for several months at Insein jail and other locations from May 2003. Many of the Generals and the leaders of the democracy movement come from the kinds of elite families who live around Inya Lake. It was during my Great Apartment Hunt that I first began to understand how the events which unfold around Inya Lake, in Golden Valley and the nearby suburbs, impact enormously upon the rest of the country.

A battered red pick-up truck drives up to my guesthouse and a large, middle-aged woman clambers out from the covered section of the truck. It transpires that she is an English tutor and does a little real estate brokering in her spare time. Our driver is a man in his thirties with thick black curly hair. We all pile into the pick-up truck. I am driven around Bahan and Golden Valley, and also to a few townships closer to the psychiatric hospital where I will be conducting fieldwork. After three days of enduring the Rangoon traffic snarls, I decide to live near the densely populated central market area. This involves a series of negotiations between the real estate brokers and the wife of the man in charge of the security office for the township. Apparently the local security chief owns much of the real estate and he takes a cut of the profits from the owners of other apartment buildings and hotels in his precinct. Finally it is agreed that I can live in the township and an exorbitant rent is also agreed. Finder's fees are given to all those involved in the negotiations. As a resident, I no longer need to register my presence in the township every night.

It was during this process of settling into my new neighborhood that I came to understand some of the constraints that apply to Burmese people in their everyday lives. In the next six months I waged an ongoing war to have the satellite moved away from Asian soccer matches and oriented closer towards the horizon, so that I could watch the BBC for news of arrests in Burma. Satellites are largely illegal; they provide access to facts that are difficult for the spin doctors of the military junta to counter. Television was introduced to Burma by General Ne Win as a conduit for the mass dissemination of propaganda. It is now used to ignore the regime's propaganda and to find out, independently, what is happening in Burma and in Burma's relations with the international community.

In my kitchen, an open drain spilled over with effluent, and the smell of shit-and-onions will forever linger in my mind and be associated with Burmese apartments. The shit-and-onions flowed through all the other apartments and into the drainage ditch, which promptly overflowed. Because I lived near a military barracks, there was some electricity for at least part of most days. The electricity often went out in the middle of cooking the evening meal and would come on three days later. On these nights my husband and I walked in the middle of the road, hoping that the moon was near full and would come out from behind the clouds. We needed the moonlight to avoid the rats, and we stayed away from the drainage/sewage ditches on the side of the road.

This downtown area was once made up of large houses surrounded by expansive lawns and high fences. The bulldozing of most of these houses has allowed high-rise apartment blocks to be hastily erected, using a minimum of rebar and poor quality materials. The drainage ditches created by the British have not been able to deal with the numbers of people who live in the city. Enormous black rats scuttle up from the ditches and over the roads, especially at night. Stray dogs, often mad from the pain of parasites and near starvation, root through the effluent and the rubbish middens located beside the ditches. Crows sit on the walls of the houses and in the palm trees above, watching this sanitary nightmare of the inner city, the remnants of the colonial imagination impressed upon a former stockade town now engulfed in global capital flows where migrant workers flood the city's inadequate infrastructure. During the monsoon season cracked and overflowing drainage ditches swell with water that covers the streets, some to more than a meter in depth, and leads to diarrhea and cholera epidemics that the regime likes to keep quiet about.

Being a resident was more than learning about the everyday life of the city. It also meant being subjected to many of the violations of privacy and individual rights that routinely befall Burmese people. It was during this period that I began to conduct fieldwork in earnest, spending a portion of each week at the psychiatric hospital, at the traditional medicine hospitals and clinics, and with medico-religious practitioners in both Rangoon and Mandalay. I became familiar with the militarized presence in my daily routines. One morning my car had a flat tire and, as my driver tried to hail a passing car, a soldier thrust his gun through the open window and into my face. He wanted "line money." Like the warlords and drug lords who control the country roads, the city soldiers and traffic police want bribes if you happen to pass their territory. I became so immune to the threat of a gun that I thought of it as "symbolic" violence: everyone knew he wouldn't pull the trigger.

A diplomatic friend told me of driving to University Avenue to take pictures of the roadblocks at "Aung San Suu Kyi's intersection." When he returned home later that evening his dog was lying dead in front of the house. Its eyes had been burned out. All of us who occasionally live in Rangoon learn to go on as if nothing much has happened. He told me this at a dinner party that evening. We continued to enjoy ourselves, knowing that again we had come up to a boundary of what is not to be known, or said. The routine bugging of my phone line was more testimony to the watchful presence of the regime. At some point I realized that I had become a resident of Rangoon.

Concerning Subversion

This book is about the psychological strategies that Burmese people conceive and enact in order to survive living under an authoritarian regime. These strategies are all about managing fear. They lead us away from social science truisms and generalizations into a gray area where strategies involving resistance, collaboration, and complicity muddy traditional motivational analyses. There is no succor here for theorists seeking answers to old chestnuts such as the free rider problem. Rather, motivations are mired in magic, millenarianism, Buddhist ethics, self-preservation instincts, and a fierce focus on family safety and mental health. Clarity is the first thing to go in a conflict situation, and Burmese psychological strategies often seem confusing, imbricating, and lacking in credibility even for those people avowing and enacting them. I use the term "karaoke fascism" not only to describe the particular modern Burmese form of oppression as it is played out in the cities, but more specifically as the label for the response made by Burmese people to a life of domination. This book is concerned with those layers or veneers of conformity that Burmese people present to each other and, most especially, to the military regime. While these veneers cover over enormous wells of suffering and injustice, they have become reality: they are the experience of public sentiment, collective affect, and modernity as a voyeuristic and hollow, class-based experience. "Karaoke fascism" is the term I have chosen that best describes the psychological survival strategies of contemporary Burma.

The refusal to allow Aung San Suu Kyi to hold roadside talks on University Avenue, leaning over her front fence, meant that a great tension settled upon Rangoon in the latter part of 1996. Young people, especially students, festered with impotence. Halfway through my fieldwork I moved to Golden Valley, better known throughout the country as the "Village of the Generals" (Sao Yin Aung 1965). My new residence was midway between the houses of Aung San Suu Kyi and her deputy, U Tin Oo. Rather than living beside soldiers, I now lived in the heart of the Generals' preferred township. Roadblocks existed on several streets, and during the fieldwork period my street was only open to University Avenue in one direction with troops patrolling the road's intersections. In this township, to which I have returned many times, we all live not only under the watchful eye of the military but with the military; together we form a strange community.

Living in the Generals' Village has taught me much about the enduring relationships between kin, school friends, age mates, and socioeconomic class. Members of the same family become monks, nuns, and military officers, doctors who work for international aid organizations, public servants, and National League for Democracy members. There is no us and them—we are all together, traveling toward an unknown and unpredictable future, strange bedfellows who love the weekend quiet of the township in the early morning mist, its spiraled laneways, and its interlinking tracks that wind through the serene monasteries and past the trees where our guardian *Nat* (*na'*) spirits reside.[2]

This quiet, the moments of peace we feel in our township, can become quickly shattered. I mention the major political players in Rangoon not because I want to engage with them, but rather, because I needed to know the broad political strategies at foot in order to interpret the wild rumors, panicked assumptions, and action strategies employed by Burmese people on the basis of what they thought these political moves were. By moving myself to a location where I was able to observe these political machinations and terror and control tactics, I became an activist-by-proxy. A key theme that runs through this book is the lack of black and white options or ways of understanding events and loyalties in Burma. I describe gray areas of complicity and collaboration, where willful ignorance of the political situation is as much a response to repression as armed insurgency. The reasons why individuals and groups choose to engage with the military regime (and the ways in which this occurs) are central to my analysis.

The flip side of this stance is that I had of course already made a decision about the ethics of military dictatorship prior to ever visiting Burma. In deciding to focus on an area of research clearly at odds with the regime's wishes, I have actively undermined, subverted, worked against, or opposed the Burmese military regime. To make such a statement is somewhat terrifying, and yet, in writing against terror and against fear, that is my position. When I am in Burma and conducting research, this is not an enviable position to hold. I scare myself. I practice self-censorship. I engage in self-talk and fear rationalization and minimization strategies. In short, I do many of the things that Burmese people do when confronted with repression. And that forms the basis of my analytical strategy in this book. I aim to intuit, as much as possible, the experience of living under the Burmese military dictatorship, in part through a shared set of physiological and psychological responses. The communication of that experience in tandem with an analysis of how those experiences are constructed by the military regime constitutes the rationale for this work.

The Cycle of Survival

I had come to Burma to understand the idioms of emotional and psychological distress used by various Burmese communities, and to explore the role of religion and medicine in conceptualizing and mediating such distress and as pathways for action. It was May 1996 and the city was clearly in distress: fear was a dominant emotion and my plans of searching out charismatic cults, sects, monks, and forest hermits in the hills around Mandalay quickly became modified as I realized that something important was happening in Rangoon.

Three times I booked plane tickets to Mandalay, and three times I remained in Rangoon. On the final occasion I made it as far as the airport before admitting to myself that the ways of life of people in a militarized capital city are no less compelling than mystic sects and magic monks in the hills around Burma's deserted ancient cities. I didn't realize that May is the culmination of the annual cycle of fear that overlies

Rangoon's topography. The BBC news reports hourly updated the numbers of people arrested in Rangoon for anti-government activities. At one stage the count was over one thousand. This book begins then, with the dying weeks of Aung San Suu Kyi's roadside speeches, and charts one full cycle of the topography of fear that characterizes contemporary Rangoon. Just as my introduction to the field was an intellectual journey of descent from tourist to expatriate to resident, so too my reactions to the militarization of Rangoon mirror those of many Burmese. For this reason, the book moves between different modes of data collection. At an epistemological level, this means that some information is gleaned from the shared circumstances of my body inhabiting the same space as Burmese bodies. Researching the experience of Burmese people under dictatorship means giving credence to shared emotional understandings between fieldworker, informant, and environment. This tension, between similar experiences and more conventional anthropological analyses, is also present between chapters and between sections of the book.

It took several weeks to become caught up in the fear that engulfed the city, and my fear, watchfulness, and self-surveillance only increased as my Burmese accent improved and as I understood more of the official propaganda, signboards, and flow of everyday conversations. I began unconsciously to stay indoors, seeking refuge from the military gaze. In Chapter 2 I explore the physical and psychological elements of the Buddhist concept of "refuge" within the running battles that daily reconfigured the urban space as a modern battlefield. I chart the major battles in this urban war over space, and the use of the bodies of the populace and students to lay claim to areas of the cities. The boundaries of the urban warfare changed hourly and confusion became not only a *modus operandi* of both sides in the urban war, but an existential condition of everyday life as the familiar suddenly became unsafe and sanctuary spaces and safe behaviors could no longer be identified.

Chapter 3 describes the affective tone set by the military. It is about fear, the most obvious and encompassing aspect of living in Rangoon. This book uses narrative and intuited data about the state construction of affect. I explore the theme of the vulnerability inculcated as the quotidian, with an examination of the vision of an incipient fascist utopia as the military council defines one kind of citizen and one kind of truth.

In the fourth chapter I describe the strangulation of civil society through censorship, propaganda, self-censorship, informers, and the surveillance and regulation of public space. Familiar, everyday knowledge, practices, and local environments become unstable and perilous through this variety of techniques overseen by Military Intelligence, the Ministry of Information, and the Department of Psychological Warfare.

That the military junta's crude forms of repression may one day soon become total and efficient is the fear lurking always in the background of the narratives included in this chapter. I chart a contiguous history of resistance to oppression that has continually sought to challenge the omnipotence of this fear through deconstructing the psychological structure of authoritarian systems of control.

Chapters 5 and 6 analyze the thin veneers of modernity and conformity that blanket the urban and peri-urban environment. In Chapter 5 I use the narratives of recovering heroin addicts, arrested and forcibly detoxified at the Rangoon Drug Rehabilitation Unit, to bear witness to the mountain of suffering that the project of modernity has unleashed. The demolition of the old cities of Rangoon and Mandalay made way for what I describe as "narcoarchitecture," the use of profits from the heroin trade laundered by the highest levels of the military regime, to build high-rise buildings and other fixtures of the modern Asian cityscape. Although it is a tacky, peeling façade of modernity born of brutality and suffering, it is the experience of the modern for two generations of children born under dictatorship.

In Chapter 6 I examine the façade with which urban and peri-urban residents cloak themselves when in the public domain. This is the creation of collective affect, the way that authoritarian regimes operate at the level of the "masses," and the particular form of active yet non-active involvement of the population in the state's social engineering project. I describe the creation of model citizens through forcible participation in state-orchestrated and choreographed events that include forced labor, army portering, and attendance at mass rallies and national celebrations. This chapter analyzes the karaoke-like aspects of the populace's response to repression and attempted absolute control at the corporeal level and the survival strategies to such repression. A short story about the body of a concrete salesman caught up in Rangoon's building boom, whose mind becomes dissociated from the material world, serves as a template for the process that Walter Benjamin has described as that familiar nexus of patriotism, modernity, and authoritarianism: the making of modernity at the level of individual bodies. In this chapter the process of giving the body over to the State as a hollow tool is shown to be necessary due to the depraved indifference to human life and human rights embedded in the remaking of Burma into an authoritarian-capitalist dystopia.[3]

In Chapter 7 I document the tension between the imagined fascist utopia promulgated by the Generals and the practical consequences of implementing this dream in an urban setting with few resources. Absurdity and a sense of the surreal often surface at critical moments, when one would otherwise be terrified or paralyzed into inaction. At such times, black humor and lampooning channel this recognition of the absurd into responses that help to minimize fear. In the tea shops and in the trusted company of friends, the significance of political events and figures are subverted, inverted, and represented as repoliticized satiric figures, devoid of some of the fear attached to the absurd and the surreal in urban Burma.

Chapter 8 corresponds to the expansion of the boundaries of my fieldwork and my knowledge of Burma past the cities of Rangoon and Mandalay and into the peri-urban townships that ring the cities. This chapter is set in the fictitious township, Nyaungbintha, or "Pleasant Banyan Tree Village." For reasons of security for informants and friends who work and live in these townships, Nyaungbintha represents an amalgam of the forcibly relocated townships of Rangoon and Mandalay. Tracing the everyday lives of women of reproductive age, I chronicle the forms of structural violence that flourish among this vulnerable population and use medical anthropological techniques to understand the links between women's illnesses, the socioeconomic situation, and the broader political climate.

The penultimate chapter of the book describes how the Burmese body, surveiled, controlled, hollowed out, and presented to the state as a mirrored signboard, releases the mind, the butterfly spirits of the Burmese population, out into the cosmos. Individual Burmese choose and enact various forms of escape from fear and from the everyday state of emergency. The resort to Buddhist, animist, miniature, and other worlds or domains of experience is documented via the narratives of prostitutes, heroin addicts, and the peri-urban poor.

Finally, in the conclusion I show that, at what eventually may be a great cost to their psychological integrity, Burmese people have escaped from authoritarianism to worlds of light and hope where they wait for the end of the regime or the coming of the fifth and final Buddha, Arimettaya. No one seems to mind which comes first.

Chapter 2
Bombs, Barricades, and the Urban Battlefield

> Benjamin shared with us other émigrés the error that spirit and cunning can possibly accomplish something against a force which no longer recognizes spirit as something autonomous, but only as a means to its own ends, and therefore no longer fears a confrontation with it.
>
> —Theodor Adorno, *Negative Dialectics*

> Our brothers in the past sacrificed to topple this military dictatorship but their demands were only met with violence, bullets, and killing.
>
> —Min Ko Naing

Scorpions

In the fiercest heat of the year, I ride a boat and then a pony cart to a small town not far from Rangoon, in the lower Burma delta. It takes two hours and I am lulled by the soft lap, lap, lapping of the brown waves against the eroded banks, and the graceful arc made by the fishing nets from the boatmen hugging the banks in their small canoes. The boat and pony cart route, though illegal, is preferable to the bone-breaking, spine-jolting ride in a covered pick-up truck on roads whose bitumen is largely washed away by the yearly monsoon, leaving potholes the size of small pagodas all over the road. The village is a typical dusty market area with dirt lanes peeling off among banyan trees and an overgrown village lifestyle that began at the river when the British created the Twante canal to create easier sea access from the port of Rangoon. Twante is a village of potters. The water pots from all over Burma come from their pottery sheds, but I am more interested in the Shwesandaw Pagoda.

The Shwesandaw Pagoda lies 100 yards behind the last row of thatched wooden houses, and one needs first to traverse the rubbish midden that fills the entire area between the houses and the pagoda. I am pleased to have finally left behind me the smell of the midden, and the pigs, dogs, children, and the sight of the poorest Twante women rooting through the food scraps and mounds of plastic bags, as I slog through sand half a foot deep on the path to the pagoda. As I place my foot on the ground I see a shadow from the corner of my eye, and I try to stop the downward motion of my leg a few inches from the ground. As I raise my foot I see an enormous black scorpion, known as a Burmese Giant Forest Scorpion, or Asian Forest Scorpion. At its maturity, a full-grown Burmese Giant Forest Scorpion is only supposed to be four or five inches in length, but this one seems at least five inches, and possible six. It is more aggressive than the Asian Emperor Scorpion and at the moment my foot is only two inches away from it, its two front pincers like giant crab claws are open and slightly raised, and its segmented tail is holding high in the air the venomous stinger on the end. I'd read that Burmese Forest Scorpion venom can prove fatal and the mode of death is usually respiratory or heart failure. I think the scorpions can achieve this just by their menacing countenance. The greenish-black monster is a fitting guardian for the impressive pagoda that rises up out of the sand only a few meters away. Pagoda steps are lined with other such deadly guardians, like the winged lions, or *chinthe* (*chin dhei*), and the ogres, or *belu* (*ba̲ lu:*), converted to Buddhism and so powerful as to prevent apparitions from non-Buddhist worlds or Buddhist hells from despoiling the sacred space of the pagoda grounds.

When I returned to Rangoon from my visit to the Shwesandaw Pagoda, I recounted my journey to a middle-aged female friend. I talked about the tranquility of the pagoda, the musical sounds carried on the wind, and the cool marble of the pagoda platform shaded from the ravages of the April midday sun. She turned to me and, with a smile, chanted a short verse about the soft twinkling sound of the bells attached to the *hti* on the top of the pagoda, the coolness of the marble underfoot, and the soothing whiteness of the lime washed walls to pilgrims who have been squinting painfully through the fierce brightness of the tropical sun.

My friend had summed up what in all my years of wandering through Southeast Asian Buddhist spaces I had been unable to: the feeling of putting ashore in a safe harbor, an aesthetic balance of the various elements of Southeast Asian life that is experienced as a release of bodily and mental tension. It is no wonder Burmese Buddhists flock to these emotional heartlands when menaced by the frightening greenish-black scorpions of the military variety.

Sanctuary

It is movement that is frightening in Burma. Staying inside, staying in one place, staying out of the cities—these are strategies of safety, but it is an illusory safety, continually torn down or made flimsy. The Generals are not content to control only the flow of information in the public domain; they seek also to dominate, reconstruct, and regulate urban space in a ceaseless breaking down of barriers that previously signaled sanctuary. The experience of fear occurs in these "open" and regulated spaces as people necessarily shuffle from one sanctuary to another. The primary mechanism for controlling space in Burma is to order the appearance, or placement, of Burmese bodies in public spaces, and the technique used to reconfigure both space and the Burmese body is what I will call "deterritorialization."

When terror becomes a means to enforce domination, violence becomes the primary force that maps social space (Feldman 1991: 35). At these times, violence spatializes power, but that does not mean that "cultures of terror" are ever uniform, monodimensional creations. A notion of physical and symbolic sanctuaries is a useful tool for analyzing the ways in which individuals experience life differentially, and at different moments, under authoritarianism. A belief in the existence of sanctuary spaces serves to remind us of the uncertainty, ambiguity, and unevenness of terror (Taussig 1987: 1992). Buddhist sites such as Angkor Wat have long been seen in Southeast Asia as sanctuary spaces. During the brutal Pol Pot period in Cambodia, Angkor Wat was looted, booby-trapped, and made into a no-go zone for Cambodian Buddhists. In the aftermath of the genocide, the reclaiming of these social spaces from areas of violence and warfare established, for some Buddhists, coherency in local worlds destabilized by violence (Skidmore 1994, 1996).

Drawing upon Gaston Bachelard's concept of the "sanctuary" as an immune space, Jean Franco argues that, in Latin America, home, church, and convent have a long history of being secure sanctuary spaces, in part because "the Church and the home retained a traditional topography and traditional practices over a very long period, and also because during periods when the state was relatively weak these institutions were the only functioning social organizations." But in Latin America, sanctuary spaces such as the home, convent, church, and even diplomatic space have at times been invaded by state sponsored violence. On the one hand, government rhetoric focuses upon the centrality of these institutions in the life of the nation. Simultaneously, however, these sanctuary spaces are cleverly suborned by the State. As Franco notes, "these convenient abstractions, which once referred to well-defined physical spaces, have subtly shifted their change in meaning . . . this process can be described as "deterritorialization" (Franco 1985: 415–16). The use of deterritorialization by military governments in both Latin America and Burma leads to the disordering of life worlds where arbitrariness now rules and no one feels safe. As one diplomat told me: "You don't know where the walls are anymore."

In conjunction with the monastery, the pagoda (or *wat*) is the primary "imagined" sanctuary space in Theravada Buddhist Southeast Asia (Skidmore 1994, 1996). Other sanctuary spaces also exist, such the home. As in Latin America these are feminized spaces in the sense that monks vow celibacy and thus are differentiated from "men." Moreover, the manager of the household in Burma is traditionally female. Unlike monasteries, almost all areas of pagodas are communal spaces available to women and families. The pagoda is a sanctuary space usually surrounded by a lush garden setting where families picnic on weekends. Lovers are sanctioned (and chaperoned) by their elders to meet in the pagoda grounds, and a wide variety of healers offer their services, including astrologers and hermit monks. Since the British invasion of Burma, however, when Burmese forces massed at their most sacred site, the Shwedagon Pagoda, the pagoda has taken on additional symbolic meaning as a political site whose sanctuary has been repeatedly violated.

During the colonial period, the wearing of shoes by Europeans inside pagoda grounds became a central rallying point for pro-independence activists. Wearing shoes within pagoda grounds became emblematic of the violation of Burmese sovereign space by the British. The National League for Democracy (NLD) has also held rallies at the Shwedagon, thus contributing to its politicization, and the junta transports school children and other coerced groups to the pagoda to witness "nation building" ceremonies. In addition to these politicizations of the premier Buddhist sanctuary space, government officials and informers have infiltrated both the monastery and the pagoda grounds.

The most significant manner in which sanctuary spaces have been deterritorialized in Burma is the colonization of the Sangha (community of monks) by the junta. Monks participated in the 1988 nationwide uprising, some immolating themselves and others turning their alms bowls upside down, refusing the military the ability to make merit and so enhance their chances of a better rebirth and erase the demerit they accrued for firing upon the demonstrators. Monks administered Mandalay and parts of Rangoon in the immediate aftermath of the 1988 uprising, and the population fell easily back into the system of Buddhist law and justice enshrined in the Buddhist Dhammatat. The army repressed a monk rebellion in 1990, and the subsequent invasion of the monasteries in Mandalay by the military effectively ended collective monastic opposition to the military regime.

As in other parts of Theravada Buddhist Southeast Asia, a great majority of the male population become monks for at least three months as a sign of respect for their families. Many stay for several years, or reenter an order upon retirement. Informers were placed in monasteries, and all monks were forced to sign a declaration of endorsement for the government and pledge not to "disrupt the stability of the State." Following this, a campaign was initiated to suborn many Burmese monks. On March 16, 1997, seven years after the Generals had begun their campaign of buying monks televisions, trips abroad, lavish new buildings, and other accouterments of modernity, political agitation by monks in Mandalay surfaced again. During the period of street rioting in Mandalay at the end of 1996, when students conducted their hit-and-run demonstrations, monks demonstrated against propagandist reports that Mandalay's most revered Buddha image at the Maha Muni pagoda had been vandalized, as well as against a series of other issues and allegations relating to the Sangha and their families. This monastic protest spread to Rangoon, where the regime began blockading monks in their monasteries. A student told me that this was one of the most infuriating aspects of the regime's control: "We Burmese people truly respect Buddhism and the monks, and we really dislike these kinds of tactics."

Barbed wire and barricades surrounded one of the oldest Rangoon monasteries, Mango Grove Monastery. Monks were warned to stay inside. More than 400 monks were arrested in the ensuing unrest and forcibly disrobed in prison. The Generals postponed the Payiyatti Sangha examination for monks and the monks were sent back to their villages from the monasteries (ABYMU 1997). The invasion of monasteries by the military, the arrest and forcible defrocking of monks in prison, and the suborning of many senior monks in the years since the democracy uprising, are evidence of the efficiency of the technique of deterritorialization. It is widely known throughout Burma that the monastery and the pagoda are no longer safe havens for those who wish to escape the politicization of Burmese life.

Refuge

Refuge is the Burmese term for a sanctuary space. The most commonly repeated mantra in Burmese Buddhism is "I take refuge in the Three Jewels: the Buddha, the Dhamma, the Sangha." U Tin U (Myaung) (2002: 25–26) explains the significance of "refuge" for Burmese Buddhists in the following way: "It is human nature to seek refuge in something. Primitive people took refuge in mountains or forests or some other physical phenomena. . . . We go to the Buddha, our precious source of spiritual pleasure, for refuge because the Buddha had boundless compassion on all beings, and showed them the right path for their welfare. . . . We go to Dhamma, our precious source of spiritual pleasure, for refuge because it enables one who follows it to find internal peace at present. . . . We go to the . . . [Sangha], our precious source of spiritual pleasure, for refuge because it provides the fertile field to sow seeds of merit that are going to yield great results." This important concept of refuge has two practical consequences in the militarized city. The first is a literal translation, where Burmese people take physical refuge in pagodas and monasteries. The second is a retreat to inner spaces of contemplation as guided by the Dhamma, meditation, and the teaching of individual monks and *sayadaws* (*hsaja do*) (abbots).

In 1990, when it became clear to Burmese people not only that the resignation of General Ne Win had failed to create a successful push for democracy, but that the "sons of Ne Win" were thoroughly entrenched in power and settling in for the long haul, one third of the total private property in Burma was transferred to the Sangha (Jordt 2002). A young man, Maung Myint Htoo, who was only a child when this happened, speculated that there was a complete loss of faith in the ability of the SLORC to manage the economy and a prevalent feeling that one's only substantive asset, land, could be arbitrarily confiscated if the regime needed funds:

I think what happened was that when the currency was demonetized and most of the buildings and property were nationalized, this happened at the same time as so many people losing their jobs and unemployment became much worse. This led to great insecurity and people gave their land to the monks because at least then it wouldn't go to the government.

The population not only invested their material resources in sayadaws, monasteries, pagodas, and meditation centers, they also flocked to these places in hundreds of thousands. Communities arose around charismatic monks such as Thamanya Sayadaw in southern Mon state, where a community of devotees had grown since he began residence at Thamanya Hill in 1980. These people lived under a kind of benevolent dictatorship of the ruling sayadaw, whose moral authority (which extended for a three-mile radius from the Hill) comes from the Buddha and whose sacred ground was not subject to many of the laws of the military council. The resulting town, Thayawady, or "Pleasant City," has approximately 15,000 residents, including 600 monks, nuns, and novices living in 45 to 50 monasteries within the sanctuary limits. During his lifetime the sayadaw was, in the eyes of his followers, a "source of protection and assistance" (Rosenberg 2002: 7–8). The town residents enter into loose but reciprocal relationships with urban populations and people from nearby towns, who bring necessary cash to the religious communities and provide a market for the sale of goods and foodstuffs grown on site (Tosa 2002).

My friend Yin Pe has an interesting take on Thamanya, a realistic view of what Thamanya could achieve for its residents. He remarked that

It's a kind of sanctuary, but there is no place where the military can't go. But there is a kind of religious or social boundary that is understood as a religious sanctuary. So it's a kind of social space where the regime is only barely in touch with what is going on, and that's what makes Thamanya so popular with Burmese people. But remember, there's no place the military can't go.

The population of monasteries, nunneries, and meditation centers skyrocketed after 1988 and even today one finds in these places the only forms of civil society beyond the reach of the military junta. In this book I will write much about the breakdown of both interpersonal trust and local civil society, but here, in nunneries in Sagaing, for example, one can find "nun-partnerships," most often between a city and a rural nun, where a special bond of trust flourishes over the lifetime of the two women as they pool their collective resources into one economic unit to ensure the success of one member of the couple at passing the Bhikkuni exams that can take up to twenty years to successfully complete (Kawanami 1994).

Although it is a less obvious phenomenon than the retreat of remote Thamanya, the meditation movement offers shelter in hundreds of meditation centers throughout the country where lay people organize themselves into Sasana groups around "lay and monk meditators, meditation teachers and donation cliques, monks' organizations, and lay voluntary committees."[1] Together they form a "moral citizenry" (Jordt 2001: iii) that has taken a superior moral position over the military regime, as evidenced by the obsessive compulsion of members of the military council towards donating to the Sangha and merit-making in general (311). Consisting of over one million "mass enlightenment" meditators, the "New Laity" is indeed a potent force in Burmese political life because they control the rationality behind the regime's use of Buddhism as a form of political legitimacy (261).

This view of the engagement of Burmese meditators goes beyond the idea of a resisting populace in its understanding of the continual process of negotiation of legitimacy that occurs at myriad local levels. While Burmese lay meditators cannot hold meetings in public spaces or engage in other kinds of activities common to Western civil society, inside the meditation centers, and on other kinds of sanctified ground, they can put pressure on particular monks to disrobe or leave their monasteries and they control significant monastic financial property and other resource transactions. This ensures that at local levels, the regime cannot ignore the forms of morality and political legitimacy sponsored by the New Laity; it thus continually seeks to remove laity from monastic grounds and place its own monks and lay advisors in positions of power within the Sangha (Jordt 2001).

Those requiring both mental and physical sanctuary come to these sanctified places, including members of the National League for Democracy who turn to the solitude of the monasteries and meditation centers when the menace of the junta threatens to become too great for sanity and when inner reserves of fortitude and mindfulness need replenishing (Houtman 1999).

A 1995 census gives the number of monks in Burma at 160,000, with 25,000 nuns and 240,000 novices from a population of forty six million (Rozenberg 2002: 13). Initiated as novices and covered in parasites and shrapnel wounds, thousands of orphans from the fighting in the borderlands are sheltered and educated in monasteries. And finally, the mentally ill, tormented by images and dreams of violence, violent portents, and the powerlessness of their situation combined with the effects of psychiatric medications, come to pagodas to find healing for the body, mind, and body politique. Daw Phyo Zar Thwin is in her mid-forties and has several children but is repeatedly hospitalized at the Rangoon Psychiatric Hospital. Heavily sedated, she tells me about her illness and how she takes refuge in the Three Gems by chanting Buddhist verses (*paritta*) in order to make merit and be cured of her illness, most especially through meditation:

I informed the police that I have a dream. My dream is about the pagoda and the graveyard. . . . It means I must read the Buddhist words and say paritta and make merit. When I read the words of the Buddha, I'm at peace. The paritta are good [powerful or effective] so I'm well in my mind. My health is good now. I like this hospital, [here] my health is better. I pity the other patients. The medicine treatment is good in this hospital. Now I don't need to take medicine. The treatment of the paritta and the treatment of the medicine are good.

As in the desperate seeking of psychiatric patients for a source of wellness in the powers that reside in Buddhist spaces, so refuge is a deeper concept than referring merely to physical sanctuary. Refuge refers also to the futility of seeking solace or sanctuary in earthly or material possessions, ideologies, or places. Craving, the result of desire, is the root of all suffering in Buddhism, and refuge from suffering and hence from human life in general, can come only through withdrawal from the world of sensation and corporeality by directing one's attention inward. Burmese psychiatric patients know that something is wrong with the place inside them that provides equilibrium and balance even though they cannot articulate it or concentrate their mind upon it, and they view the pagoda as both the center and symbol of wellness for themselves and their world. The inward absorption of consciousness creates, for Buddhists, a subtle body that overlies the crude, rotting carcass that the consciousness of humans inhabits. Mindfulness is the tool that allows insight into the futility of earthly concerns and this is what Burmese Buddhists mean when they say that they take refuge in the Buddha, the Sangha, and the Dhamma.

When I think of these two meanings of refuge, I recall a conversation with a group of young male political refugees in Melbourne, Australia. In a discussion regarding the 1996 hit-and-run demonstrations, several generations of political refugees reminisced about their various experiences of hiding in monasteries. One man, born in Chin state and a former student at the Rangoon Institute of Technology, told me about the various monasteries in Rangoon where monks were known to have hoarded arms and ammunition, and where students had been allowed to assemble and create their protest banners. U Aye Hlaing took a sip of beer and continued with the conversation, recounting incidents involving a monastery near Hledan junction that sheltered students fleeing from the military during the 1996 demonstrations. "Oh yes," interrupted my friend, Angelay. He had fled the country after the 1988 strike. Around a mouthful of fruit he said, "We hid in that monastery too." These exiled students understand that the refuge of the pagoda space is temporary and illusionary. Unlike the hundreds of thousands of Burmese who flee to these sanctuary heartlands for years at a time, the political refugees know that for them refuge cannot be obtained through Buddhism. Each of these generations of student activists turned, instead, to destabilizing the regime's topography of fear, imbuing the cities with new landscapes of resistance. Pagodas and monastic communities played their part, but only as a reappropriated staging ground for a new round of urban guerrilla warfare.

Military Fear

Like the Tatmadaw (armed forces), the Burmese Forest Scorpion lies in plain sight, its matte surfaces absorbing the tropical sun. But armament alone is not sufficient for a feeling of safety. Urban Burmese wonder why military sites and homes need guards, barbed wire barricades, and towering cement walls. What do they have to be frightened of? Like Burmese people who flock to pagodas and monasteries, the Generals seek places of refuge from the fury of the populace that cannot always be contained, especially among the younger generation, the children of dictatorship.

On December 25, 1996, in the midst of the hit-and-run student demonstrations in Rangoon, two bombs exploded during an exhibition of the Chinese Tooth relic at the Kaba Aye Pagoda. Five people were killed in the explosion and seventeen injured. Secretary No. 2, Lieutenant General Tin Oo, the fourth most powerful member of the ruling council and Commander in Chief of the Army, had left the site only a few hours earlier. Four months later, a letter bomb exploded at his home, killing his daughter and blowing off his hand. It is not known if he was finally successfully assassinated in February 2001, when a helicopter in which his delegation was traveling suffered engine failure and plunged into the Salween River (Head 2001: 1).

The city abounded with rumors of Japanese gang involvement after the two initial attacks, but in 1998 the military arrested forty "aboveground destructive elements" whom they accused of conspiring to bomb buildings and conduct political assassinations (Human Rights Watch 1999). Political assassination through bombing is a well-known occurrence in Burma and all Burmese can recite the death of the entire pre-Independence cabinet of General Aung San when a grenade was thrown into a session of parliament. Perhaps, then, the military regime has much to be fearful about at the level of personal safety.[2]

Fleeting Resistance

It is September 1996, and the end of the rainy season is upon us. Weddings, banned over the rainy season and Buddhist lent, begin to be planned. Normally, romance is on the minds of Burmese at this time, and the festival of lights is much anticipated throughout the country. But not this year. Not in Rangoon and Mandalay. The blue skies signal that political action is no longer planned in monasteries, universities, and military headquarters. It has begun to happen. I realize that I've stopped taking field notes. What is a field note anyway? All I have now is snatches of conversations and partial views of incidents; there's no time for analysis. I have no sense of the overall plan, just fragments:

- 29th September—500 people have been arrested and a violent scuffle breaks out outside Aung San Suu Kyi's house.
- Ma Shwe told me of the rumors about the bomb blast that felt like an earthquake last night: "The military said that the communists and the KNU did it. The military drag out the Communists whenever it is convenient." She continued, "I couldn't sleep and I heard a great big explosion, and I wasn't sure if that's what it was, but then Ma Pyu

told me that it was an explosion early this morning on the 25th, at 1:30 a.m. No one was hurt during the explosion but the government is repairing it urgently; they repaired it all night but there's been no news about it."

- Ma Theingyi sidles up to me as we walk past the rubbish middens. I hardly register her comment; so intent am I upon breathing through my mouth and trying not to be sick from the fumes of a hundred kilograms of food scraps moldering in the tropical midday heat. Ma Theingyi is quiet, but insistent. A rough hand grabs my chin to force eye contact. She hisses, "My friend is a doctor who works in the general hospital. He said that last night at midnight, two Indians came in; they had been beaten by monks. There is a lot of "security" near the mosques." She says nothing else all the way to the noodle stand and back to the house, content with expelling the dangerous knowledge from her body.

- Across from the Nurses Institute, two monasteries are surrounded by barbed wire to keep the monks in. Two mosques have been damaged.

- Again, thousands of people are out on the streets; everywhere small confrontations are occurring. Everyone is discussing it openly—the fear has finally broken the surface.

- Tanks have gone from the Sule Pagoda, but still on the major arterials like U Wizara and Pyay Road. Shwedagon Pagoda Road is blocked, as is the street parallel to it. Tanks also at Thura and Thuwanna stadiums (stadiums being used as forced assembly locations and military hubs).

- Yesterday, a bomb scare at the airport, but it seems to be "security as usual."

- Student demonstrations at Medical Institute No.1, the Dental Institute, and the Rangoon Institute of Technology.

- *Time* magazine has been banned for the last two weeks.

- The military council is engaged in a desperate attempt to channel student demonstrations and surfacing anger into the old religious hatreds against Muslims and people of South Asian ethnicities. The "ants" invading the belly of the Maha Muni pagoda Buddha image and the "planned renovation" of the Buddha causing outrage by monks. Then the incredibly persistent and widespread rumor that a woman, whose brother is a monk, was raped by two Muslim men. Two mosques destroyed today in Pegu and many soldiers and tanks there standing guard. CNN reports that in Malaysia a Burmese monastery is damaged.

- The Maha Muni pagoda now closed in Mandalay and rioting in two nearby towns.

- Rumors of 700,000 people displaced in Shan State and dying of cholera.
- Rumors of students and monks arrested when trying to make their way to Rangoon to join in the hit-and-run demonstrations.
- Aid personnel working in Nyaungbintha have returned to the city by 2 p.m. because they'd heard that the troops had been ordered to shoot if there was any trouble and that the bridges to the city were to be closed at 2 p.m. Businesses all over the city are closing a few hours early.
- Rumors of an official curfew in Rangoon to be announced, like the ones in the minor cities.
- 11 p.m. and 4 a.m.—forty trucks go to change the guard at University Avenue, 100 soldiers.
- Students resorting to smaller and more numerous hit-and-run tactics.
- A nonviolent sit-in at the American Embassy.
- Every day now there are sporadic demonstrations across the city. Head of the junta, Than Shwe, accuses Aung San Suu Kyi of inciting unrest.
- Roadblocks go up around the city's universities which remain firmly closed.
- 22nd Oct—approximately 400 students went down University Avenue at about 12:30 a.m. Around 4:30 a.m. on the 21st, the barricades went up on University Avenue.
- Two bombs go off—one at Taungoo and the other near an electricity plant.
- 2nd November—today I drove down University Avenue past four trucks loaded with troops. Many MI with sunglasses, sport shirts, and two-way radios.
- There are tanks across from the Tatmadaw Hall. There are wire barricades near so they can block U Wizara Road if necessary.
- 6 Tanks on Pyay Road with machine guns mounted surrounded by armed troops.
- Friday December 13—the annual marathon is cancelled. Rangoon Institute of Technology convocation cancelled, school exams cancelled, even down to 3rd standard; many high schools closed.
- Roads around the capital are sealed off; many suburbs are entirely cut off from downtown.
- Rangoon Institute of Technology students started demonstrating today, so 8-mile junction and Pyay Road have been closed, creating utter havoc and grinding all traffic in the city to a standstill.
- My friend and unofficial research assistant, Maung Ko, was in a panic this morning because his brother, a student at RIT, was arrested last night, but then released this morning.

• 2000 students demonstrate at Hledan, 600 march through the downtown area.

Despite the propaganda, censorship, intimidation, and climate of fear
that prevailed in the cities, it became clear to the military junta that the
National League for Democracy was growing in strength and that Aung
San Suu Kyi would not be silenced or exiled. The roadside speeches
given on weekends by Aung San Suu Kyi and other senior NLD members
caused ever larger crowds to gather in front of her house. When she
arrived, with flowers in her air and microphone in hand, the crowd went
wild. Cameras flashed, and even the photographing of participants by
military intelligence failed to diminish the size of the crowds. Estimates
began to reach 10,000 per weekend, even in the midst of the most crippling forms of repression of civil society. The junta acted by placing
roadblocks and armed troops at either end of University Avenue, making it impossible for Burmese to attend Aung San Suu Kyi's talks. As she
was still under house arrest, she could not leave her house to give
speeches in other locations. The frustration of the populace was palpable, but nowhere more so than in the universities where an impetus to
rage was barely concealed and where groups of students began to mobilize from the depths of desperation and the heroism of youth.

The Political Geography of Rangoon

On a day when the sun was beginning to heat the city and the mist began
to burn off early in the morning, I sat in the midst of traffic, gridlocked
by sudden road closures, and made the following list of sites and symbols
of military control and locales where people try to carve out sanctuary
spaces for themselves:

Military departments and other military sites, jails, the psychiatric hospital, social
welfare department "homes," USDA [Union Solidarity and Development Asso-
ciation] offices, government "donated" buildings such as Ne Win's pagoda and
the Tooth Relic pagodas, bomb blasts at General Tin Oo's house, American
Embassy, People's Desire Signboards, and the Tooth Relic pagodas; road closures, forced rallies, showground: "the corral" named by the NLD as the OK
Corral because that is where they are initially interned when the mass arrests
occur, Military Intelligence with their distinctive pressed longyi and sunglasses,
two-way radios and cameras, Lon Htein [riot police]. Other important '88 sites,
i.e., the White Bridge, Inya Lake, teashops, a landscape of violence and resistance. Symbols of sanctuary: pagodas, some parks, meditation centers, monasteries where you can live permanently [*Dhamma tai*'], pilgrimage sites, mystic cults,
NLD flags, university campuses.

These changing sites of control form the basis of the unmarked topography of Rangoon, a chronicle of events that now overlays the landmarks

from the previous period of dissent, the 1988 uprising. The list demonstrates how an urban geography is continually being reconfigured and reconstituted by violence and the struggle for power in Rangoon.

The ceaseless changing of the urban landscape is nothing other than a technique of terror. There are three components to the creation of this form of urban terror: firstly the placement of soldiers in areas generally regarded as public areas; secondly the blocking off of public areas using the weapons of urban warfare; and finally, the channeling of the urban populations into specific militarized no-longer-public areas of the cities. It is a key method of deterritorialization, the making of the world into an unsafe zone, and the removal of the sense of security from the long known and the long remembered and the achingly familiar (and now lost) landscapes of childhood.

The weapons of urban warfare serve two purposes in the militarization of the city. First, they are the means by which bodies are moved to different locations and restricted from others. This includes the bulletproof vests, bayonets, and guns of the soldiers and the crowd barricades, barbed wire, and roadblocks that limit pedestrian and vehicular access. These military accouterments are always in evidence, but not always in use and this is precisely their second function. Symbolic violence manifests itself in the presence of these munitions such as tanks brooding at intersections or the entranceway to parks or government sites. Like the mobile threats of violence contained in the propaganda signboards, these weapons common to battlefields and war zones lie by the side of the road or are positioned in alleyways as a sign of both the contemporary character of the urban space, and the battle readiness of the armed forces.

The Tatmadaw maintains a continual visible presence on the streets of Burma's cities. Hiding behind barricades and bushes, or peering out of public buildings and construction sights, Burma's army appears to be on the watch for anti-government behavior and always listening. Their presence is most effective during the peak hour traffic jams when they peer into car windows (tinting car windows is illegal). To see armed soldiers lining the streets and manning barricades is to be continually reshocked by a sense of dis-ease, of a continuing wrongness about the environment in which one is living. When a car pulls up at a city intersection, conversations fall silent. We wait in silence as a soldier's gaze sweeps across us. The major intersections have an electronic timer that counts down the seconds until the light changes. We watch and watch and watch the countdown and then, finally, the light changes, the car splutters back into life, and we let out our collective breath into the relieved space where time begins again as we resume our journey and our conversations.

This continual military inhabitation of civilian areas ensures that "public" and "private" have no meaning in Burma. Streets are routinely closed; parks, stadiums, and sports grounds become staging areas for tanks, troop carriers, and bayonet-wielding troops in formation. Some streets become open in one direction only, and others have a series of armed soldiers manning barricades to ensure that only residents use those streets.

Greenwood (1994) has constructed a map displaying the landmarks of the 1988 pro-democracy uprising and its bloody suppression that includes the "white bridge" remembered by students for the particular atrocities that occurred there. In the present political geography, the bodies of soldiers move through spaces no longer available to civilians and the bodies of civilians are routed into configurations demarcated by violence, both real and symbolic.

At each of these strategic infrastructure, communication, and political sites the junta positioned soldiers, tanks, and barricades. This deployment was in response to the open resistance shown by National League for Democracy supporters and by student demonstrators staging hit-and-run protests in December 1996. The immediate effect of sudden road closures and the militarization of the capital is to reroute civilian life. Commuting to daily workplaces involves negotiating roadblocks, tanks, and resultant traffic gridlock in a city that had almost no vehicles only ten years ago. Channeling the population into certain routes with the aid of crowd barriers, barricades, and barbed wire, the regime began shepherding Rangoon residents beneath the watchful eye of the State. A student who participated in the 1996–97 hit-and-run demonstrations described the situation as:

Students have to take their responsibility to be active under these conditions, but our mothers and our relatives, even though they are scared of the tanks and the troops, they know that they are only there because of the students. They know about the student demonstrations and why they [the tanks and soldiers] are here. So they show empathy to the students because they realize that we are risking our lives for them. They know that there are military tanks and soldiers stationed all around the city, but people just go about their daily business, because they are conditioned to this.

The new political geography imbues the city with disorientation, a continual changing of previously accessible streets or buildings and the sudden appearance of tanks and soldiers. In addition, curfews and barricades maintain the control of these spaces by controlling the movement of civilians. The continual spatial reconfiguring significantly increases the degree of confusion and flux felt by individuals, families, and wards. For example, the presence of soldiers and guns is immediately disquieting and disordering. The apparent randomness of their arrivals and departures, street closures, and appearance of barricades, creates an existential sense of disorder, as previously stable geographies become moving landscapes of "no-go" areas. Like a giant's game of chess, the bodies of soldiers, civilians, protestors, and onlookers are positioned by the two opposing sides to stake their claims upon urban space. By massing, if only for short periods in key areas around the city, the student demonstrators illustrate that when resistance is present, rather than the State using violence as a means of demarcating areas of control, violence itself becomes the only arbiter of space. The sense-destroying character of violence becomes the only constant or predictable element of the urban battle, a battle in which power becomes spatialized through the mobilization of the bodies of Burmese soldiers and the enforced removal of civilian bodies from areas claimed as belonging to the State.

These unmarked and changing sites, then, of both military domination and brave but fleeting resistance to the regime, constitute a contested landscape which people must traverse everyday. It is no longer possible to try to establish sanctuary spaces. When active resistance to the regime's reconfiguration of space occurs, all pretense at the maintenance of security and the warding off of fear and vulnerability disappear.

Nodes of Violence

Resistance points arise and are quickly repressed by the regime as it moves in the army to occupy spaces that the students and resisters have temporarily claimed as theirs. The architecture of the city is such that junctions become the practical sites for street protest and government repression. Road junctions are points of assembly and mass protest and as such are examples of changing sites of resistance. Junctions are important ways of orienting oneself in Rangoon, and soldiers and civilians alike are well aware of the way their city functions as a battlefield and the strategic position of road junctions in the war zone. The circular neighborhoods that require local knowledge to navigate spill out into large multi-road junction points, the location of monasteries, bus and trishaw "gates," markets, tea shops, and photocopy and telephone stalls. Several local neighborhoods converge at each junction and together these junctions with their attached neighborhoods form the political nodes of street protest and information dissemination. It is no coincidence that propaganda signboards denouncing internal opposition and democracy politics, and lauding the efforts of the Tatmadaw, line the roads of the junctions. Two of the most famous in Rangoon are the Kokaing junction, the nearest intersection to Aung San Suu Kyi's residence, and Hledan junction.

An assassination attempt was made against Aung San Suu Kyi at the Kokaing junction during the period of street unrest, and violent conflicts have occurred between NLD supporters and the government at this site. In 1997 Union Solidarity and Development Association [USDA] members were transported to the junction in Tatmadaw vehicles and police looked on as an iron bar was used to smash the glass of Aung San Suu Kyi's car. One of the occupants in the car was injured: blood could be seen streaming down his face before the car was able to pull away (Amnesty International 1997).

This incident was a dramatic but typical example of the violence perpetrated by the paid USDA members whom the regime ferries to the sites of planned violence and intimidation. On November 2, 1996, I and my friend Shwe Shwe were near Aung San Suu Kyi's residence on University Avenue. This was the day on which the regime decided Aung San Suu Kyi's roadside speeches were going to be banned. We went in a taxi to better preserve our anonymity. Violence and coercion were being used to dissuade people from entering University Avenue. "Drop me off by the side of the road past the tea shops, then you can go up Thanlwin Road," said Shwe Shwe. "I'm scared to leave you here," I said, "it looks too dangerous." "I'll be okay," she replied, "I want to see Her." As we drove off I saw monks being jostled and pushed back by the military using their rifle butts, and young men trying to defend themselves with umbrellas as the soldiers beat them with batons to force them away from the area.

The other important junction is Hledan junction. This is a busy and populated intersection because of the nearby market and its function as a major bus terminus. The residents of Hledan are particularly anti-military; it is one of the few areas of dissent the junta did not forcibly relocate in the aftermath of the 1988 Strike. In December 1996 students staged a sit-in that was broken up by police using water cannons. The usual summary arrest without representation, charges being laid, interrogation, and lengthy jail terms for political prisoners followed this incident. The following statement was given to a diplomatic friend by Daw Tin Tin Myint, who witnessed these events and who sheltered students involved in the sit-down strike:

In Hledan we are united. We also support the opposition. We all support the students, that is why they [the SLORC] hate us so much. In the end there were only 150 students in the triangle sitting very quietly and thousands of people shouting. Then I heard: "Are you going to sit there all night? Do something, fight them." There were only one or two voices, they were MI, and they started to throw stones [at the military, in a bid to cause the army to rush the students]. Then the water cannons came and the arrests. People came running up the stairs. Everyone opened the doors so that they could hide inside their homes.

The military said: "We are very disappointed you hid them. Next time, if you open your doors, you will lose your homes." Now they're not allowed back in if they leave their houses, so they are eating dried food.

I had ventured up to Hledan junction earlier in the night and noted an unusually strong contingent of international media crews. With an uneasy feeling about the situation, I went to the house of a friend to wait out the events. Anthropologist Christina Fink, traveling in Burma to speak to people willing to talk about fear and political violence, participated in the events of Hledan junction that evening. Knowing that my access to Burma was certain to be revoked if I attended, I read with interest her description of that evening's protest and the participation of Hledan locals in the resistance moment:

When a friend and I arrived at around 7 p.m., the junction, usually full of traffic, was blocked off by military barricades in all five directions. We could hear people making speeches and the audience shouting its approval as we made out way through the wide circle of perhaps 2,000 standing people. . . . I and a dozen other westerners present were approached by students eager to tell us why they were protesting. . . A group of students circulated around the area distributing water and sweets donated by local shopkeepers, while others picked up rubbish. . . . But as the night wore on, and armed soldiers and riot police began moving closer, the atmosphere changed. Many students and onlookers became afraid and silently slipped away . . . the troops and riot police began inching towards the students, clearly hoping to intimidate them into leaving without having to use force. By 2 a.m., there were only 100 students left sitting in a tight triangle, praying as they faced the Shwedagon Pagoda. On the pavement, there were about 150 students and locals armed with chair legs, determined to fight back even while the students in the centre had called for non-violent resistance. The remaining onlookers, including myself and the other westerners, had moved up to the balconies overlooking the junction. After giving a final warning, the troops trained water cannons on the silent students and stormed the area. Everywhere shattering glass, screams and wails could be heard as people were injured and arrested. We made our way into people's apartments, where we sat out the rest of the night in utter silence and darkness, though some of the Burmese girls in the room could barely stifle their sobs. In the early morning hours, we were able to slip out. (Fink 2001: 92–93)

It was not until 2003 that I chanced to meet Zin Maung, a man in his late twenties who had spent three years (1999–2001) in hiding from the regime before crossing the border to Thailand in 2002. He was a participant in the 1996–97 demonstrations and tried to also create student demonstrations in 1998 before going underground. Zin Maung's view of the student demonstrations differs from those of the onlookers in part because he needed to get to a point "beyond fear" before he could act. He was inside the grounds of the Rangoon Institute of Technology (RIT) and one of the group of people who made lists of missing students and demanded that the RIT Rector approach Military Intelligence (MI) to have the forty locals and eighty seven missing students released. The students were released around 1 P.M. and they told their fellow students about the previous night's demonstration:

ZM: Around the eleventh and twelfth of December there started to be a gathering of around 1,000–2,000 students. They decided to go for a march into the city to follow up their demands. That night I went home to [a distant township] but some of my friends remained to march into the city. They marched into the city and to the Sule Pagoda. It was around 3 a.m. in the morning, and other people started to join in. They didn't realize so many members of the public had joined the students until they got to Pansodan Bridge and then they looked back and saw that already there were 5,000 or 6,000 people. After they had passed the zoo and the south gate of the Shwedagon Pagoda, they were blocked by the Tatmadaw. They blocked us in from behind and in front. On one side was military headquarters and on our other side was the Dhammayoun.[3] They began to crack down on them, to beat them with "rubber tou'" (*ra ba dou'*).[4] Then they arrested them and took them to Kyaikkasan. You know the Kyaikkasan stadium?

MS: Yes, that's where they put people who are arrested en masse. Can you tell me about the demonstration in which you participated the following day?

ZM: We had already decided to join a protest outside the university on the streets. We opened the gates [of RIT] and the Lon Htein [riot police] blocked the road. There was around 100 Lon Htein with the Tatmadaw behind them, confronting about 400 of us students. More and more students gathered at the campus, including students from Hlaing campus. We had also just heard that students from Kyimindine campus were preparing to demonstrate. We all got into a bus to go downtown to start demonstrating, but we knew that we could be arrested at any time because the Lon Htein blocked our way with rubber tou'. They told us we had to stop within 200 meters otherwise they would beat us. I was in the middle of the students.

MS: Were you wearing a mask? How were you feeling?

ZM: We had no other choice. They could beat us if they wanted to. We didn't care any more, we had nothing to lose. No matter what was going to happen, we had already accepted our fear and the possibilities, and so we didn't even cover our face because they already knew who we were. It was the sort of mind set, "Whatever happens, happens," you know, whatever, we had nothing more to lose. I felt no fear at all, perhaps because they had suppressed us for such a long time. I don't know. Also, there were a lot of people standing in the street, shouting encouragement to us.

MS: What do you remember they shouted?

ZM: "Don't be afraid, we are here beside you."
"Don't do what the nawata [SLORC] tells you."
"Don't be afraid, we are with you, your mothers are with you. You are our children, the sons of the nation."
"Don't you hurt the sons of the nation. Don't touch our students."

Then they sent our teachers to reason with us. They didn't try to dissuade us, they said instead that they had experience with what happened to their students in 1988 and that the army has us surrounded and will crack down on us, so please, just disperse. The standoff went on for about three hours and then we heard there was a group of students gathered at Hledan junction, only about 300 or 400 and they needed help so we decided to disperse and each make our own way to Hledan to join the main demonstration group.

MS: What happened at Hledan?

ZM: They started spraying us with a fire hose, and some of the girls who were protesting, they "lost their longyi" [that is, members of the army or riot police grabbed the women's longyi and as they are only tucked into their waist, they were able to disrobe them, a shocking thing to happen to a woman in public, and generally believed to be the prelude to rape]. People saw what was going on from their balconies all around the junction and they became very angry and they began to throw their pot plants off the balconies onto the Lon Htein below. Removing the girls' longyi is so insulting. They began throwing everything off their balconies at the Lon Htein.

MS: So what did you do?

ZM: Well, we ran forward, then we ran back, depending on where the fire hose was spraying, sometimes we would charge forward together towards the Lon Htein, other times we would fall back because the fire hose was on us. This was around 5 p.m. We began shouting slogans and then the army trucks arrived [these are the covered trucks that take prisoners to Insein prison. It signals that the riot police are about to close in, arrest the students, and put them into the vans and take them to the interrogation cells of MI.] So we dispersed and continued to gather at junctions around the city to chant slogans. The army kept sending in their trucks to find out who was shouting slogans and arrest them.

The series of sit-down strikes such as the one at Hledan junction, and the well organized hit-and-run protests occurring all over the city, effectively reversed the regime's topography of militarized and "no-go" areas. The street protests also temporarily collapsed laws such as those forbidding freedom of assembly and official nightly curfews. I witnessed several of these flash protests and noticed a remarkable thing at one in Ahlone Township on December 15, 1996. The protesters gathered in a knot and stood about sixty meters away from a roadblock manned by soldiers who were madly scrambling to get to the scene of each strike. Approximately eighty soldiers stood in front of twelve troop carriers with their weapons aimed at the students. They covered the whole street and there were sometimes several rows of soldiers lined up in formation. The surprising element for me was the number of people who came to watch these demonstrations. About half of the onlookers stood within firing range. I listened with amazement as for the first time since 1988, Rangoon residents began to speak to each other in public about what was occurring. Fear was evident in the conversations and the body posture of the witnesses but the character of the fear was that of anticipation, a barely repressed hope for change. I remember thinking that I was well within the range of the new SLORC weapons but I doubt many of the people there realized their range.

The response of the military to this event was not only to arrest demonstrators, but also to commandeer more space and to populate it with more soldiers and more of its weapons of crowd control, such as barricades. Truckloads of troops from up-country began to arrive in Rangoon and near hysteria ensued as residents began to see the similarities with the repression of the 1988 uprising: "It's just like '88," and "Look, they're bringing the troops in again like they did just before the Strike," and "It's happening again," were just some of the ways my friends expressed their fear of a repetition of the 1988 uprising.

On December 8, 1996, the Australian Broadcasting Service reported that two major roads near the "disturbances" remained closed. On that occasion I wrote the following field note:

The whole area from Parami, Pye, Kaba Aye, and U Wizara is blocked as well as many side streets. Security forces remain on patrol after "crushing" a demonstration by students. Security around the scene is tight and the university is barricaded off. 260 people were arrested, almost all released. More than 1,000 took part in the protest.

Very few people I spoke with in these confusing and frightening weeks had eyes that remained dry as they recounted the heroism of the students. Many wept openly when describing how the student protests represented physical proof that the hope and desire for change is profound, widespread, and defiantly alive. The most gratifying element of the defiance was the sheer youth and inexperience of the students. These young men and women were born under dictatorship, and some had parents who were likewise born under dictatorship. That they have both internalized the desire for democracy and not succumbed to the grinding propaganda and seduction of a military-controlled modern future is knowledge that breaks through even the most hardened psychological barriers of the older generations. Such knowledge causes hope, long since banished, to rise up through the cracks in emotional firewalls, like the soft scuttle of rats whose heads dart up through the cracks in the cities' sewage system. Feeding off the fear generated by the civil unrest, hope, courage, and patience were refueled, and a reenergized public settled down to wait for the next battle in the War against the Generals.

Chapter 3
Darker Than Midnight: Fear, Vulnerability, and Terror-Making

The meeting concluded with [the] chanting of slogans—the National Objectives must succeed, must succeed; objectives of the USDA [Union Solidarity and Development Association] must succeed, must succeed; and internal and external destructionists must be crushed, must succeed (sic).

—*New Light of Myanmar*

Ethnography in an Authoritarian State

Ethnography conducted under conditions of fear and terror defies traditional methods of data collection.[1] My fieldwork interpretations and the very framework by which I determine whom to interview and why are consciously embedded in a belief in the need to write against terror (Taussig 1987). I am an activist-by-proxy, as is evident to me through my avoidance of the Burmese Generals and my continual worry over their anger at my writings.

Linda Green (1999: 6) has argued that fieldworker and informants inevitably share experiences. Returning from the field, the anthropologist has not only the analytical tools of the discipline at his or her disposal, but also "the language of people's practices," practices the anthropologist has witnessed or participated in. In my case, the shared experience includes being frightened, confused, and disoriented, and suffering from a general loss of perspective. Green (1998: 6) argues that anthropology can help to bring about a more just world if the "complex links" between analytical and experiential varieties of knowledge are explored.

Like Green, I have adopted a methodology appropriate for this type of fieldwork. I also place myself, as one opposed to human suffering and authoritarianism, in the ethnography. With Scheper-Hughes (1992) I share a disdain for anthropologists who write ethnographies that are essentially autobiographies. This is certainly not my aim. I have included my own observations, fears, and experiences as a way of intuiting affective dimensions of the lives of Burmese with whom I associated, and I privilege the subjective and emotional content of the relationship involving informant, ethnographer, and environment.

Another similarity between my own and Green's (1998, 1999) work is that my aim when planning and commencing fieldwork was not to write about the state construction of affect. I had intended to understand how the cultural construction of mental illness is influenced by life under an authoritarian regime. I had assumed that violence would enter my informant narratives, and (following Nordstrom and Robben 1995) I was interested in violence as a dimension of daily existence. But my original aim gave way to a different one.

I arrived in Rangoon in May 1996 at the height of the yearly cycle of urban militarization, during the mango showers that signaled the imminent arrival of the monsoon period, and the cessation of many military activities until the end of the rains. I became fascinated by what I have called *military time*, that is, by the temporal topography of fear in Rangoon. The tension generated by the military spectacles was heightened by the "roadside talks" given each weekend by Aung San Suu Kyi. She had been released from house arrest one year earlier, and a public alliance was developing between her party, the National League for Democracy, and an increasingly bold student movement. This conjunction of events meant that Rangoon was ablaze with rumors. Most of the events recounted in this chapter occurred between May and December 1996 in urban and peri-urban Rangoon.

It is not ethically feasible to conduct a detailed ethnographic study of Burmese everyday life at this time. Physical danger threatens participants in this study if their names are revealed. Jail terms await those who speak with foreigners, host foreigners in their homes overnight without permission, or gather in groups to speak about politics. Accordingly, in narratives, informant statements, and life histories, I use fictitious Burmese names and identify individuals only by approximate age and sometimes by occupation. I have used names common among the ethnic Burman majority population, not to make any kind of political statement, but to protect informants by avoiding references to ethnic identities. In Rangoon I draw material from a close circle of female friends in their twenties to late forties, and in the forcibly relocated townships that ring Rangoon and Mandalay, I include material from mainly female acquaintances of the same age range. I also include data from patient interviews at the Rangoon Psychiatric Hospital and the Rangoon Drug Rehabilitation Unit.

What I cannot include here are many of the rich details of everyday life that anthropologists learn from engaging in participant-observation fieldwork. Such detail was certainly available to me, but it would have been irresponsible of me to be known as having more than a passing acquaintance with particular Burmese. Although I ate, shopped, and spent time at pagodas with Burmese friends, such encounters were not frequent and never took place more than once at any given location. This situation and the restrictions placed upon foreigners by the military government mean that there are holes in the data that I hope to be able to fill at a later date. For example, I lack data from military interviewees. I must admit to being too scared to risk talking to military personnel. For the same reason, I avoided known democracy activists and instead focused on the majority poor populations of the largest cities. Like my informants, my understandings of the mechanics and construction of fear and violence are partial and fragmentary (Seremetakis 1991).

I do not pretend to depict an unbiased or total picture but rather I try to present an anthropological analysis in which, through my own experiences of fear, I intuit the experiences of Burmese people whom I have come to know well. In so doing, I argue that emotional knowledge arising from similar (never identical) circumstances can be important, in this case, necessary, for an analysis of fear in everyday life. This is because fear is a subject that cannot be discussed openly and that is usually acknowledged only in its absence. As Jennifer Leehey (2000) has found in Burma, it is in spaces of absences that meanings proliferate. Such absence can even be read at the bodily level; for example, as Burmese people sit motionless and expressionless at forced mass rallies. Unable to support the regime or to openly resist it, they hollow out their lived experience and present themselves as lifeless wooden dolls for the regime to use. For the anthropologist to interrupt this rigidly controlled self-construction and ask about fear is not ethical; it disrupts the reconfiguring of time that Burmese people assiduously enact, as I show in the following section. It is my contention that fear is inherently temporal and that time is an aspect of everyday life that can be controlled and, indeed, is carefully manipulated by the regime's propagandists.

Demarcating the Battlefield in Time and Space

Since the failed democracy uprising in 1988, the Burmese military council has been hard at work creating what it considers to be a Buddhist authoritarian utopia. Accordingly it has renamed Burma the "Union of Myanmar," with "Union" being a euphemism for the coercive process of subjugating Burma's many ethnic minorities under the control of the military council. From 1989 to 1997 the council was known by the acronym SLORC (State Law and Order Restoration Council). As of late 1997 it has been known as the SPDC (State Peace and Development Council). An important factor in the creation of imagined communities is what Benedict Anderson has described as "temporal homogeneity" (Anderson 1991). In the case of the Union of Myanmar, however, it is violence that has become a temporal marker and that creates a shared system of meanings and understandings. Allen Feldman argues that etching bodies with the power of the State changes the concept of time for the affected individuals, that time becomes a mimetic and recursive faculty. But in defining the manner in which individuals perceive time, Feldman also believes that the State is cut off from a secret history of the body, that it is not privy to this sense of time, this "clandestine history of alterity" (Feldman 1991: 80). Through violence and the promise of violence, the Burmese State creates new "national" boundaries within which temporality is altered. The sense of time that the military regime creates includes the historicizing myths of State power and dominance that we see embedded in State monuments and spectacles such as Armed Forces Day.

However, the clandestine history of alterity in this new state of emergency is also visible in the scars, broken teeth, and other bodily markers of imprisonment and torture inscribed on the bodies of Burmese. It is also evident in the way in which Burmese conceive time as flowing differently from the birth of the state of emergency, the eighth of the eighth, nineteen-eighty-eight, the day known as "the Riot" or "the Strike."

"The Strike" is a temporal marker evident in language, illness, and life histories. Although the failed pro-democracy uprising occurred over several weeks, many Burmese mark the "Four-Eights," the day that the military opened fire upon the protesters, as the day that marked the end of a certain way of life. Prisoners were released from jail (as there were no wardens present), property was damaged, work ceased, and many people, especially students, left the country for fear of their lives. Some of these students fled to the jungles where many contracted malaria and some subsequently died. With the formation of the SLORC, whole neighborhoods were disassembled and relocated. Thus, to many people the end of the demonstrations meant an end to their old way of life, neighborhood, some of their friends and family, their land, occupations, and so on (Lintner 1990a). Universities remained closed for several years and the economic crisis deepened leading to more unemployment. A year before the uprising, on September 5, 1987, the regime had seized the assets of many people and devalued the currency by 60 to 80 percent, pauperizing whole communities overnight (Carey

1997: 7). Members of the upper class suffered under the new regime, the class most intimidating to a fledgling dictatorship. In the forcibly relocated townships there were no services or amenities and, of course, no jobs.

Not only are events dated as to their proximity to the uprising (such as "It was one year after the Strike"), but time is also conceived to move differently. Time no longer "flows," it now "pools." There is no sense of progression from one season or cycle to the next, rather there is a spinning out of the same set of circumstances into the future. The population comprises a nation in waiting as Schwarz (1994) suggested of Indonesia during the Suharto era. The population is waiting for democracy, freedom, and employment, but it is also waiting for violence. For example, during the rainy season, political action is "planned" rather than enacted. Burma is heavy with the continued expectation that "something will happen." The time framework is conceived in terms of "waiting on events." There is a Burmese term, *mou: khoude,* which means both to take shelter from the monsoon rains and also to suspend operations, especially military operations, for the duration of the rainy season. The rainy season is a tense period, during which people wait for a sudden moment, when, as one Burmese civil servant explained to me, "a spark could ignite." Since 1988 the urban landscape has become charged with the possibility of violence and the uneasy silence of waiting.

Military Time

The military maintains fear and an atmosphere of emergency through two temporal methods. One is by creating a fear of the Other, whether a neocolonial presence, a foreigner, an internal traitor, or simply change and difference. Vigilance (*nou: kja: hmu*) is the term the regime uses most often to denote a continual heightened level of wariness in the face of threats by the Other. Burmese are admonished to stay on alert, to be ever ready for unspecified acts by "Others." Failure to do so could lead to a loss of independence such as happened under British colonization. The second temporal strategy adopted by the regime (having tried to paralyze the population into inaction) is to point out that the only safe pathway for the Union of Myanmar is progress, as defined by the military. The regime claims to be the ultimate arbiter of what must be preserved in Burma and what must give way to their dystopian, authoritarian view of "progress." To this end, institutions such as the Ministry and University of Culture were created to preserve an essential Burmese identity, and progress is presented to the populace at annual military spectacles that display both the consumer objects and military infrastructure that will create a secure and modern nation.

Burmese, then, experience time in a variety of ways and these experiences are discontinuous. In the public sphere, State discourse about progress and modernity has as its aim the overriding of other forms of purposive action. But not only must the population go forward in time in the manner dictated by the regime, Burmese people must live in a continual state of battle readiness, always prepared to leap into the breach to defend the Motherland against traitors and outsiders. The temporal aspect of fear, of always living in the current state of emergency, is twinned with exhortations to the population to look towards the past only in the manner prescribed by the various self-appointed "Culture" experts. Certain aspects of ethnic Burman and Theravada Buddhist history are preserved for posterity in State spectacles and rituals in which the military plays a pivotal role. Only one version of the past, present, and future is imagined, a monolithic temporality that brokers no dissent, no chronological deviance. In the following section I describe the affective dimensions of these authoritarian strategies.

The State Construction of Affect

The sheer weight of fear imposed upon Burmese leads them to respond outwardly with inertia. A number of emotions including suspicion, distrust, and fear have been described as part of the inner experience of living in a state of emergency. Margaret Lock has pointed out that such emotions can be profitably analyzed via an examination of the politics of embodied emotion (Lock 1993: 139).[2] I am particularly interested in the collective, communal aspects of affect. Arjun Appadurai, for example, has made a study of the "community of sentiment" generated through the conscious application of praise to "create a chain of communications of feeling, not by unmediated empathy between the emotional 'interiors' of specific individuals but by recourse to a shared, and relatively fixed set, of public gestures" (Appadurai 1990: 107). The bonds of sentiment which praise creates are an example, not only of the cultural construction of affect, but also of the politics of everyday life as they are constructed and operate in the public domain (110). The political construction of affect thus lies at the intersection of experience, body, politics, and discourse. In the previous section I have argued that violence has become an arbiter of such domains, and in this section I wish to pursue the effect of violence, namely, the State's construction of fear and terror, upon Burmese people.

Linda Green has written of the circulation of objects and symbols of war, terror, and domination in the Guatemalan altiplano and has captured the affective tone created by such routinization of oppression in conjunction with the lingering emotional effects of terror and torture such as grief and economic impoverishment (Green 1999). In a similar way, Delvecchio Good and Good (1988) have written of the affective tone set and mandated by the Iranian state as one of mourning and sobriety.

Both Taussig and Jenkins document how the state constructs terror through the personification of affects such that they become "things-in-themselves" (Jenkins 1991: 153, Taussig 1992: 5). [3] Terror becomes a self-perpetuating force that must be collectively denied in order for individuals to survive this particular form of psychological warfare. Taussig argues that "paranoia" is also constructed by the state through techniques of silencing and by the "strategic use of uncertainty and mystery" (1992: 16–17, 26).

The Burmese military regime deliberately creates a number of collective affective states as voiced in the "People's Desire" ideology. The State is conscious of its ability to manipulate emotions. In fact, the Department of Psychological Warfare within the Ministry of Defense is devoted to the State construction of affect, its collaborator in propaganda being the Ministry of Information. A series of affective tones are set, including the need for defense and alertness against foreign invasion and the defilement of Burmese culture and morals. Opposition leader Aung San Suu Kyi, a victim of assassination attempts, incarceration, and "house arrest," has written about the emotions that the Burmese regime so successfully generates. She comments that in Burma there are many kinds of fear, including "fear of imprisonment, fear of torture, fear of death, fear of losing friends, family, property or means of livelihood, fear of poverty, fear of isolation, fear of failure. . . . It is not easy for a people conditioned by fear under the iron rule of the principle that might is right to free themselves from the enervating miasma of fear. Yet even under the most crushing state machinery courage rises up again and again, for fear is not the natural state of civilized man" (1990: 184).

Fear is the most common emotion constructed by the regime. At times its generation is an incidental, unplanned side effect of the regime's policies, but the majority of the time, the regime deliberately uses strategic and symbolic violence to engender fear and terror. Propaganda and State spectacles are strategically used to make the regime's claims to absolute authority more persuasive to the Burmese people. These strategies perpetuate fear among the general population, a major element in the disabling of fifty million Burmese by a small military elite.

Fear

Fear is most commonly experienced as a distortion and disorientation of perspective. It gives everyday life a surreal dimension that emphasizes negative aspects to such a large extent that thoughts involving the future are flattened and silenced. These thoughts are replaced by wild, black fantasies that colonize both the waking world and the dream world. Fear is intimately associated with time. As a response to a future possibility, it is inherently temporal. In generating fear, the military confuses, distorts, and controls time with the aim of stopping Burmese people from imagining futures other than the one mandating their incorporation into an authoritarian state.

This disorientation coincides with the topography of fear and terror I mentioned above, climaxing at times of military spectacles and mass arrests. For example, during the tense months of the military buildup of forces in Rangoon and Mandalay (December 1996 to March 1997), I, along with many Burmese, experienced an array of feelings triggered by the State's strategic use of symbolic violence and aggression. Such tactics included the prominent deployment of tanks around the city as well as barbed wire, roadblocks and barricades, checkpoints manned by soldiers with flak jackets, and bayonet-wielding troops ostensibly searching the city for land mines. At such times of urban crisis, fear creates thoughts, scenarios, actions, and nightmares that are out of proportion to the actual likelihood of an individual being caught up in political violence.

My first indication that political violence was creating terror came from a conversation with a friend, Ma Khin Nu, a young woman recently graduated from university. She lives a carefully regulated life, chaperoned by her mother and grandmother. After a few weeks of getting to know each other well, I ventured the subject of the political situation. I made the following field note of our conversation:

Last night I asked Nu Nu about the "situation." She whispered that she was very afraid. She was very disturbed by my questions and couldn't get to sleep that night. The next morning she told me that she hadn't slept at all and was worried about what she'd told me. She had told me only that she is afraid because of the love she bears Aung San Suu Kyi and that (her eyes glinted as she thought about telling me this) she knew Aung San Suu Kyi's phone number. Sometimes, when she is sure no one is listening, she recites it to herself. This is her personal form of resistance, and revealing it to someone for the first time has terrified her and left her sleepless.

This conversation was in some ways a watershed in Ma Khin Nu's life. Realizing that she had trusted someone, over the next year she began to covertly listen to the BBC broadcasts (in Burmese) on a short wave radio, involving her family in her subversive activities. Aung San Suu Kyi's telephone number is forbidden knowledge by the regime, but once she acknowledged it as such, it became possible for Ma Khin Nu to seek out other forbidden forms of knowledge. Although still fearful, in imagining an alternate future Ma Khin Nu came to believe that the regime's control in the present might not be hegemonic.

My second indication of the State's construction of terror came from a conversation with a middle-aged friend, Daw Shwe Shwe, who has been involved in active but extremely careful resistance to the regime's policies for many years. Relatives and members of her circle of friends have been imprisoned for daring to agitate for democracy and she knows well the fear generated by opposing the regime. She spoke of the everyday dimensions of fear in urban Burma: "Paranoia is so widespread you don't think about it anymore. We all live in this delusion. It's blanketed all around us, you surround yourself in this abnormal world where this is not an abnormal way to live."

These two conversations, coming within a few days of each other, posed a difficult anthropological problem: how could I access Burmese experiences of fear when speaking about it only serves to compound people's fear? Burmese people don't talk about fear, a strategy that enables them not to think about it, and not thinking about fear is crucial to successful functioning on an everyday basis.

Burmese people consider expressing emotion, especially by allowing emotions to play across the face, distasteful. Expressed anger, in particular, is considered a likely sign of madness. It is crucial for their survival that Burmese show only "appropriate" emotions when in public. Because they find feigning enthusiasm for the junta exceedingly difficult, the vast majority of Burmese I have met survive by adopting a blank exterior persona: listless eyes in wooden bodies. I think of this persona as, in Madeleine Albright's phrase, a "Burmese Daze" (Albright 1995). Not only is fear inaccessible through participant observation and the eliciting of interview data, it also raises serious ethical questions for the anthropologist. Is it ethical to ask questions about a subject that will heighten fear, cause insomnia and worry, and break through the carefully constructed mental barriers that filter the regime's propaganda and fear-making exercises?

Urban Burmese are well aware of the ways in which the military council deliberately constructs affect. Many are aware of the existence of the Department of Psychological Warfare and of the identities behind the pen names attached to the flood of propaganda writings in the media. This subject came up in a conversation I had with several student-activists in the context of the effect my questions were having on them in this atmosphere of "terror as usual." The ethics of fieldwork in such conditions are extremely difficult, and the consequences of unintentional, naive, or unethical behavior can be magnified a thousand-fold. During this particular conversation we spoke about the ripples of fear that my questions generated. One man said to me: "Your talking to me produces this kind of fear (*sei' chau'cha: de*). This feeling gives me goose bumps. It is a little scary because the more you think, the worse it becomes. It is based on information that you receive."

We discussed this subject for a few minutes, as well as the literal translation of the term used to describe fear in this instance. In direct translation the term *sei' chau'cha: de* means something arising from nothing, in the sense of a small stream or brook that emerges from a tiny hole in a rock or boulder. *Sei' chau'cha: de* implies a tiny release of fear that does not emerge as a result of anything physical or an actual event but, rather, arises from thinking—from the mind. I have found that the only ethical way to speak to Burmese people about political violence and fear is to make clear that I wish to discuss this subject and that such discussion will likely cause those with whom I speak worry (*sou: jeinde*) and will lead to the resurfacing of memories and fear. I then leave it for informants to choose whether or not to go ahead with such a discussion at a future date, and we continue with our present conversation, knowing that what we say now will not generate a small stream or trickle of fear. At a later date, and after weighing the risks and consequences, informants can choose whether to speak with me about more sensitive topics, cognizant of the fact that such conversations will most likely lead to the bubbling up of fear and other emotions that are usually tightly suppressed.

In stark contrast to this approach, the State deliberately constructs affect. Burmese experience this as the intentional evoking of a small stream of fear to serve as a constant deterrent to behavior disallowed by the regime. The following statements given by the students illustrate their understandings of the creation of affect:

The government makes people feel this because of the propaganda it puts out. It causes a lack of sleep, a weakness (*thwei: chau'cha: de*).

When people are arrested the government puts them into separate cells so that they can feel this. So you don't know what the other person is saying and you are always worried about what they are revealing.

This is how they work—by putting informants around everywhere. They make you feel paranoid. Your family and teachers become paranoid about you because the government makes them responsible for you.

It is clear from these statements that the State constructs affect through its use of propaganda, its tactics of arrest, incarceration, and interrogation, and its strategic placement of informers. The final statement refers to the continuous declarations of the danger posed by students and other internal subversive elements to the security and well-being of the nation and by their links to wider, chaotic groups (such as expatriate pro-democracy groups). These pronouncements have occurred at the same time that the government created a law stipulating mandatory jail terms for parents whose children, and teachers whose students, take part in anti-government activities. This has resulted in teachers and parents monitoring their children's activities, and the students have interpreted this as a lack of trust and a "paranoid" attitude on the part of adults.

Just as the State constructs the affect of fear trickling like a stream through the mountains, so does the ethnographer working in cultures of terror. To attempt to address this dilemma I have adopted several strategies. The first is to deemphasize the importance given in recent years in the anthropological literature to text and speech within narratives. Gaps, silences, and omissions are key markers of the experience of fear. Like pain, fear is primarily felt; it breaks down meaning, inhibits actions, and defies the ability of language to hold its experiential weight. Robert Desjarlais (1992: 90) has recognized that in Nepal pain "clings to the body." I cannot articulate so finely how fear is sensed in the Burmese context except to say that I believe it is buried, as deeply as Burmese can manage, within the body. Fear is not normally revealed, except through its absence. From those few informants who entrusted me with their safety and the safety of their families, I have collected narrative data on this subject.[4] These individuals understood that consciously articulating their feelings about fear would bring it to the surface, that it would trickle through their conscious and sleeping moments, and that they would live with their new sense of disquiet in the weeks and months ahead. Their testimonies were often given in their homes on sunny afternoons, or in deserted places, when fear seemed farthest away.

In the following sections I demonstrate a second strategy for transmitting the experience of fear in Burma by juxtaposing Burmese silences with my own feelings of fear. My aim is to intuit, through my experiences, how Burmese people may be experiencing fear. Although I felt solidarity with Burmese friends at being cowed by the same regime, I am less vulnerable than they and thus able to articulate my feelings of fear. I did not need to construct such elaborate filters to perception because I was free to leave Burma and could eventually shake off the affective tone set by the military. Although fearful, the community of sentiment generated in the everyday life of dictatorship is, in the final analysis, only temporary and intermittent for me. I am free to imagine a future that is not controlled by the dictatorship.

A Fieldworker's Fear

Within a few months of living in Rangoon, I was caught up in fear, evident in my own suspiciousness, covertness, and nightmares. Toward the end of my fieldwork I made the following field note:

The drink truck is labeled "Loi Htei," but every time I see it my heart seems to stop momentarily, and in that silence I force myself to look again, and I realize that yet again I have made a false connection between a drink company (Loi Htei) and the dreaded Riot Police (Lon Htein). Often the riot police dress up in other uniforms, such as traffic police at the Kokaing junction. As everyone knows, however, traffic police and regular soldiers are reed thin, but these guys have muscle and are twice the size.

The Lon Htein often manned barricades at the corner of my street, armed with machine guns sometimes fitted with bayonets and wearing bulletproof vests. I recalled Feldman's statement that "interspersed with mimetic violence are beatings that serve to diffuse the boundaries between the real and the imaginary" (1991: 122).

This fear increased when I came into direct contact with the institutions that support the regime, as the following incident illustrates. In late November 1996, when the junta was still permitting Aung San Suu Kyi's speeches, I was visiting the Traditional Medicine Department, where I had (I thought) established a degree of rapport with senior staff. The Director seemed very agitated. He asked me if I had been going to Aung San Suu Kyi's house and, when I replied in the negative, if I had been involved in subversive matters. He then refused my request to speak to patients alone, saying that perhaps my Burmese was not good enough to understand the subtleties of the language. I offered to bring along an interpreter to assist with those patients who spoke dialects. The Director replied that many different English interpretations are possible for every Burmese word and that an interpreter may give me politically subversive translations. Later I made this field note:

When I returned from the Traditional Medicine Department I felt shaken up, as if I was an insignificant Hobbit facing an overwhelming evil, both in size and wickedness. This feeling was not in perspective at the time, but moments such as these became common as I passed soldiers in various parts of the city. My husband noted that we always avoided that main road leading to the Shwedagon Pagoda because of the silent intimidation involved in walking past the military barracks. But U Wizara also became a road I wanted to avoid because of the stop checks and the military presence, as well as being the address of the Traditional Medicine Department, which also felt like a dangerous place to me now.

Such exaggeration of danger becomes clearer when it is articulated by groups or collectivities. When the government closed the universities, parents began sending their children into the countryside to stay with relatives. There was terror and panic and a rush to leave Rangoon, even though at that time military forces had beaten only a small group of students and sprayed them with water cannons. When Maung Tin, a young man I knew from Mandalay, called his mother to tell her he would be staying in Rangoon for an extra week, she whispered urgently, "Come home now!" and hung up the phone, too terrified to speak any longer. I do not mean to downplay the actual atrocities perpetrated by the dictatorship but, rather, I want to draw attention to the powerful impact that the State construction of terror can have on everyday life under conditions of dictatorship.

The State's deterritorialization of fear by techniques such as the reconstruction of urban space using the bodies of soldiers and the weapons of urban warfare (such as tanks and barricades) is exacerbated by rumor. The desire for knowledge in urban Burma is primarily fulfilled by the passing of rumors. By trading rumors individual Burmese can accrue social capital (status, prestige, respect, and personal power). Moreover, in Burma rumors are extremely important because they are one of the few forms of mundane information that allow individuals and families to speculate on outcomes, to gamble on courses of action, to assess options, and to weigh probabilities. De Certeau (1985: 143) notes that rumor crystallizes and reifies diverse opinions, that it "is always injunctive, the initiator and result of a leveling of space, the creator of mass motions that shore up an order by adding make-believe to make-do or -be. Narratives diversify; rumors totalize. Although there is always an oscillation from one to the other . . . narratives are becoming more private and fading into out-of-the-way neighborhoods, families, or individuals, while rumor is rampant."

In urban Burmese spaces, rumor has become a dominant form of discourse for several reasons. First, rumor presents an impression of clarity. It is a sense-making device in the disorienting environment of the everyday state of emergency. Second, rumors construct a shared social geography, a kind of city code intelligible to those who live within the temporal and spatial boundaries of the state of emergency. Third, rumor creates a sense of intimacy that is otherwise impossible under the regime. Narrative is personal and embedded in one's own experience and therefore inherently dangerous to voice in public. But rumor is always about others and about events with which one is not necessarily connected. As De Certeau notes, rumor is rampant in the public domain. It is, however, also a carrier of terror, often confirming the individual's worst fears. The numbers of demonstrators or opposition members arrested, the number of riot police or tanks, as well as the number of people killed or tortured, can be exaggerated in the rapid and whispered exchange of rumors.

Perhaps the most disorienting dimension of the State's construction of fear and terror is the penetration of these emotions into the dream world. For several weeks after leaving Burma, I continued to have violent nightmares, dreams that were revisited during the writing of this book. One night after dining with an American and a British friend, both interested in the Burmese political situation, and we were followed first on foot and then by car, by Military Intelligence (MI). The agents were obvious and unguarded in their surveillance, and it was not difficult to escape them. The incident, however, caused me a sleepless night and a mad scramble to get my field notes safely out of the country.

On another occasion, my husband and I photographed the military roadblocks on University Avenue that barricaded Aung San Suu Kyi's compound. Returning to our apartment, we had an afternoon nap, and we both dreamed vividly. This was how I described my dream to my husband: "We were having an afternoon nap and they [MI] followed us, and I woke up (as I did in actuality), and you'd been shot to death, and I had several bullet wounds. That's when I knew that being here does bad things to your mind." My husband awoke at the same time I did, also shaken by the vivid violence of his dream. He dreamed that after taking the photographs we were followed by Military Intelligence, who burst into our room. Despite the ardent efforts many Burmese make to escape the politicization of their lives, such markers of the regime's oppression as soldiers, murder, and military intelligence impress themselves so deeply on one's experience that, even in sleep, they are inescapable.

Fear itself is finely nuanced in urban Burma, although the regime is almost certainly unaware of the multi-textured effect it is creating. For example, fear translates to terror and panic at certain moments, but at other times it is tinged with menace, hope/excitement, certainty, and rigidity. By certainty I mean the feeling engendered when you stand in front of a soldier with his rifle aimed at you and you know, with certainty, that the man at the other end of the weapon, himself a tool of the State, will kill you if you advance any farther. This knowledge feels viscerally lodged; it is not a stomach-churning feeling, but more like a cold, sharp stone lodged among your vital organs. At other times when one is confronted by the regime's weapons, fear translates into rigidity, a paralysis. Fear can also register in reaction to an omnipresent menace, for example, when you drive or walk past an open gate or turn a corner and are confronted by a physical manifestation of State power, such as a tank. But it is not simply the tank, a brooding store of potential lethality, that menaces; it is also the military personnel with their reflective dark glasses, helmets, and boots who generate menace. Your eyes involuntarily move over the reflective surfaces to the matte gun, which seems to absorb your gaze. It is hard to stop staring at it. In that instant you are once again assailed by the renewed realization (made dull by the continuous nature of the state of emergency) that this is not a joke, not a game, and not an inflation or paranoid turn of thought. You are shocked with the renewed realization that these men are prepared to kill you.

Pressed Down

The various kinds of fear, whether tinged with anxiety, certainty, men-ace, or rigidity, can all lead to rage. When people's (especially young people's) dissatisfaction with the regime reaches a crescendo, as it did when the regime curtailed Aung San Suu Kyi's roadside speeches and again when the universities were closed, there is a great need to control this rage. As James Scott (1992: 63) has commented: "In any established system of domination, it is not just a question of masking one's feelings and producing the correct speech acts and gestures in their place. Rather, it is often a question of controlling what would be a natural impulse to rage, insult, anger, and the violence that such feelings prompt . . . Conformity in the face of domination is thus occasionally—and unforgettably—a question of suppressing a violent rage in the inter-est of oneself and loved ones."

Frustration can lead to another dimension of fear, in which "hope/expectation" is implicit and terror is tinged with surprise and suspense. The fear that many Rangoon residents experienced during the student demonstrations in December 1996 was colored by anticipation of a pos-sible end to the continual "waiting for something to happen" feeling that even now continues to pervade life in the state of emergency. Such anticipation is only possible if one believes that there are certain ways of behaving and modes of action that are safe from military scrutiny.

I am aware that this is a contentious issue in the literature (Nordstrom 1997), and scholars have argued that to be extremely afraid, to be in what Taussig (1987: 121) calls "the space of death," is to be too terrified to do anything at all (see also Daniel 1996; Scarry 1985). But that extremity of fear is not what I am referring to here. Instead, I am describing a situation in which the playing out of dangerous and fright-ening events breeds hope that change may occur. As described below, such hope is extinguished in cases where one is "beyond fear" (*lei'pja nge de, lei'pja lwin de' chei je' cha: de*). For example, when events result in the arrest of individuals, all hope is gone.

During the student demonstrations in December 1996, a frisson of quiet excitement existed, a barely repressed hope that things might change. This hope was palpable in the urban atmosphere. I asked many students about the combination of fear and excitement. They used the phrase "scared but hopeful" (*kjau'to. kjau'de, da bei me. hmjo lin.che' shi.de*) to describe the feeling they sensed in the broader community. For example, students described how members of the public took their license plates off their cars so as not be traceable by the regime. This was common practice in Rangoon, having occurred every weekend earlier in 1996 when people attended Aung San Suu Kyi's roadside talks. The license plates came off again in December, and cars drove up to student assemblies and left fruit and other food before driving off quickly. One student said, "On the sixth of December, someone drove by quickly and dropped 60,000 kyat onto our car bonnet then quickly drove away."[5] Another student noted that during the demonstrations taxi drivers all over Rangoon made it clear that they were not charging students fares. This allowed students to mobilize in different places all over the city. More importantly, it allowed them to disperse quickly without being followed.

Students agreed that being scared and being excited or filled with hope are compatible at certain times. One student observed, "During the uprising I was scared and worried all the time. But also, there is some hope that maybe, one day things will change and this can make it better." Another student noted, "I have been shot at and I have been scared. But you can overcome that because you are also excited. Because you are hopeful." Such conversations inevitably came back to a discussion of how one remains balanced on such emotional roller coasters. How does one attempt to not be scared all the time? Many Burmese respond by talking about "sense" (*khan za: hmu*), which I translate as the construction of affect. Burmese talk about the "sense" that the military council creates and how they strive to change or ignore this sense. In one student's words:

I was scared [during the demonstrations] all the time, because so many things were happening, but also hopeful when we were doing activist things. We also had to try everyday to change our sense. We played guitars. We listened to music. We are always trying to change our sense.

Burmese people have thus become experts—under monarchical and feudal rule, British colonization, and military dictatorship—in convincing themselves that so long as they act and speak in a few limited ways, they are safe from the daily onslaught of fear-making generated by those wielding political power. By not engaging in activities known to be dangerous (such as associating with the National League for Democracy, talking to outsiders, and so on) individuals remain free to explore other openings for action. Universities and monasteries are examples of spaces where, traditionally, a higher degree of liberal thought and action has been permitted than in the public domain. Not surprisingly, these are the areas where the regime has concentrated its surveillance and repression. The December 1996 student demonstrations resulted in the junta again closing the universities and cutting off access to many monasteries in Rangoon and Mandalay. The fear-tinged-with-anticipation evident in the 1996 student demonstrations speaks to the ability of some Burmese to imagine a future free from military control, and to plan action in the present to achieve such a future.

The student demonstrations, like the "Four 9s" planned revolution, ultimately succumbed to the regime's improved methods of domination.[6] Burmese people commonly use the gesture of the thumb pressed into the palm when referring to the military, symbolizing the "over-the-top" force that the regime uses, its brutality. This gesture is accompanied by the use of the phrase "pressed down," indicative of the experience of feeling trapped and pinned down. A Burmese psychiatric patient told me that he felt as if "the whole world pressed down on me." This is the sentiment expressed in the gesture. People also express a feeling of claustrophobia, described to me as "being in a fish bowl." One woman recounted "the intimidation of waiting outside her [Aung San Suu Kyi's] house—like being in a fish bowl, the way they succeed in making the frightened feel even more frightened." A journalist described to me the enormous fear involved in waiting outside Aung San Suu Kyi's house as like "running the gauntlet." It is a fear of constant and intense surveillance.

On Being Beyond Fear

Being extremely scared or frightened is experienced in Burma as a shrinking of the soul (conceived and represented as a butterfly). The decreasing size of the butterfly spirit (*lei'pja*) within the body is caused by excessive worry. The following excerpt from an interview I conducted with a tertiary educated, urban man, Ya Kyaw, in his early thirties, illustrates this concept:

YK: If you are too scared, you become worried about everything. You can't sleep, you can't eat. Your soul shrinks inside your body (*lei'pja nge de, lei'pja lwin de' chei je' cha: de*). It becomes smaller and then bad things can easily enter or be absorbed because there is no resistance to it.

MS: What kinds of entities?

YK: Ghosts, witches, black magicians.

MS: What kind of bad things can happen to you when you are in this state?

YK: You collapse, you can't travel, you have family problems, and you break things.

Two men who attended the central university campuses in Rangoon and who were active in the 1988 "Strike" as student leaders and organizers also exemplify this kind of extreme terror. One young man, thirty years old, articulate, witty, and urbane, spoke to me of his escape from Rangoon:

[I felt extreme fear] when I was trying to leave Rangoon. I had been arrested and was trying to escape before they arrested me again. I was on a boat and the Navy stopped our boat. (I was already sort-of arrested). I was pretending to be a sailor. I was registered on the manifest as a sailor. They searched the boat. I pretended I was a clerk. I thought I was really finished. It was very unusual. The Navy doesn't search this kind of boat. I tried to be calm and normal so that it wouldn't look suspicious. I was also worried for the other two students on the boat. And then they let the boat go. I think they bribed them. Oh, I felt so relieved!

The second young man, thirty-two years old, is diminutive, subdued, and thin almost to the point of being gaunt. He had been tortured by military intelligence because of his student activism. During the interview he sat quietly with arms folded and legs crossed at the ankles. We were sitting among friends, eating papaya and drinking beer. During our conversations, especially when others were discussing their shared experiences, his eyes become a little unfocused and he seemed to draw in upon himself. He spoke succinctly, quietly, and slowly of the time he most felt extreme fear or terror:

[I felt like this] during the 1988 Strike at the Bohtataung Pagoda. The Lon Htein put me into their covered van on the way to Insein Prison. I had a very high degree of fear at that time. I thought that all my lives were finished. I thought I would die or be disabled and I thought my life was finished. All of my hopes totally collapsed. I had nothing left.

In previous sections I have been concerned with fear and anticipation, but it is clear from these vignettes that there comes a time when all hope is extinguished and only vulnerability is left. In anticipation-fear, Burmese believe that forward momentum can be maintained if certain pathways are avoided. In vulnerability-fear, however, Burmese people do not know which direction is safe and feel that any movement may bring unwanted consequences. I turn now to a consideration of this continual state of dis-ease, the feeling of vulnerability.

Fear and Vulnerability

A defining characteristic of the 1962–88 socialist regime of General Ne Win was the arbitrariness of punitive actions visited on the population and the resulting feelings of vulnerability that such arbitrary cruelty generated. The current regime also tries to create a sense of arbitrariness and unease through its terror-making tactics and the strategic use of political violence; it attempts to enshrine disorder and chaos in the context of an everyday state of emergency. Such a strategy has disastrous consequences for Burmese because the vulnerability they feel leads to paralysis—a lack of desire or ability to move in any direction.

Their fear of surveillance, of being "crushed," and of being unable to suppress rage, culminates in inaction and in alienation for the Burmese, who have become a nation of individuals unable and unwilling to trust each other.[7] Most Burmese born after 1950 fondly remember school as a time of few cares, when trust was never an issue between friends. After leaving school however, they seldom form friendships based on trust, and political conversations take place among old school friends and some family members only. These breakdowns in interpersonal relations also inhibit the formation of, and trust in, community organizations that might serve as friendship and support networks. Aung San Suu Kyi (1997a: x) has written that "the greatest obstacle in the way of peace and progress in Burma is a lack of trust: trust between the government and the people, between different ethnic groups, between the military and civilian forces. Trust is a precious commodity that is easily lost, but hard indeed to take root."

The military dictatorship thus effectively manages to isolate Burmese people into small knots of friendship. The sense of isolation people feel is commonly expressed as "they're [MI] always listening, you can't trust anyone" (*thwei: a: lwe de', sei' macha ja.bu:*). As Daw May Ohn, a professional woman, told me:

If you speak about politics people become silent or make a silly laugh. If you don't call it fear, then what do you call it? Just now, when someone bought our things, we stopped our conversation. I don't want them [my friends] to know what they don't need to know. It's a formula.

This situation has become so serious that Burmese people in their teens and early twenties don't even consider trusting other Burmese, as illustrated by this excerpt from an interview I conducted with Ma Win Win Mae, a young middle-class businesswoman:

WWM: The people who don't have strong feelings for any particular party and who want promotions, and who want to "make face," they inform a lot.

MS: Who to?

WWM: They can inform to the people who are in charge of any government department and with whom they are friendly. They cannot inform to people who don't know them.

MS: Is it hard to make friends and trust people?

WWM: I never think in terms of trust and not trusting. I make friends with everyone, just chitchat. I give the impression that I am very kind and friendly. But I

don't have anything on a deep level with them . . . because you don't trust anyone except yourself. If anyone tells us, in a taxi, for example, that the government is very stupid, or something similar, you just keep quiet, you just listen to
it. You'd better not trust that the taxi driver is a supporter of [opposition] politics. Maybe they are from BSI [Bureau of Special Investigations] or SB [Special
Branch]. Vegetable sellers and taxi drivers that are really informers, they are
legal informers. These kinds of stories are very common. I've never met such a
person, but it's best to stay very quiet if you want to stay well.

Alienation and vulnerability are perhaps the most common ways
urban Burmese experience fear on an everyday basis. They feel vulnerable to economic forces, to the arbitrariness of institutions, to the military, and, of course, to arrest and interrogation without recourse, to
which almost all of the population are liable.

The Generals' disastrous economic mismanagement forces people to
engage in the informal economy in order to survive. Official salaries and
pensions are not adequate for the necessities of a family's survival. Commodities such as fuel are rationed and often run out, meaning that fuel
is one of many essential items that must be purchased on the black market. By making such purchases on the black market, people save money,
which can then be used as "line-money" (bribes) to facilitate business
ventures, access to education, and employment opportunities. An enormous amount of fear is generated by the knowledge that at any time a
Burmese person can "legally" be arrested for his or her illegal black
market transactions. The higher up the social and employment ladder
one is (if one is a public servant), the more access one has to the informal economy. The risks are higher because of the amount of money
involved, but the opportunities for making money are also greater. This
financial and economic uncertainty leads to feelings of vulnerability and
a tendency for people to stop making plans for the future. Families are
always living in the present, uncertain when or if they will suffer the ire
of the military. Most Burmese agree however that the degree of arbitrariness of enforcement of economic illegalities is slightly less now than it
was under the capricious Ne Win junta.

A related sense of vulnerability is created because of the complete lack
of trust Burmese people have in their institutions. This may have long-
term effects upon the notion of civil society in Burma. What has tran-
spired in the banking sector is a good example of distrust leading to
disengagement from institutions. The military regimes have, at various
times, wiped out the higher denomination currency notes, closed banks,
and refused to allow people to withdraw money. This has provided the
junta with hard currency but led people to invest in gold and store it
in private homes. As Ma Khin Nu told me, prior to the 1988 currency
devaluation, her wise grandmother had converted her kyat to gold bars
and even now continues to hide them under her bed.

A general lack of law and order is also experienced in institutions other than banks. Because all institutions are nationalized, people consider them to be compromised. A few examples are germane. The enormous fervor over lottery tickets in Burma is evidence of both a strong belief in the miraculous and the desperation of even the poorest families in the forcibly relocated townships, who spend money essential for family survival on Thai lottery tickets (the Thai lottery is illegal in Burma). Ma Mya May, a teenage mother working as a prostitute in a relocated township, told me that: "If you want to smuggle things, or participate in the illegal lottery, you have to pay the local LORC [security office], the police, and so on. You always give line money."

Daw Thida Aung, a doctor in her thirties who works in the same township, told me that about 50 percent of her patients participate in the lottery. They buy one ticket at a time, for 10 kyat:

Some families "go crazy" and spend 10,000 kyat. People generally prefer the Thai lottery which is illegal but which gives much more prize money. It's illegal because they often can't repay the money and so people lose their money. The military, police, and doctors sell the tickets. You ask a trishaw driver where to buy it.

The involvement of the police and the military in bribery, corruption, and the black market has led to a complete lack of faith in "security"-oriented institutions. During 1996 inflation ran at around 40 percent per year, but this figure escalated dramatically in the latter half of 1997 and 1998 when the "Asian economic crisis" reached Burma. Civil servants' real salaries dropped dramatically, leaving them particularly reliant upon corruption. For example, urban residents on a daily basis encounter traffic police, who are among the civil servants most loathed by the public. Their salaries are so low they are reduced to stopping cars and blatantly demanding money from motorists. For several years now, the traffic police in Rangoon have said to motorists, "Give me tea money," meaning the amount of money generally spent at a teashop (anywhere from 15 to 40 kyat). This amount began to increase in 1997. U Ba Pe, a friend in his fifties, recounted to me a conversation he had had on the way to work that morning when stopped by a traffic officer. He said to the traffic officer: "Do you want tea money?" U Ba Pe was quite surprised to receive the reply: "No, not tea money, it's too little, give me beer money. Give me 500 kyat."

The vulnerability produced by a breakdown in institutional integrity has become routine, just another exigency of everyday life. U Min Oo, a sailor in his late thirties, commented on this in December 1996, during the student demonstrations. I asked him, "Are people frightened?" To which he replied:

It's about 50–50. They have Suu Kyi legally in jail so now everyone and the students are saying everyday, "Why, why, why?" Now I think things will be quiet. I think it's not the end. I think it's the beginning. [He points to the left] That's the President's Old Place—Ne Win's place. Things were very bad then. Now it is run by military men: his sons. So nothing has changed. The government is like an old song, you know? If you want something done, you pay money, they're mostly police.

Those who work within the regime also experience vulnerability and are forced to rely on cronyism and patron-client relations to secure positions. U Khin Maung Din, an educated man in his forties, explains this vulnerability as follows:

The problem is that a lot of these people who are in the government at the moment, their parents worked under the BSPP [Burma Socialist Programme Party] and people who are obscure would become a Minister later on. That's how Ne Win ruled the country, calling people from that kind of level. They became generals and thought they'd made it because they're smart. So if you have the right connections you can rise up. If there's a government change, then what they've worked for, all the contacts, they will lose it all. I'm talking about mid-rank officers; that's how they think.

Here U Khin Maung Din has expressed the need for public servants to establish personal ties within the bureaucracy and notes that careers are made or lost depending upon the fortunes of one's allies. There are, however, other aspects to public service life that contribute to insecurity on the part of public functionaries. Officials must do nothing wrong, which they accomplish in two ways: they adhere to the public service maxim "Don't do anything, don't get involved, don't get fired," and they strive to be "slorcier than the SLORC." This phrase means that public servants must appear to be even more zealous in their support of the State than the military junta itself. Especially at the higher levels of the government service, an extra degree of fear exists. The regime places low ranking officers at various levels within the public service both to ensure the loyalty of civil servants and to actually get things done, since nonmilitary personnel are too frightened to take any initiative whatsoever.

Vulnerability is thus generated through involvement in the black market, in the public service, and via an increased sense of insecurity due to a lack of faith in Burmese institutions. The greatest sense of vulnerability, however, is produced by people's lack of recourse to a fair justice system, as U Khin Maung Din explains in the following interview segment:

MS: Do you think the government controls people through fear?

KMD: (Yes), they do.

MS: How?

KMD: You have no law and order here, they can do whatever they like—they can arrest you and impose a sentence without any proof. That's how they do it, and people know that this is the case. There's no regulation that says I can't do it, there's no regulation that says I can do it. . . . I am not safe because there is no rule or law saying what I'm doing is right, or what I'm doing is wrong. . . . You are never safe because you can't do anything right. You're not safe, but I don't live in fear because of what may happen someday.

MS: Is this why you haven't become involved in the opposition?

KMD: I'm scared. I don't think this is the right climate to get involved. My father is dead against it. I have a skill, and I market it, it's all I have. The image I see of a politician (Ne Win doesn't go out or give public speeches), I just see him as a dictator with a gun. I'm scared because of the repercussions which would come to my whole family. My sister lost her job because my father was active in politics. I don't want my father to be pulled in for interrogation. My mother is not well. I know this is a dictatorship and I know well what a dictatorship is. . . . Sometimes our phone gets tapped. They can just come and take you away. This is what dictatorship is, and I hope by now, Monique, you know it too.

There is a seeming contradiction between U Khin Maung Din first denying he lives in fear and then, when pressed, revealing that he is scared. Denial is the most common reaction to fear in Burma: convincing oneself that there is no need to live in fear on a daily basis is essential to well-being. Another common reaction to questions about fear is laughter, again part of the process of ensuring that fear remains buried inside. Despite people's ongoing attempts to suppress it, however, fear rises readily to the surface where it is experienced in all of the varieties described above.

The powerlessness of Burmese people to control the situations that give rise to fear only compounds their sense of vulnerability. Two generations of Burmese have now grown up with the terror of the regime coming in the middle of the night to "search and seize," as U Winn explains:

When they [the military] come to your house, they come with a prison van. They normally inform the local authority. The local authority has power. They make them step out and then they seize them and come and surround the house and burst into all the rooms. They search and ask lots and lots of questions. "Put all your jewelry in a locked box." They take an inventory of all the things in the house, apprehend whomever they want to and take them away for interrogation.

The family never gets told what's going on until they see them [the detainees] back again.

As in most of Southeast Asia, Burma is full of stray dogs that bark and bite with little provocation. Sometimes these animals are crazed with hunger and pain, and the term "mad dog" has come to be used as a slang term for Military Intelligence. The barking of dogs at night has taken on an additional, sinister meaning related to Military Intelligence, as one veteran political opponent, U Aung Than, explains: "We never eat properly, we never sleep properly. We are always listening for the dogs barking because they [MI] come to get people at night."

The most common response to the State construction of fear and terror is silence: not silence in the sense of absence but in the sense of a numb calmness in the eye of a storm, a temporary relief from the surrounding terror. This numbness (silence and inactivity) is a conditioned response that allows Burmese to keep fear in the back of their minds and to focus carefully on the immediacy of everyday occurrences. In May 1996 I drove past Aung San Suu Kyi's house as people were arriving (including international media crews) for her weekly roadside speech (the speeches were stopped by the military later that year). I asked the fifty-year-old woman I was with, Daw Khin Me Yi, an English tutor, about the "situation." She answered, "Burmese people really want democracy," but she doubted it would ever happen. "Burmese people are not brave. Some are afraid, some are cowards." I asked her if the feeling in Rangoon now was one of fear, and she responded, "Yes, of course. And we have been trained to [fear] for twenty six years."

Another professional woman of the same age, Daw Myaq Thi, suggested that there are two main conditioned responses to terror. The first is the absolute lack of expectation. She stated that Burmese have learnt to get rid of "expectation" as a response to events. The second conditioned response is that of emotional flatness, a calm that emerges from the panic occasioned by terror of the military coming to arrest you:

"Please let it be a dream." You try to pray, but can't find the beginning, can't find the end. You swear it's the truth. If you were in a normal situation, you wouldn't be able to stand this sort of thing but if something is already happening and you are facing this, surprisingly you go very calm, ready to face the situation.

Such calmness surely is a serious long-term consequence of living under an authoritarian regime. This phenomenon of the mind becoming very calm is a significant strategy adopted by Burmese people to ameliorate the panic, vulnerability, and alienation characteristic of contemporary urban Burmese life. It is not difficult to imagine this same strategy being adopted on an enormous scale by those forced to participate in the regime's spectacles, such as mass rallies and in forced labor. My hypothesis was confirmed by Daw Myaq Thi. I asked her if she had noticed the blank, featureless expressions and rigid comportment of the participants in the mass rallies, and she replied, "Yes. Tens of thousands of them. Can you do this by just pretending? It comes from the heart."

Darker Than Midnight

Two generations of Burmese have now grown up in an environment of alienation. They try both to construct a blank exterior to their persona and, often ineffectively, to numb their thoughts and senses to the ongoing intrusion of authoritarianism into the most intimate domains of personal and interpersonal life. Their experience of fear in its various intensities and varieties is difficult for outsiders to access and understand. Expressing fear brings no concrete advantages; it only brings closer to the surface that which Burmese people struggle every day to suppress.

There comes a time in many Burmese people's narratives when silence represents the inability of language to convey experiences. However much Burmese people manage to erect barriers from the fear generated by the junta's strategic use of political violence, there are times when nothing can stop the fear. At such times of extreme terror—search and seize raids, when standing in front of armed troops, at arrest and imprisonment—there is no future imaginable and no possibility for action, only despair. The Burmese are no strangers to political repression and to despair. Although there may be few words that can hold their burden of fear, there are many proverbs to describe the despair of powerlessness and a lack of hope. As one old Burmese proverb asks, "What is darker than midnight?"

Chapter 4
Sometimes a Cigar Is Just a Cigar

> The armed forces have not been created for the purpose of persecuting the people, nor for the purpose of exercising power with weapons. The army is the servant of the country. The country is never the servant of the army.
>
> —General Aung San

> Amnesty International, Asia Watch . . . foul-air propaganda machines raising hue and cry about "violating human rights."
>
> —*New Light of Myanmar*

Nightmares frighten us because, for a little time, we are unable to tell what is real and what is the product of our imagination. This process began to colonize my waking world. The city became a surreal juxtaposition of the sinister and the mundane. Statues, buildings, government institutions, even the "undercover" uniform of MI—pressed longyi and aviator glasses—began to scare me. I started to read Rangoon's architecture as fascist. I explained my dilemma to a visiting American psychiatrist, David Iserman. In the middle of one of my bleak imaginings he turned to me and murmured, paraphrasing Freud, that "sometimes a cigar is just a cigar."

Undoubtedly, sometimes a cigar is just a cigar, but the possibility that it may not really be a cigar, or that it has the potential, at any moment, to transform itself into more than just a cigar, keeps Rangoon and Mandalay residents awake at night. Burma is not a fascist state, it is instead a potential or incipient fascist state, and it is that never fully realized potential, always present in propaganda and the constant threat of violence, that is frightening in the extreme. The thought that military control could become complete and efficient and penetrate every sanctuary space is the *über*-fear that lurks always in the shadows of the tanks, government institutions, and propaganda signboards. The Burmese historical experience of oppression generates practices of resistance to this fear, and it is the methods of both creating and containing that fear that I am concerned with in the following pages. Let us leave then for a few chapters the running street battles between the army and the students and the desperate search for sanctuary, and delve instead into the world of fantasy, nightmare, dreamscape, illusion, and deception, in order to understand what Georges Bataille (1979) described as the psychological structure of fascism.

Incipient Burmese Fascism

Since 1945, over three-quarters of the new states that have emerged have undergone, at some time, direct military rule (Kennedy and Louscher 1991: 1). Military dictatorships are very common in Asia as well as most other parts of the world. In the case of Burma, an incipient fascist state, the Union of Myanmar, has been emerging since 1989. Peter Sinclair (1979: 90) maintains that fascism is not a revolutionary force, but one in which business and industry cartels support such regimes for as long as possible. He argues instead for a definition of fascism as "the Marxist interpretation of it as the defense of the ruling class interests during a period of crisis" (88). It has two key elements: the maintenance of a climate of continuous mobilization, necessarily using the armed forces for this purpose, and the incomplete and ineffective use of totalitarian strategies of control through terror. He defines many countries as undergoing a period of incipient or potential fascism where these two key elements are met in conjunction with an appeal to, and use of, the middle strata of society. Viewed in this way, fascism is a class-based political system, not characterized by the revolutionary fervor of the goose-stepping masses, but by a particular mode of control, not fully actualized, although certainly envisioned, in many developing capitalist countries.[1]

Why is it necessary to describe Burma as an incipient fascist state? For three reasons: first, the present experience of authoritarianism is consistently compared by the National League for Democracy and other opposition groups as akin to their historical experience of Japanese fascism. Second, if we are to describe Burma as really nasty, horribly brutal, really authoritarian or very dictatorial, or perhaps as ruled by Asian military despots like Suharto or Marcos, where is the massive social reengineering project? Where is the accounting for more than four decades of civil war in the borderlands? Where is the attempted genocide of dissenting minority populations? Where is the scope of the authoritarian project and the breadth of cruelty and suffering to be recorded if not in the label of fascism? This is not just crony capitalism, not just an oligopoly of capitalist interests centered in the hands of a cadre of Generals, and not just a venal impulse grown to national proportions. There is, for example, a deep and unfeigned reverence for Buddhism exhibited by the Generals and there is no room for such claims to moral legitimacy in regularly corrupt, nepotistic, late capitalist dictatorships. And finally, almost all forms of control through repression historically adopted by fascist regimes are clearly apparent in the methods of the Burmese military regime. In the remainder of this chapter I flesh out these reasons why Burma is best characterized as controlled by incipient or potential fascism, and how the fear of a future imprisoned by a perfected military state is magnified in nightmare, rumor, and the voices of the mentally ill.

There Are No Fascists Here

On November 10, 1998, Lieutenant General Khin Nyunt, head of the Burmese military intelligence unit, spoke at the opening of the Burma-Japan Bilateral Conference on Information Technology Co-operation in Rangoon. "We shall never forget the important role played by Japan in our struggle for independence," said Khin Nyunt . . . the most powerful general in the SPDC. "In the same vein, we will remember that our Tatmadaw [military] was born in Japan.". . . The term "fascist" and mention of the cruelty of Japanese troops were missing from the general's words. . . . As long as the junta, which has been accused of being neo-fascist by its own people, holds the power, and the Japanese government healthily supports so-called humanitarian aid to the junta, the antifascist revolution will no longer appear on the leaves of Burmese history. (Moe Aye 1998)[2]

Moe Aye wrote this reminder of the sanitizing of Burmese history texts ten years after the failed pro-democracy uprising. It is part of a program of rewriting Burmese history that combines the pandering of the regime toward aid donors such as Japan with the desire to separate skeins of the past so that a new history can be woven, one where it is not possible to find threads that link Japanese fascist methods of control with contemporary forms of oppression.

Anson Rabinach (1977: 160) argues that this kind of authoritarian control arises when structural weaknesses occur during global capitalist change. That is, he posits an ideological vacuum existing at certain global historical moments, such as in the aftermath of the Second World War: "The fascist form of state intervention took root only when certain types of national development made impossible a "normal" transition to monopolist capitalist hegemony." And indeed, Mary Callahan (1998) demonstrates the progressive militarization of Burmese institutions during Burma's turbulent 1950s at a time when pocket armies and gangster politics were in decline and forces controlling large areas of the country were becoming united under the control of the Socialist Party (not the Tatmadaw). Similarly, Martin Smith (1999) shows the development and changes to the pocket armies in the borderlands throughout the 1950s and the eventual metamorphosis of soldiers into minority leaders, drug lords, and, in cases such as that of Khun Sa, a final transformation into "legitimate" urban entrepreneurs that enter into joint ventures with the members of the military council.

There is much good historical and political analysis of these turgid years that birthed the present regime and its "accent of violence" (Bataille 1979). Of course, at the level of daily knowledge there is a less nuanced articulation of the mechanics of the historical transformation of oppression into its modern modus operandi. I am concerned here with this everyday operating knowledge of oppression that Burmese people carry around with them. Burmese people unceremoniously dump into one category of oppressors all of those who have practiced repression against them. There is a collective cult of martyrs that includes those who rebelled or agitated against the British and sued for Independence (such as Saya San, Bo Aung Gyaw, and Aung San) and those who died in the fight for democracy against the Burmese junta (such as Phone Maw). From the period of resistance to British colonization, through the period of resistance to Japanese fascism, and onward through more than four decades of military dictatorship, a collective historical memory of resistance has been formed and articulated by urban and educated opposition groups. Rather than present a simplified history of a complex and turbulent past, I turn to the makers of this contiguous history of resistance to oppression to explain in their own terms their contemporary experience of repression as of the same order as oppression in the past, in particular, the brutalities of the period of Japanese fascist occupation.

Three of the most prominent expatriate organizations are consistent in their version of this history of resistance. The All Burma Federation of Student Unions (ABFSU) maintains that "In Burma, a common democratic ideology links student movements and popular struggles. This link was formed through the fight against colonialism and fascism, and strengthened through the national independence movement and the ongoing revolution against the military dictatorship" (ABFSU n.d.). Similarly, the All Burma Student's Democratic Front (ABSDF) draws attention to the cult of oppression-fighting martyrs of the last century, a group of martyrs separated historically but linked by their practice of resistance and desire for an independent, free Burma. They state that "In tribute to the memory of the martyrs who sacrificed their lives in the struggle for independence, anti-fascism and democracy, the ABSDF will work together with other allied resistance groups" (ABSDF 2001).

In 1999, on the fifty-fourth anniversary of the resistance to Japanese occupation, the Burmese government-in-exile, the National Coalition Government of the Union of Burma directly compared the military regime to the Japanese fascists in the following way:

> Though the alien fascists could be expelled, the "domestic fascists" clique of the army, changing their title from time to time, are ruling Burma again with militarism, ever since Gen. Ne Win seized the state power from the civilian government in 1962. The SLORC (State Law and Order Restoration Council)/ SPDC (State Peace and Development Council) military clique has been misusing patriotism, practicing the system of monopoly over the country's finance, economy, and politics, using the so-called Union Solidarity and Development Association in like manner as Hitler had used his Brown Shirts. It has created special military intelligence organizations, like Hitler's Gestapo secret police organization, to control the whole society, including the armed forces, with fear. . . . The domestically made fascist military dictators of today shamelessly changed the name of the Anti-Fascist Resistance Day, which has its inception in the Burmese armed forces led by Gen. Aung San and the historic victory of the people of various ethnic nationalities of Burma over the fascist dictators, to Armed Forces Day, disregarding the role of the people. (NCGUB 1999)

Within Burma, the similarities of experience between aspects of Japanese fascist and contemporary nascent fascist rule cannot be stated so blatantly. National League for Democracy members, U Win Tin and Aung San Suu Kyi, have both made these historical connections in public speeches. U Win Tin gave a speech on Writer's Day, 1988, in which he carefully noted that: "Writers' Day was first held in the very dark days of fascism under the Japanese. But at that time we were allowed to make speeches. And we certainly did. . . . It was celebrated under fascism, under the AFPFL [Anti-Fascist People's Freedom League], under the Union, even under the BSPP [Burma Socialist Programme Party]. Not until this year has it been missed. . . . However great the darkness that hangs over us, there is still the light of democracy." U Win Tin's comparison of the "very dark days of fascism under the Japanese" to the "great darkness that [now] hangs over us" was considered a very clear commentary on military rule and such statements led to his arrest and sentencing in 1989 to fourteen years imprisonment.

Similarly, the speeches made by Aung San Suu Kyi and the NLD Central Executive Committee reconstruct a collective history of resistance to oppression and make clear that, to borrow from Negt (1976: 46), the "historical experience of the present" for the National League for Democracy, the only in-country opposition group able to express any form of nonviolent public defiance, is demonstrably the Burmese experience of Japanese fascism:

On page 83 of the book "History of the Resistance to Fascism," General Aung San wrote "On the 27 March, 1945, our whole nation organised and commenced the resistance movement against fascism as is known to the world today." This story of resistance to reclaim sovereign power that began in 1945 is of tremendous importance and stands out as a landmark in Burma's history. The overthrow of fascism was not only a symbol of the unity of all the peoples of Burma, it was the fore-runner in the obtaining of our independence on the 4th January 1945. . . . It is important that our children and the future generation should be made aware that the 27th March is not a commemoration of the Armed Forces but a commemoration of the resistance to fascism. . . . The real reason of our victory in the fight for independence from fascism was because the people and the political leaders were united. Similarly, the situation today calls for the whole country to learn from the past. . . . Because the army is composed of sons and daughters (jewels) of all the peoples of the country from every walk of life, fascist policies and systems must not be applied. (NLD 1999)

This reading of the past and the present is vehemently opposed by the military regime who have tried to erase the period of Japanese fascist rule from the history books, largely because of the repeated links drawn between this period and the decades of large and small accounts of suffering caused by the junta that together provide the moral basis for ongoing resistance.[3] The *Guardian* (1989) reported that: "The junta felt 'very-much insulted' by Ms Suu Kyi's comments on Wednesday, broadcast by the Voice of America, accusing military rulers of fascist behaviour. 'It is a well-known fact that we abhor both fascism and imperialism,' declared the spokesman." Aung San Suu Kyi was placed under house arrest for six years for such comments.

Perfecting Control

If we grant then, that the historical experience of oppression in the present includes Japanese fascism, it is possible to further understand how the *über*-fear of the emergence of an efficient, monolithic fascist system of control is the stuff of urban nightmare. Sinclair (1979: 99–100) is one of a group of theorists who saw in fascism a novel marriage of capitalism and totalitarianism: "The novelty was that, in presiding over the development of industrial capitalist societies, both Italian and German fascists tried to use a totalitarian strategy of control. The central feature of totalitarianism is the ideal of total power or total domination." He quotes a variety of definitions of totalitarianism, such as the desire for unlimited control (Buchheim 1968), and the "subjection of all life to the intervention of the state" (Kogan, in Woolf 1968: 11). For Arendt, totalitarianism is "a form of government whose essence is terror and whose principle of action is the logicality of ideological thinking" (Arendt 1958). Under such a system "even the private world of 'experience, fabrication and thought' cannot survive" (Sinclair 1979: 100).

Sinclair (1979) notes that in Italy there were many members of the ruling class who benefited from Fascist rule, even though they were subject to totalitarian controls. Such a view precludes the obvious political repression against any members of the elite who oppose the regime. It was most often the other social classes that felt the impact of such repression more strongly and more effectively in Nazi Germany and Fascist Italy. But above all, the methods of control instigated by fascist regimes were hopelessly ineffective in the sense that almost no one believed the ideology and went along with it only in the most perfunctory manner: "Neither Nazi Germany nor Fascist Italy was a monolithic society controlled by all powerful authoritarian leaders. Almost every commentator on Italy has noted the incompleteness and ineffectiveness of many totalitarian strategies. In the case of Germany . . . even within the Nazi Party there was no all encompassing central control and state officials retained much of their old power by virtue of their indispensability. The Party . . . was staffed primarily with incompetent functionaries who were in no way prepared to serve as the revolutionary elite of an industrialized and technically advancing nation" (Peterson 1969).

This attempt to use totalitarian methods of control is also characteristic of incipient fascist regimes and in urban and peri-urban Burma there are four key ways in which this control is experienced: at the level of community organization and through the use of propaganda, censorship, and informers. I turn now to describing how the fear of a future imprisoned by the military state is magnified in nightmare, rumor, and the voices of the mentally ill when they are confronted with these attempts at total control.

Local Knowledge

The collective history of resistance to oppression is created by monks, students, and an educated urban elite, and it does not necessarily represent the remembered past of the majority rural population, or the many minority groups who remember their own markers of oppression. Ardeth Maung Thawnghmung (2001: 328) cautions that "the same autocratic and repressive military leaders who are perceived by a particular sector of population as 'illegitimate' may at the same time be favorably seen by another segment of the citizens." She provides significant evidence of the "economic legitimacy" held by the state in the early years of the revolutionary government (1962) as it worked hard to forge ties with the rural population and create agricultural policies favorable to them. Rural support for the regime is highest in areas where "a specific rural development program creates better economic conditions for rural residents" and "when farmers are convinced that abuses and mistreatment by the local government . . . took place without the knowledge of the central government" (Ardeth Maung Thawnghnmung 2001: 330).

In contrast, in the villages in which I have worked in Ayerwaddy, Yangon, and Bago Divisions, I have not come across favorable views of the regime, perhaps because villages within several hours transportation of the major cities are increasingly ensnared in peri-urban and urban day laboring and other forms of movement and commerce that bring them into contact with urban and peri-urban officials, whose power greatly eclipses the kind of local leaders that the above study focused upon. Similarly, at pagoda and other rural festivals in central Burma, I have not heard of the beneficial protective role of the State with regard to local leaders that is well documented by this author, but I have been given several life histories by teenage girls working as prostitutes in Burma, who had been sold into slavery in Yunnan and were rescued and smuggled back to Burma by young Tatmadaw men. Ma Yi Yi told me that

Last year [1996] I was given a drink by a client and I don't remember anything else until I woke up in a truck. I was crying because I was so thirsty. We (myself and another girl) were put in a room and a Chinese man came and told us he'd paid for us. I had to sell heroin during the day and at night . . .

Ma Yi Yi breaks off as tears pour from her eyes and through the wooden slats to the dry earth below. Ma Aye Yee takes up the story on behalf of her now seventeen-year-old sister:

She had to sell herself at night to Chinese men and sometimes to Burmese traders. After three months she was selling heroin one day near the checkpoint and a young Tatmadaw man asked her why she was doing it. She was too embarrassed to tell him, but he guessed and asked her where she was working. That night he and his friend went to the house [brothel] and paid for her services and also for the other Burmese girl. They took them across the border and gave them money to get a bus all the way back home.

We cannot infer either a commitment to totalitarian methods nor a complete disdain for state ideology and methodology by soldiers such as those who risked their career and their personal safety to rescue Ma Yi Yi from slavery. Many of these young men were forcibly recruited and remain in the armed forces because of the fear of reprisals to themselves and their families (Fink 2001: 145). Like the foot soldiers and bureaucrats of the European fascist regimes of the past (Peterson 1969), there is no hegemonic army here, just 400,000 people committed, to various degrees, to state ideology and to receiving a pay packet.

Ma Yi Yi's drugging and kidnapping occurred in a car parked by the shore of Kandawgyi Lake in central Rangoon. She and her family live in a relocated township on the outskirts of the city. In these peri-urban areas the new structure of the townships is panoptic, and to walk to the market or the school, or to play chinlon in the lengthening shadows of the afternoon, entails being visible to the government and security offices that overlook the public space.

For the majority of urban and peri-urban Burmese, the regime is able to exercise an astonishing degree of surveillance and control over individual, family, and community life. Burmese recite the well-established chain of command that they have been taught as follows: "NaWaTa, PaWaTa, MaWaTa, YaWaTa." This translates as

State Law and Order Restoration Council,
Provincial Law and Order Restoration Council,
Township Law and Order Restoration Council,
Ward Law and Order Restoration Council.

The Ward Law and Order Restoration Council, or Yawata, represents the military regime at the level of actual communities and has become the keeper of records, chronicling all births, death, marriages, movement and residency, and the "volunteer labor" of Burmese who are divided into zones of influence known as Wards.[4]

The Yawata provide a crucial political function in their day-to-day monitoring of the events that occur within each ward. Perhaps the most important of these from the perspective of the regime's continuing ability to maintain power is the monitoring of urban space. All movement must be reported to and permitted by the Yawata and the location of each person in Burma must be recorded by the Yawata each evening. The LORCs (another term for the Yawata) in both the ward where an individual usually resides, and the ward in which a person plans on spending the night, must be notified. This rule also applies to expatriates and tourists.

Communities considered rebellious by the regime and communities whose houses stood in the way of the government's urban renewal scheme have been disassembled and forcibly relocated to rice fields bordering the capital cities. The control of space in the newly relocated townships is close to absolute, and monitoring ward activities during the day is an easy task due to the panoptic geography of the township. Ward officials are aware of the number of prostitutes such as Ma Yi Yi working in their area, and one thirty six-year-old woman who prostituted herself in order to provide for her four children in the wake of her husband's sudden death told me that the Yawata stopped neighbors from stoning her roof. "Leave her alone," they told the Ten House Leader and the street residents, "She's doing this job to stop her children from starving."

Although they may see most things that go on during the day, at night the Yawata need to rely upon intimidation to control movement within their communities. During the student demonstrations in December 1996, the Yawata in Rangoon enforced an unofficial curfew. A male in his early twenties from Insein township, Maung Htay Hlaing, told me that on the night of December 8, "at 11:30 p.m. I went outside to see what was happening. The Yawata told me to get back inside." And during another unofficial curfew in March 1997, a young female friend, Ma Thanda Win, told me, "They haven't declared any curfew in words, but the elders have told young people not to go out at night. Everyone now has to inform the LORC if they want to travel at night, even within our ward."

Micro-control at the ward and township levels is a tripartite strategy of control. The Yawata is the most feared, but the ward leaders and the GONGOs (Government Organized Non-Government Organizations) such as the Union Solidarity and Development Association also investigate and report upon the most intimate levels of personal and community life. Leadership within the wards is similar to the traditional Burmese concept of the headman and Rangoon and Mandalay residents refer to "the head-man of our street." Every ten households in the cities have a "Ten House Leader." Similarly, every street has a "Street Leader" and every 100 houses, roughly one block, have a "100 House Leader." This is a hierarchy of control below the Yawata and answerable to it. In each ward a battle occurs each time a leader or Yawata official is appointed. In the 1990s, some townships managed to have NLD members appointed to these positions, and the character of a ward is often indicated by the political persuasions of its leaders.[5] The presence of "community leaders" means that a steady supply of individual and family misdemeanors is available to the Yawata and hence to the Mawata, Pawata, and so on up the chain of hierarchy.[6]

In the townships in which I have worked, the Yawata have continually hindered my movements, followed me on motorbikes, and made people repeat the questions I had put to them. The Yawata complained to higher authorities that I had been seen with a camera and that I declined to sign the "visitor's book," that is, I refused to be complicit in my own surveillance. This all occurred on occasions when I had been given official permission to be in those wards and to take pictures "surreptitiously." One senior health official told me, "They have been trained to act like that for thirty-five years. It's a hard habit to break." It is the fear of reprisals and loss of both position and "face" that prompts ward officials to such zealous surveillance rather than any belief in the necessity or national benefits accruing from the implementation of forms of totalitarian control.

Propaganda

It is of course ridiculous to think that the state might become monolithic and that all members of the armed forces and state institutions might wholeheartedly believe the regime's propaganda and act accordingly. But late at night, when neighbors' dogs begin barking, or when a phone line repeatedly goes dead in the middle of a conversation, or when one suddenly confronts an armed soldier or tank, it is not so hard to envision. Burmese dreams are not filled with these images all the time; they seep in with increased militarization of the cities in response to student, monk, and NLD agitation. Local officials become more zealous, government officials become overly suspicious of all motives, and rumor increases in the atmosphere of heightened propaganda and suspense.

In the final chapters of this book I describe the religious and miraculous frameworks that many Burmese people turn to in such times of physical, emotional, and spiritual crisis. No such succor was available to me, but in order to keep control of my own fear I needed to find a way of distinguishing the elements of the militarized city that were designed to terrorize, as opposed to those that engendered unexpected fearfulness, and finally to sort out my own phantasms from the nightmarish reality of this unacknowledged civil war. The problem was that I was conducting fieldwork at the Rangoon Psychiatric Hospital and my head was so full of their subversive narratives that I felt sure my thoughts could be overheard by the soldiers, bureaucrats, and the intelligence apparatus of the city. I was sure that I was somehow leaking subversion. My dreams were filled with Aung San Suu Kyi, pagodas, generals, murder, gun battles in the borderlands, and all the other political markers apparent in the disordered life worlds of suffering patients. In public, under the gaze of the regime, these stories were dangerous knowledge, proof that the social and individual bodies are intimately entwined and that the political situation penetrates the dreams of all minds, regardless of their soundness. Even in madness there is no retreat from the crushing weight of terror.

Consider, for example, the life story of a kindly looking gentleman, U Sein Htay, who is in his mid-forties and spoke to me shortly after his arrest by the Yawata for fighting. The officials committed him to the psychiatric hospital, where he was found to be positive for codeine, an illegal substance in Burma. As with the majority of patients incarcerated at the psychiatric hospital for violent acts, U Sein Htay is an ex-soldier. The Yawata officials testified that the man went armed with a sword and a "double-hook" weapon to the local army barracks to ask if he should sleep there or at home. U Sein Htay denies that he intended violence and refused to be admitted to the hospital:

I am a retired Tatmadaw man. I left the Tatmadaw in 1969. I performed my duties as a Tatmadaw man in the armed forces. When I was in the Tatmadaw I gave up [lost] one eye [in the fighting]. I came to this hospital because I was arguing with another person out the front of the Yawata office and people thought I was mad and sent me here. . . . I will tell you the story of my short life. When I lived in [name withheld] township, I sold spectacles. The neighborhood ignored/shunned my family because they decided I was mad. I was put in Insein jail twice. But it wasn't my fault, and I was able to return home. When I returned, my wife wasn't there. So I looked for her and when I found her, I lost my identity card. Finally, everyone thought I was mad and so they sent me to this hospital.

U Sein Htay's patient notes are extensive. In his initial interview with the staff of the Rangoon Psychiatric Hospital he claimed to have been hearing multiple confusing voices for over a year. Sometimes these voices tell him to assault people. He also claimed that the Yawata were trying to kill him and his children. The sister on his ward labeled this a delusion and proceeded to tell me about other delusions, including that U Sein Htay had heard "political" voices. He claimed that the National League for Democracy had seized his children, but one son had escaped and remained in the village. He also believes that he knows Khun Sa (the world's most notorious heroin drug lord, who surrendered to the regime in 1996 and is now a Rangoon-based "legal entrepreneur"), and asked him if he were now aligned with the government. He also claims to be related to a man who was a former Minister of Railways and that he has been traced by his enemies through the radio.

The current sociopolitical situation, including corruption and nepotism that makes "contacts" necessary for survival, as well as the enormous burden of fear produced by Military Intelligence, provide the subject matter of U Sein Htay's tormented mental state. Other key figures and elements in the political landscape such as Khun Sa and the National League for Democracy contextualize his experience of illness. The content of the delusions related to me in the nation's psychiatric wards mirror the content of the State propaganda and the dreams of its citizens. That successive military dictatorships have adopted panoptic surveillance and methods such as placing informers in public sites to gather information about the activities of Burmese people is something that is of concern not only to patients suffering psychotic illnesses such as U Sein Htay, but is a concern made evident by the self-censorship practiced by Burmese people in public space.

Since 1994, the face of urban Burma has changed dramatically. Multistoried buildings made from modern materials, bridges, department

Figure 1. The People's Desire signboard. (Colin Rieger)

stores, and other staples of the modern city have emerged from a frenzy of construction. One of the most remarkable changes is from the use of bicycles and pony-carts to cars and pick-ups, the installation of phone lines to many parts of the country, and the increasing electrification of the nation. Anderson (1991) defines rapid changes in forms of communication, transportation, and construction as central elements of modernization in Southeast Asia. Such changes have occurred alongside a transformation in the way the intelligence and "information" apparatus of the State functions. Manual surveillance is still intensive, but a range of supra-panoptic methods are additionally now used by Military Intelligence from their new headquarters. A state-of-the-art "spy center" exists that can intercept phone conversations, facsimiles, e-mail, and other electronic communications (Selth 1997). Amid these changing forms of both intelligence gathering and the delivery of state ideology through repetitive propaganda, Burmese people are continually having to make distinctions between what is real and meaningful and what are lies in their everyday lives.[7]

These new forms of intensive surveillance and the effective targeting and relentless bombardment of the population with propaganda are thus primary methods by which the regime maintains control (see Figure 1). Like a blunt instrument, this propaganda becomes effective because of its magnitude and its continual repetition. The Chinese government is an old hand at this kind of ideological indoctrination. In Burma, the difference lies perhaps in the nakedness with which violence is threatened and the increased vulnerability of the population to such propaganda. Without access to alternate forms of information, the sheer volume of this propaganda threatens to trip Burmese up in the "facts" of their nation's history and current political situation, and thus through a combination of silencing the public sphere and filling it with repetitive propaganda, the regime creates gray spaces of confusion in which complicity may begin.

Maung Hmon Gyi, a student involved in the 1996 hit-and-run demonstrations, described to me, with a sense of shame, the confusion he felt when confronted with the onslaught of propaganda initiated by the regime in the years following the repression of the 1988 country-wide uprising:

HG: When I was in high school, around '91 and '92, I became very confused about government propaganda, especially with regard to the reconstruction of the country by the SLORC which had begun to appear in the newspapers. They said they wanted to maintain our national culture. I also read news about the people who were trying to destroy our country. As I was reading this news, or propaganda, every day, I began to believe little by little that what they were doing was right.

MS: Can you explain a little more about this?

HG: Now I am regretful about this period. What the government was doing was to make people vacillate, to be indecisive about the influence of foreign culture that was entering Burma. When the government opened up the country in 1996, foreigners came in who were not very neat, who did not dress or act in ways that were culturally appropriate. The government propaganda attacked this, especially with regard to the influence on young Burmese girls and women and the way that they dress. I thought that this was a good thing, because Rangoon girls were beginning to act in a wanton manner, and as a young man, I thought this was a good thing for the government to do, because I thought foreign culture might destroy the country.

MS: Were many people confused by the propaganda?

HG: I can't speak for everyone, I think about 80 percent of the population were also confused. Of all the people I knew, many of us were unsure, indecisive. But it only lasted for a year or two. . . . Later, my brother who was at RIT told me not to be fooled. He said, "If you are interested in politics, then you should read about history and more about politics. Find history books and read them, read translated works." He encouraged me to read and think critically about government propaganda. Later, after I had read history and analyzed these books, I realized it was all for show, they were not doing it to maintain our national culture. On the one hand, the propaganda was attacking the problem, and on the other hand, they themselves were opening brothels and enjoying themselves.

They were making money from all their brothels in the border areas. They were very hypocritical about tourism, in particular.

Maung Hmon Gyi was fortunate to have an older and politically active brother to call upon when the propaganda became seductive. For myself, I found comfort in documenting the forms of attempted totalitarian control. It became a way of easing the tension between the juxtaposition of the confusing verbal and optical onslaught of propaganda with the heretical statements loudly and publicly voiced by the mentally ill. I avoided the State's institutions and public space as much as possible, censoring my own thoughts, not completely believing that the treasonous statements in my head could not somehow escape my mental high walls and barbed wire barricades and be picked up by the vigilant ears of the regime.

Censorship and Self-Censorship

The arrest of western journalists has become a commonplace means of stopping alternate truths existing in the public domain. On September 29, 1996, a photographer who had been given a press visa to enter Burma was placed under "hotel arrest" and a white board was used to erase his video footage. In December 1996, during the student demonstrations, a Japanese journalist was hospitalized after suffering a beating at the hands of the military, and other journalists and activists have been bodily searched for film that has been confiscated. Propaganda is most effective when a simultaneous process of silencing other forms of media is occurring. Even more important than convincing the population of its own version of the present/future (and each individual's place within this dystopia) the government must block out all alternate forms of information which would otherwise allow Burmese to construct their own visions of the future.

After each of these incidents of arrest and detention, the regime did its best to "disappear" evidence. This includes the jailing of Burmese and the expulsion of foreigners. The *New Light of Myanmar* ran a story in August 1996 stating that "Action [had been] taken against Win Htein and accomplices for subversive acts to destabilize [the] nation" (NLM 1996g). This concerned an interview that U Win Htein gave journalist Evan Williams where he pointed out to the cameraman a pair of MI following U Win Htein on motorbikes. He was sentenced to seven years jail and was moved from Insein jail to Myitkina jail in northern Burma, away from family and friends who could provide him with food, medical supplies, and psychological support. Official media stated: "Win Htein and the others were sentenced for malicious acts aimed at destruction of the peace and stability of the state. . . . Win Htein agitated and organized members of the NLD . . . to provide news and figures that would be detrimental to the agricultural plans of the state" (Reuters 1996: 5). In 1998 Daw San San, a prominent NLD leader, was jailed for years under a 1923 Official Secrets Law for giving an interview to the BBC (Lintner 1998), and six political activists, four of them former members of the All Burma Democratic Student's Forum (ABDSF), were sentenced to death (*Financial Times* 1998). Disappearing alternate versions of the truth continues apace in Burma.

The junta is particularly wary of visual images because of the strong belief that seeing is believing. For example, most Burmese will take as true reported sightings of ghosts and visions, as well as the performance of magic, miracles, and so on. It is hard work for the ruling council to make people disbelieve images, and therein lies the power of television. The regime was particularly startled to learn that within a few hours of the mass arrests of NLD members at their 1996 Annual May Conference, video footage and a mounting tally of the number of arrests was being aired by media outlets around the world. Even more annoying, the BBC and VOA routinely report these numbers in their Burmese language broadcasts. The vast majority of Burmese who cannot speak English are thus able to hear news about their country, news that is otherwise censored within Burma.

Through this episode the Generals became aware of the speed with which international media services can generate news. Subsequently, journalist visas became tightly controlled and the regime began holding a monthly press conference so that it could feed the international media outlets its own version of the truth. These press conferences were halted after several months when it became obvious that the attending journalists would not refrain from asking difficult political questions and writing about the regime's refusal to answer such questions. The most recent strategy is to deny visas to most journalists and to publish on the Internet an "Information Sheet" to disseminate their vision of the Union of Myanmar to an international audience.

The control of international broadcasts is thus of great concern to the military junta and it occasionally blocks the BBC and VOA radio signals to stop alternate truths entering Burma. The regime has issued a two-volume tome entitled *A Skyful of Lies,* the title referring to the satellite and radio transmissions from the BBC and VOA. In the neighborhood in which I lived for several months (an area containing army barracks and high ranking military officials), the satellite dish positions were hurriedly altered during the periods in which mass arrests of NLD members and suspected supporters occurred. The dishes are rotated such that they can no longer receive the BBC as the regime conducts "surprise" spot-checks to arrest people for watching the BBC. The common belief on the streets of Rangoon is that there are only three thousand legally registered satellite dishes in Burma, and the thousands of other dishes are thus illegal. I bought a "receiver box" (satellite receiver) during the June 1996 arrest period, and it took Burmese friends several hours to find an electronics shop that would admit to selling satellite receivers. The receivers had been dispersed to relatives in the various townships in preparation for the stores being raided by the government. These manual methods of control rely upon the fear that rumors and propaganda create to stop Burmese watching and listening to information from outside.

A more effective means for making alternate versions of the truth disappear takes the crude form of "ripping out, inking over, and blacking out" Burmese written expression. Anna Allott has written a history of press censorship in Burma. Beginning with the Press Review Department of the U Nu government that began censoring material in 1961, an ongoing period of denial of freedom of speech and expression has occurred (Allott 1994: 5). Allott documents the arrest of newspaper editors, the cessation of all publications in 1963, and the creation of the Ministry of Information newspapers and journals. In addition, the combination of the formation of the Press Scrutiny Board (1962), the Printers' and Publishers' Registration Act of 1962, the Printers' and Publishers' Central Registration Board (1975), arrests of editors and writers, and author Blacklists led to a situation in which, by 1982, "the process of Censorship in Burma had settled into a routine that appears to be in place today, when nearly all manuscripts . . . of books have to be submitted [to the government] before printing" (11–12). She concludes that "the majority of pieces published in Burma today do not have any overt or hidden political message, as most works with even a hint of such messages are refused publication. The consequent trivialization of Burmese imaginative literature has been immensely discouraging to all serious and independent-minded writers. Some feel that they can now only produce work that is intrinsically without worth" (3).

Leehey has documented the censorship of anti-government sentiments when they break through into public discourse, particularly through the satirical methods of clowns and cartoonists. Using the medium of cartoons she shows how "the very existence of the cartoons reveals a shared, not-quite-public spirit of opposition" (Leehey 1997: 154). Leehey's analysis of the cartoons underscores the conflicting realities and alternate visions of Burma and its population which, despite the best efforts of the junta, continue to exist in the public sphere. The cartoons raise questions about the impact of economic changes and the new "development" projects which are underway. They satirize SLORC propaganda, and point to the gross inefficiencies of the state bureaucracy. On a more subtle level, these cartoons reflect the Burmese recognition of the grotesque absurdity of the world they live in, the reality they are obliged to accept. They reveal a world in which surface appearances cannot be trusted, and norms of morality and rationality are being steadily eroded . . . they suggest a sense of isolation and powerlessness. And yet, they are also hopeful, for they show that the SLORC has not succeeded, in the words of one observer, in turning the people of Burma into "mindless sheep." (Leehey 1997: 154)

The hands-on approach to destroying visual images, reducing international broadcasts to static, and destroying literary and artistic works that may contain guarded political or economic commentary is undoubtedly crude but effective. However, the long-term and ultimately more efficient result of such manual censorship involves the waves of panic, fear, suspicion, and rumor that such censorship evokes. Each time an act of censorship is witnessed or rumored, many frightened Burmese begin a process of self-censorship. The regime's spokesperson, Lieutenant Colonel Hla Min, told a journalist about the high degree of self-censorship among the artistic and literary communities that ensures that the Press Scrutiny Board is less and less often presented with work it will censor. Hla Min stated that: "the people are very used to the old socialist habit [of censorship]. They don't want to give strong recommendations to the government" (Mockenhaupt 2001: 74). Functioning in the same way as propaganda dissemination and intelligence gathering, self-censorship is a significant victory for incipient fascist systems of control, bringing efficiency to these mechanisms of domination.

Informers and Informing: Dissolving Boundaries

Zin Maung, the young man who had told me about his participation in the 1996 student demonstrations, also told me about his activities in 1998 that forced him underground and eventually to the Thai-Burma border. In relating this story to me, he tried to stop himself from shuddering a few times, and it was always when he mentioned Military Intelligence. Few people who have been followed by MI can say the term in a normal register, and some of us unconsciously cover our mouths when we talk about such things. Zin Maung's relationship with MI is not one of presumed surveillance, it is instead a continuous fleeing from their operatives through a variety of deceptions:

ZM: In 1998 they held university exams that had been postponed from 1996. We were only able to study for two months for the exams and without attending any classes. A letter was sent to the houses of students who had been enrolled at the university campuses and informed them of the upcoming examinations. The timing of the exams caused divisiveness among the students. We split into two main groupings. One group concentrated upon passing their exams, and the other group worked to support the calling [by the NLD] of the convening of the People's Parliament. We organized and made statements. Because there weren't any university classes, most people had to have private tuition and most of the private tuition schools are around Hledan junction, so we focused our activities there and concentrated on giving leaflets and other statements to students around Hledan junction. . . . We distributed leaflets in those schools but we also distributed them on the buses around the junction. We put them on the seats and on the floor. Spies from MI infiltrated some of these private tuition schools.

MS: Is this why you went into hiding?

ZM: My group, we didn't stay at our homes anymore. We were running from our very good reputation now, as we had formed an underground student union. We rented a large house and we stayed there and made all our propaganda. We produced a lot of propaganda. A lot of people were being arrested because of it. There were only a few of my generation left, only two of us, the rest had already been arrested. Because Daw Aung San Suu Kyi was calling for the convening of the People's Parliament, we made flags and pamphlets. At the end of the exams, about 300 students gathered at Hledan junction in 1998 to support the convening of the People's Parliament. Our group became very well known, and we had links with lots of other student groups and we had made flags and banners. MI had already infiltrated one of these other groups, and that's why I had to go into hiding.

In Burma, there are only a few shops that sell microphones and in that one "line" [i.e., row in a market or a particular street] MI are always hiding there, waiting for students to come and buy microphones and following them. And on 31st Street is the only place where you can buy the banner and pamphlet paper, the A-4 sized paper, and MI is always there watching us; they know that students have to go there. We had to escape from them lots of times after we had gone there to buy paper or microphones. So many times I had to escape from them after I had bought paper. I used to have to take three taxis. When the taxi comes up to the traffic lights, I just jump out and take another taxi. I was a little scared each time. . . . Of course in Burma, we always know that frightening things can happen, so we have to try and be wary, to try and be smart, so although you're scared, you still have to do this.

A variety of crude yet powerful forms of information censorship and dissemination thus operate in urban and peri-urban areas, but the experience of student activists is exceptional and the great majority of the population are paralyzed into inaction by the nightmare scenarios of their own making that involve the merest possibility of falling under the surveillance of the regime. Nothing creates more self-censorship and fear than the possibility of one's actions and words being reported to the regime. Informers are thus the key to the military junta's maintenance of control. Their existence creates extraordinary levels of fear, covertness, suspicion, and self-censorship. In effect, the Burmese population takes upon itself the task of the military. It becomes unnecessary for the regime to place informers in all public places and to use recording and listening devices to stop political planning and dissension. The level of fear in Rangoon and Mandalay is such that the mere possibility of informers and "bugs" is a powerful force for self-censorship.

Individuals are regularly threatened and coerced to become informers if they work in hotels or other facets of the economy where they might encounter foreigners or political activists. This situation has led to people informing in case the government finds out about a piece of information which that individual did not volunteer to the government. Informing becomes not only a pragmatic strategy, but also a necessary form of self-preservation. A hotel worker, Ma Mya Mya Thein, related to me that:

Sometimes MI come to the . . . [Hotel] and ask me a lot of questions, For example: Monique—what time did she leave? When will she come back? I don't like them [MI]. Sometimes they pretend to be beggars, sometimes they pretend to be fools . . . they take photos of people and sometimes they come in the middle of the night, at midnight, and arrest people.

This young woman's personal experience with MI makes it logical for her to assume that informers are everywhere. The strategic placement of MI in areas where Burmese congregate (such as tea shops, trishaw "gates," post office and telecommunication centers, markets, and universities) serves to further this belief.

Foucault (1975: 201) argues that the modern form of deployment of state power consists of making citizens believe that the exercise of such power is permanent. The almost unanimous perception in Burma that informers are everywhere, all of the time, is certainly a triumph of the panoptic model of state power. But more than this, it is the belief at certain times in the omnipresence and hence omnipotence of the regime that constitutes a triumph over the spirit. Such beliefs lead to an ever narrowing circle of friends whom an individual can trust. These basic survival skills are learned very early in life as U Chit Swe, an educated Burmese man, explains:

You will never discuss any politics with anyone. You will tend to talk to very close friends you went to school with about politics, but no one else you meet. They have informers. I don't think someone I am going to open my heart to is going to be an informer. Informers are probably effective at the level of blue-collar workers, [shrugs] but I wouldn't discuss politics with anyone on the street. Informers become informers because they're paid. I don't think [about censoring myself] a lot. I don't work in an organization for that reason. . . . I don't want to be stumbling across informers. But for my friends who work in government offices who have responsible positions or official ranks, they have to be very careful because the government plants informers there. So they are forced to deal with these people. You have to be careful when talking to these people. All these [new] hotels and restaurants have informers. They are forced to take on five percent government employees, take them on and employ them. Partly also because the government is calling themselves security conscious, they need to know everything. Knowing everything makes them feel secure, that's why they need informers.

U Chit Swe comes from a well-connected family and has lived all his life within the limits imposed by government censors and the necessary forms of self-censorship. Like Ma Mya Mya Thein, he practices self-censorship in public and even in private unless he can be sure of the loyalties of his relatives. This lessens the fear of being caught, but it also creates confusion about what is real and true and leads to a situation where it becomes impossible to separate understandings of passive resistance from those of complicity and acceptance. Such a separation is not currently possible in Burma because of the confusion generated by fear and the multiple strategies that Burmese must adopt at any one time to reduce their burden of fear.

Perhaps the regime really can listen to most of our conversations, perhaps it really can efficiently monitor phone, fax, and email correspondence, and perhaps it does have informers in every tea shop and worksite. Self-censorship is proof that the *über*-fear of actualized fascism lurks in Rangoon, Mandalay, and their satellite townships. It is true that, in the torpor of the early afternoon, when the stomach is full of rice, tea shops provide relief from the heat, and monastery and pagoda grounds give shade among luscious tropical foliage, a cigar seems like just a cigar. But Burmese Buddhists know that dreams and mental illness give way to worlds where knowledge exists in other forms. At night, when the moon is behind the clouds and the dogs are barking, the shadow of fascism and its attendant methods of totalitarian control seem eminently feasible and sometimes, when despair strikes, inevitable. At such times a cigar is not just a cigar.

Chapter 5
The Veneer of Modernity

At a time when the mother land Union was on the brink of being burnt down to ashes by hellfires in the 1988 disturbances, the State Law and Order Restoration Council (Tatmadaw) saved it in the nick of time. It then endeavoured to avert the terrible fate in store for the nation and build it up into a mountain of gold.

—*New Light of Myanmar*

Disneyland for Dictators

It is only a one-hour flight from the modern Thai capital of Bangkok to Rangoon, but the difference is extraordinary. There is perhaps no other country in the world that has closed its tertiary institutions for most of the last decade; where a lost generation of youth turn to heroin if they're wealthy, and prostitution and smuggling if they're impoverished; no other country where the border areas are frenzied frontier posts of enormous hundred-room brothels, exit gates for Burmese slaves, sites for amphetamine factories and heroin refineries, and river crossing posts for weapons, teak, tigers, bears, rubies, Buddha images, and other items of Burma's dwindling natural and cultural heritage. This frenetic trading and smuggling of every imaginable trade good has been occurring for many years and contrasts with the scarcity of western trade goods allowed in Burma's legal economy since Ne Win's military coup in 1962. Not too many years ago, 555 cigarettes, whisky, lipstick, or ballpoint pens were all you needed for an extended stay in Burma. But after the 1988 Strike, the military junta selectively encouraged the flow of global capital into the country, reincarnating Burma as a giant fascist wonderland, a Disneyland for Dictators (Ryle 1999: 8).

The incipient fascist imagination that seeks to build the country up into a "Mountain of Gold" does so of course through a betrayal of the masses. This process was described last century by Ernst Bloch as a "swindle of fulfillment" (Rabinach 1977), a process that has caused enormous confusion in Rangoon since 1990 when the economy was selectively liberalized. In the cavernous marble monstrosity known as the Tatmadaw Museum, the top floor is dedicated to what can only be described as an orgy of kitsch that the regime calls its vision of modernity. It consists of exhibits that show how the military will continue to control the Burmese economy in perpetuity. Nowhere more clearly than here can the envisaged utopia be glimpsed, and it is a frightening vision. Purple and khaki army boots with heels and sequins for the army of the future and plastic dummies covered in fake blood depicting the regime's pacification of minority groups are typical of the exhibits whose subject matter fills the nightmares of Burmese people, who understand little of the transnational dimensions of the regime's finances and feel helpless to prevent this orgy of kitsch from dominating their waking reality.

The practical consequences of instituting this nightmare of centralized control is a dual process of transforming the city into a form of mass culture that I describe in this chapter as the thin veneer of modernity. The other half of the process is the transformation of the city's residents into "mass ornaments" (to borrow from Kraceaur 1975), the forced implementation of which I describe in Chapter 6. A veneer is a covering of a finer substance, and mass culture now swathes the capital cities—a landscape of gilded pagodas and gold paint that tarts up the wizened pagodas and moldering downtown terraces for the sensual pleasure and seduction of foreign companies with hard currency. In this chapter I use the narratives of young male heroin addicts to peel the veneer of imitation gold leaf from the modern city and expose the mountain of suffering below.

The Veneer of Modernity

In 1994 there were twelve hotels licensed to take foreigners in Rangoon. A year later the international business media were working themselves into a lather about Burma as the next recipient of massive amounts of global capital. The air of optimism is summarized by Philp and Mercer (1999: 30), who note that investors seeking the next Asian "tiger" economy have set their sights upon Burma, "a country Catley (1996) has referred to as 'the next frontier.'" A far cry from the twelve guest hotels in 1994, by the beginning of 1996 there were 8,000 hotel rooms to be found in Burma (EIU 1996) and the regime had created 946 licenses for private tour guide businesses and a further 410 for various tourism enterprises (Ministry of National Planning and Development 1997, quoted in Philp and Mercer 1999: 30). Alongside this prodigious growth in tourist infrastructure is the corresponding creation of golf courses and tourist precincts that are the focus of the new tourist industry.

This period of liberalization of the economy involved many international companies, such as Pepsi, Singapore Airlines, and Mitsubishi, setting up offices and production facilities in Burma. One night, at the Australia Club, I heard a familiar ringing. It took me a few seconds to realize that it was a cellular phone ring, a sound I hadn't heard since leaving Bangkok airport. Rangoon was changing fast, I mused, over a gin and tonic at a new jazz nightclub for business people. A Canadian newspaper, the *Globe and Mail*, ran a story in 1995 entitled "The Golden Smile of SLORC," proclaiming that "since 1990, foreign companies have invested $3.9 billion in, and committed another $1.9 billion to, projects in the country . . . with a growing number of friends in Asia, SLORC has reformed the country at its own pace and won billions of dollars in investment and trade. . . . The investment boom has taken Myanmar from the brink of insolvency to a foreign-exchange surplus of at least $400 million" (Stackhouse 1995).

The Asian financial crisis finally reached Burma in late 1997. Businesspeople in Rangoon were initially unconcerned, as the Burmese kyat is not linked to other currencies. The problem was with the other nations of Asia that immediately cut their losses in Burma, as it represented from the outset a high risk venture with profits expected only in the long term. The mobile phones stopped ringing, the expensive houses in Golden Valley became vacant, rents halved, and the black market value of the kyat plunged as the regime turned up the printing presses. A reshuffle of the regime and its reincarnation as the State Peace and Development Council (SPDC) did nothing to arrest the slide into bankruptcy.

The empty and already moldering hotels and shopping malls in Rangoon stand as testimony today to this brief period in the mid- to late 1990s when it seemed as if the military regime was actually going to be able to effect a successful transfer from military dictatorship to Asian Tiger. This caused ambivalence at first, then confusion, and finally the realization that all incipient fascist masses must finally arrive at, that the new urbanism of authoritarian regimes is a betrayal of the working classes, as young Maung Tun Tun ruefully explains:

I will divide this [question about modernization] into two. One, what happened, and two, what I felt. People have two feelings. One is that they demolished historical buildings and public buildings and then put up the Sakura Tower and many other buildings like that, so people feel very sad. At the same time, people think that in the movies, other modern cities and states always have those tall, flashy tall buildings, so they are confused between these two views. They think that Burma also needs those kinds of buildings in terms of modern city-states, because they've seen those kinds of cities in movies, so we have mixed feelings. So we are confused about whether or not this is a requirement for a modern city-state, like with tall buildings and towers.

This was around 1996, but the perception about these tall flashy buildings had changed by 1998. In 1997 we all began to get a really bad feeling because it became clear that we weren't the people who were going to be able to use all these new things like electronic supermarkets and international hotels. The grassroots majority of the population changed their view because they quickly realized that this new modern city had nothing to do with them. It's not for me, and we started to see the reality and get really upset with the way the regime had operated. When we first saw all the construction, we thought, "OK, this will be our big city, a big new modern city." But afterwards, what we realized was that only the elite class and a few foreigners can use our city now.

Like Maung Tun Tun, by the beginning of the new millennium almost no one could still believe in the utopian dream of a worker's paradise promulgated in the State media, especially as the economy continued to crumble from its peak in 1997. The May 2003 arrest and incarceration of Aung San Suu Kyi at Insein Jail and other "secure facilities," created an international fury that facilitated the signing by the U.S. president of the Burmese Freedom and Democracy Act of 2003, which effectively closed down the Burmese garment industry, a major export earner. But the regime limps onward, even ordering fifty new tanks from the Ukraine (DVB 2003). The kyat continues to sink as inflation soars in an inverse relationship to the scarcity of electricity, food, oil, and onions. Why hasn't the junta of the new millennium become so completely bankrupt and unable to pay its public officials, satisfy the military, alleviate chronic food shortages, inflation, lack of fuel and hard currency? How has it been able, even in its darkest moments of utter bankruptcy, to intensify its repression and expand the military, its intelligence apparatus, and its array of weaponry?

The answer lay in Hla Hla's wide eyes when she tried to describe to my group of friends the horror that is Patpong Road in Bangkok for a good Buddhist woman. She had recently returned from a trip to Bangkok to visit her husband and had seen these horrors for the first time. We had gathered together to welcome her back and hear of her trip. She had witnessed in graphic detail the age-old way of getting money fast, through exploitation, depravity, and a complete disregard for the people, environments, and cultural heritage as they are traded for a quick buck. Similarly, outside Rangoon there are now a variety of global outposts where hard transnational capital facilitates and provides incentives for the production of heroin, *ya ba* (methamphetamine), the Asian "leisure" and entertainment industry, and the proliferation of organized border crime.

The military regime is a major player in these outposts, and it is here that it garners the all-important hard currency that it uses to remake the capital cities in its dystopic image. The Burmese state has been the progenitor of some of these outposts, while others have grown up in order to resist the military regime. Thai baht, Chinese yuan, and U.S. dollars have been exchanged for drugs, natural resources such as teak, natural gas, and precious minerals, and, most important, Burmese bodies.

The subject of Bangkok's Patpong Road is simultaneously fascinating and horrifying to my circle of friends; they want me to explain, over and over, why it is possible for morality to be suspended in such "pleasure grounds." I give a short lecture on why it is possible for similar amoral areas to exist along Burma's fringes: about the way that Burma has never really been a "country," but has been more a series of suzerainties whose composition has changed enormously in the past 1,500 years. I give the example of the roadblocks that still exist throughout the country and the various "fees" that need to be paid for landing one's boat at a jetty or parking a pony cart near a market. These practices remain from the days when warlords divided the country into personal fiefdoms and the Independence government of the mid-twentieth century controlled only the major cities. I explain about small kingdoms, like the Shan princedoms, the Arakenese kingdom, and the Buddhist kingdoms of Toungoo and Nan in the Thai borderlands (Wyatt 1994). Small states such as these were perpetually in need of labor and smuggling, waging war to gain slaves, corvée labor, and other practices were used to bolster the wealth of the fiefdom, ensuring that for most of its history, the imagined entity of "Burma" was riven with internal skirmishes. In the modern era these suzerainties flourish or decay depending upon the relationship the ruling war lords or drug lords have with senior members of the Burmese junta.

My friends find it very hard to believe that these outposts exist and that the cities are modernized in part through the hard currency they generate. They can believe such things might by possible in Thailand, but it stretches credibility that everything they have been taught for years in the State media is totally false. They can believe that in Rangoon's outlying suburbs there are women working as prostitutes, and they know that the Generals are building new golf courses and sweatshops and that they play golf with the drug lords in the middle of the peri-urban slums, but they just cannot envisage the scale of these gaudy leisure and production zones rising out of the same jungles, forests, and coral atolls which they are repeatedly told by the regime are the historical birthright of all Burmese people.

The Golden Façade

The hard currency procured and laundered by the military council has been used to coat the cities with a golden façade, yellow peeling paint which, like the regime's claims to a worker's paradise, has eroded to reveal the grim reality below. This process in not new but historically familiar, as authoritarian states move from pre-modern to modern, a fact made clear to us by Walter Benjamin and members of the Frankfurt School.

Walter Benjamin includes in his description of the modern phantasmagoria of the twentieth century a form of demolition and rebuilding in European capitals known as the "new urbanism." The new urbanism involved the reconfiguring of urban space and the replacement of existing social and physical relations with a landscape imbued with a "totalitarian aesthetic." Susan Buck-Morss (1989: 90) comments that Baron von Haussmann's "slum 'clearance' simply broke up working-class neighborhoods and moved the eyesores and health hazards of poverty out of central Paris and into the suburbs. His system of public parks and 'pleasure grounds' provided the illusion of social equality, while behind the scenes his building projects initiated a boom in real estate speculation whereby the government expanded the private coffers of capitalists with public funds. . . . In fact, the plan, based on a politics of imperial centralization, was a totalitarian aesthetic."

The transformation of Paris via a totalitarian aesthetic bears many similarities to the destruction of the old quarters of Rangoon and Mandalay in the 1990s, a destruction that is aptly described by both Baudrillard and Benjamin as a form of terrorism imposed upon a population. The demolition of homes, neighborhoods, and sites of religious and cultural tradition and significance occurred as a consequence, almost a side effect, of a totalitarian architecture that imposed a new landscape upon urban residents, a landscape glorifying the control and authoritarian vision of its leaders who rule from the center toward the peripheries: "For Benjamin, this was the very form of fascism, that is to say, a certain exacerbated form of ideology, an aesthetic perversion of politics, pushing the acceptance of a culture of death to the point of jubilation" (Baudrillard 1993: 186). In Burma this process is referred to by the regime's primary architect of terror, General (now Prime Minister) Khin Nyunt, as the "huts to highrise" scheme (*New Light of Myanmar* 2002).

Following Ne Win's military coup of 1962, the regime confiscated a large number of buildings in central Rangoon, and the SPDC has extended the reach of the regime by turning the wealthiest suburbs of Rangoon into heavily restricted or "no-go" areas. Guards armed with automatic submachine guns patrol these "VIP" zones. Traffic is rerouted around these newly militarized edifices and the homes of the Generals with their guard towers, barricades, and barbed wire palisades. In Bahan, the central suburb that contains the Shwedagon Pagoda and many other important Buddhist sites, new pagodas such as "Ne Win's pagoda" (Maha Wizaya) have arisen.[1] This period of nationalization of private property occurred under a military-socialist program, and it was not until the incarnation of the SLORC that the "sons of Ne Win" completely abandoned socialism in favor of an incipient fascism that conjoined capitalism with authoritarianism.

In the run-up to "Visit Myanmar Year" (which began in November 1996), the capital cities underwent a façade change where buildings were whitewashed and pagodas painted with yellow paint to mimic gold leaf. Monasteries have been enlarged and marble and gold paint adorn Bahan as testimony to the regime's commitment to Buddhism. A prolific period of pagoda building has occurred since the inception of the military council in 1989 (Brac de la Perrière 1998; Lubeight 1995; Schober, 1995; Singer 1995), where institutions such as the Rangoon Psychiatric Hospital as well as residential areas have been relocated and reincarnated as sites of new Buddhist infrastructure. Plaster and brick Buddhas several stories high preside over the outer suburbs of the city and establish, in these townships, the preeminence of the SPDC as the architects of urban and suburban space (see Figure 2) and the patronizers of Buddhism.

Locals are conflicted about this. On the one hand they are delighted to have more opportunities to make merit, but on the other hand these monuments were constructed in part to create merit for the dictators, and individuals make decisions about whether they will patronize the new elements of their landscape based upon the strength of their political versus pragmatic priorities. Few Buddhists would argue with the advantages of Buddhifying the local environment, but many Muslim men whom I know believe the golden façade project to be an inordinate waste of money and a further marginalization of their status as Burmese citizens in an increasingly Buddhicized state. "Pah!" is all my friend Ule can manage to spit out each time he drives past one of the new pagoda complexes north of the city limits.

In order to create a Buddhist tourist wonderland, the regime has accepted millions of dollars from Japanese, Taiwanese, and Korean Buddhists seeking to make merit through helping to recreate the hundreds of eroding and earthquake damaged pagodas that litter the Pagan plain. Archaeologist Pierre Pichard describes the gaudy renovations as "catastrophic," because, "spurning professional assistance from international archaeologists, the junta has proceeded with plans that use cheap techniques that are damaging the temples and the priceless painted murals

Figure 2. The golden façade. (author's photo)

inside. And it is rebuilding damaged temples using new materials that stand in stark contrast to the historical structures" (Covington 2002: 1). The creation of this simulation of the past included demolishing the village of Pagan and relocating the villagers to "New Pagan," well outside the archaeological zone. The sound of goat bells clanking as pre-adolescent boys herded them with long sticks in the shadows of the pagodas has been replaced by the huffing of white tourists furiously pedaling rented bicycles in the glare of the midday sun as their tires sink into the soft sand of the paths between the pastiched stupas.

Like the ancient pagodas of the Pagan plain, even the Shwedagon Pagoda has fallen victim to the regime's "golden façade" projects. The stairways at the four cardinal directions have been enlarged with marble stairs and teak roofing. Perhaps the most symbolic "modernization" of the Buddhist faith in Burma is the installation of an escalator so that pilgrims no longer need to walk barefoot up the many stairs to the central pagoda platform (which is a way of gaining merit) but can now watch others labor up the stairways as they ascend slowly on this wonder of modern technology. The only other escalators I know of in Burma are in Sino-Burmese department stores. The Shwedagon's escalator is a key symbol of the junta's ongoing goal of making Buddhism a voyeuristic, commercial experience, devoid of its potential for political resistance. We should not mince words here. These projects are part of the imprimatur of a fascist imagination upon the Burmese landscape, a huge public works program throughout the country that involves the building of roads, railways, bridges, dams, "model" villages, and "model" towns through the "donation" of money and labor.

Relocating, Rebuilding, Renaming

Following the overthrow of the Burmese monarchy in the Third Anglo-Burmese War in 1885, the British required a standing force of 30,000 soldiers and a further 30,000 military police in order to quell the uprisings that continually occurred in the wake of the British government's reign of terror. The burning of villages, the forcible relocation of villagers, the persecution of headmen and their families, and the on-the-spot hangings of Burmese found to be in possession of weapons were the preferred terror tactics (Maung Htin Aung 1967: 266–68). An English soldier wrote the following lines of a poem to express his sense of shame at these atrocities:

Under a spreading mango tree
A Burmese Chieftain stands,
His hour has come; a captive he
Within the conqueror's hands;
And they fasten around his sturdy neck
A noose of hempen strands.

Under a spreading mango tree
A lifeless body swings.
Though bound its limbs, a soul is free
And spreads on joyful wings
To solve the perplexing myst'ries of
Ten thousand hidden things. (Maung Htin Aung 1967: 267–78)

In recounting this poem, Maung Htin Aung notes the ways Burmese people refused to allow the topography of domination to settle upon the memories of these atrocities. He writes: "Burmese villagers quietly built little pagodas on the sites of the executions and kept alive the spirit of nationalism so nobly demonstrated by the guerrillas."

Once again a topography of domination has settled over the country, and its psychological dimensions include the renaming of the nation, townships, and streets so that the familiar landscapes of childhood no longer exist; the new cities consist of differently named streets, buildings, and gathering places where one is always a "stranger." Colonial buildings are being phased out as the seats of government as Ministries are relocated to concrete and glass tower blocks that squat along the main arterial roads (Philp and Mercer 2002: 30). In this way, the colonial past fades to political irrelevance, except as refurbished tourist locales, as power becomes vested in the marble and cement blocks so beloved of centralizing regimes. Even the nation has a new name. It is rare now to hear "Burma" or "Rangoon" in urban everyday speech. Colonial names are replaced with names more appropriate to the new nation. War heroes and victorious warrior kings and monarchs are used to rewrite familiar locales with bronze and marble figures more suited to the political ideology of the times.

This process of selecting aspects of the past compatible with the imagined future of the nation is most clearly manifest in the museums, memorials, and other "trophy" sites. Not least is the complex built to house the newly "found" white elephants. During the time of the Buddhist Kings, white elephants signified the purity and morality of a particular monarch's rule and white elephants have begun miraculously popping up all over the country, supposedly proving beyond reasonable doubt the moral fitness of the SPDC. Such sweeping claims never go unchallenged for long. A queue winds around the building where the elephants are housed as Burmese people wait to see with their own eyes the junta's pachydermic claims to legitimacy.

In a malicious mood during the heat of the 2002 dry season, I conducted an experiment over a month by asking a variety of car, jeep, and taxi drivers about the color of the "White" elephants. Without exception they turned to me with just a hint of a wicked grin and slapped the dashboard before mercifully turning their attention back to the oncoming traffic. The dashboards were all reddish-brown. I've never seen a white dashboard.

The demolishing of existing structures and the rapid construction of new edifices most often precede the renaming of roads and parks. Whole city blocks disappear in a matter of days, the population loaded onto trucks and forcibly relocated to the new townships that the government has established on rice fields outside the major cities. One hot morning at the beginning of May 1997 my friend Shwe Shwe and I were walking in a relocated township north of Rangoon when she grabbed my arm and whispered "Shhh!" as she pulled me into a squatting position. We slowly raised our heads to peer above the low bamboo trellis. "Look!" she hissed, "The Tatmadaw are relocating these people. See the tin they've been given for a roof and the planks of wood?" A lanky soldier, his rifle slung over his shoulder, his lips red with betel juice, was supervising the unloading of these gifts of construction materials from a green army truck. They are the compensation paid by the regime for the relocation of the family from a quarter behind the main market in Rangoon. There are seven members of the family headed by the patriarch, U Ba, and over the next month his son Taw Win and daughter-in-law Thin Thin Yu scramble to have bamboo walls woven and a thatched roof completed in time for the monsoon rains that begin in June.

Physically uprooting families like that of U Ba is a devastatingly successful policy in the short term as it disables people's information and friendship networks, adding to feelings of alienation and psychological isolation. Rewriting and rebuilding the landscape does not erase people's memories, however. Underneath the government names there are local names. For example, although Rangoon residents navigate by a building known as the IBC (the optimistically named International Business Center), there is not a soul in Rangoon who does not know that the large white structure has been built on the site of the "White Bridge" (known throughout the country as the "red bridge"), a scene of brutal repression by the military during the 1988 uprising. University students were raped and murdered here, "so that the white bridge ran red" with their blood (Greenwood 1994).

Relocating, rebuilding, and renaming are, however, effective strategies in the longer term because both life spans and memories are comparatively short in Burma due to high infant mortality, maternal mortality, the prevalence of diseases due to bad or nonexistent sanitation, high accidental death rates, and other poor health indicators. In addition, knowledge has most often been handed down orally, especially during the Ne Win period and the first years of the SLORC regime when paper was extremely rare. Knowledge has traditionally been written on palm leaves and kept in monasteries that, until the British colonial period, were the primary source of written education. It is unusual to find paper and writing implements in Burmese houses (with the exception of the educated elite in the cities), and as of 2003 there was once again a growing paper shortage. A large percentage of the population (28.1 percent) were born after the 1988 uprising (CIA 2002), or remember it as children.[2] The concept of Burmese memory is such that events that occurred more than about a decade ago quickly reach the category of "a long time ago" or "a long time in the past." Thus the demolishing of structures, neighborhoods, and lifestyles and the rewriting of history to erase the red stains from the White Bridge, eventually wins out in Burma (see, for example, Figure 3).

Through the renaming, rebuilding, and relocating of familiar landmarks and the heavy presence of the army and weaponry, the military council imposes a new spatial configuration on Rangoon. A second political history is simultaneously being written as the old city is destroyed by these "artists of demolition" (Benjamin quoted in Buck-Morss 1989: 90). The bulldozing of Christian, Hindu, Jewish, and Islamic burial sites and places of worship constitutes a reconquering of the dead (following Robben 2000). The cemeteries tell a truth about Rangoon's

Figure 3. The demolition of Rangoon. (Dominic Faulder)

colonial past, of the large numbers of people from India and China who were resident in Burma under British colonization. A 1931 Union of Burma census showed that 52 percent of Rangoon's population of 400,000 was Indian (Brac de la Perrière 1992a: 231). This retrospective victory over a history of Buddhist kingship enrages the Generals and they plough through the ghosts and bones of the dead for no ideological or propaganda purposes but for the simple reason that some of them believe the ferocious nationalism and xenophobia extolled in their own propaganda.

Narcoeconomy

The "huts to high rise" scheme and the creation of urban and transportation infrastructure requires billions of kyat, money that the regime does not have in its coffers. That is why the most drastic changes to the Rangoon and Mandalay urban environments have been the result of the "narcoeconomy" (Bernstein and Kean 1996). Such narcotics include heroin, amphetamines, and opium. Although the regime is directly implicated in the production of narcotics, the term "narcoeconomy" refers to the laundering of these profits by both the military and the drug lords of Burma such as Khun Sa and Lo Hsing-han (Davis and Hawke 1998; *Economist* 1995; Lintner 1990b, 1991, 1993a, 1994a, 1996a,

1998). The shareholders and capital contributors to many joint ventures are the Generals and the drug barons. François Casanier, a research analyst with Geopolitical Drug Watch in Paris, is the source that many investigators turn to when they want statistics on the breadth of the narcoeconomy. He has stated that "All normal economic activities . . . are instruments of drug money laundering . . . and no drug operation in Burma can be run without the SLORC." Casanier found that the national company, Myanmar Oil and Gas Enterprise (MOGE),

"was the main channel for laundering the revenues of heroin produced and exported under the control of the Burmese army." In a deal signed with the French oil giant Total in 1992, and later joined by Unocol, MOGE received a payment of $15 million. "Despite the fact that MOGE has no assets besides the limited instalments of its foreign partners and makes no profit, and that the Burmese state never had the capacity to allocate any currency credit to MOGE, the Singapore bank accounts of this company have seen the transfer of hundreds of millions of US dollars," reports Casanier . . . funds exceeding $60 million and originating from Burma's most renowned drug lord, Khun Sa, were channelled through the company. "Drug money is irrigating every economic activity in Burma . . . and big foreign partners are also seen by the SLORC as big shields for money laundering." (Bernstein and Kean 1996: 2–3)

One tires of seeing drug deals go down in Rangoon between teenage boys and men in their twenties. As one veteran of the Rangoon Drug Rehabilitation Unit told me, "heroin is easier to buy here than candy." In Yankin township, for example, there is a large number of military and public servant housing complexes. The children of this non-poor class, the "middle strata," can afford to buy clothing, western appliances, and other accouterments perceived to be associated with modernity, including heroin. In this township heroin is sold on virtually every street corner with little pretense. I have seen small bags of white powder changing hands countless times. The dealers smile at me when they realize I understand what is occurring. When I mentioned this to two patients at the Drug Rehabilitation Unit, one told me that "All levels of people use drugs here. I got drugs from tea shops, then private houses, and then finally by the roadside." The second man, Maung Chit Hlaing, told me about his arrest and incarceration for a month in 1994:

At that time, things [drugs] were easily available in Yankin Township. [I used then] not because my friends persuaded me to do so, but because I followed in their steps. The people who live in Yankin Township are mostly government servants so their sons use while their parents go to work.

Burma's banks solicit funds for money laundering, taking a 40 percent cut on the clean money. Bernstein and Kean document the relationships that Generals Khin Nyunt and Maung Aye have with the most powerful drug lords in the country, such as Khun Sa, Lo Hsing-han, and their family members. Companies run by the drug lords, such as Asia World, have initiated joint ventures with the regime, such as a "twenty-five-year contract . . . for a new wharf at Yangon Port, which handles more than 90 percent of Burma's exports. With the SLORC's blessings, one of the world's biggest heroin traffickers will thus soon operate a port sending ships loaded with cargo to the United States and countries around the world" (Bernstein and Kean 1996: 3).

Despite the development of infrastructure that creates profits for the military and drug lord cartels, no such infrastructure is being created for the urban youth who contend with enormous unemployment and underemployment. These are children of the military and the upper echelons of the public service. Maung Zali Maw, a university student, told me about the reasons for his addiction and that of his circle of friends:

I started using drugs in 1993. I didn't think this drug could affect me so much. I just tried it for fun. I also tried other drugs as a youth. That doesn't mean I was only interested in drugs, but I'm in close proximity to heroin. I used drugs not because I was bored but because school time is just so much fun. We were just drinking and smoking for fun. As a student here it's quite free at school and we skip classes to have fun. Not all the people who skip classes are drug addicts. If you make friends with drug addicts and are persuaded by them because you are interested, [then] you'll try [heroin]. . . . Here the rate of heroin addicts is high because the number of people who like heroin is high. The reasons that people are forced to use drugs are: proximity to drugs, their background, and their family and social problems which make them upset. Also related to these factors are the cheap price and high supply. There are drug addicts at all the universities and things [drugs] can be bought there.

Maung Zali Maw's sentiments are echoed by Maung Mhu Aung, who attests that "Generally there are a lot of drug addicts in Myanmar as there are a lot of drug sellers. There are some other reasons: there is not much leisure here such as swimming pool facilities, tennis courts, without charges. If we could get those, youngsters wouldn't head that way. But now they charge in every way so people head for drugs." Maung Aye Maung believes that "the reason why most young people use drugs is so many are unemployed and bored, hanging around and injecting heroin with their friends."

These young men are inmates of the Rangoon Drug Rehabilitation Unit, where they were transferred after their arrest by the police for drug use or suspected drug use. Here they are forcibly detoxified for six weeks, either cold turkey or with the aid of a tincture of opium. Not many of the fifty young men I interviewed here have any intention of giving up heroin when they are released. The plentiful supply makes it difficult for recovering addicts to stay away from the drug, especially when they are in the company of their peers. The two main reasons given for reusing heroin upon release from the Unit are peer pressure and social problems. Readjusting to everyday life is very difficult, especially in the absence of any counseling or life-skills training. A twenty-two-year-old man, Maung Paw Tun, who had been through the program many times, reused heroin after his latest admission to the Drug Rehabilitation Unit as a form of self-medication for "unhappiness" and "disappointment" (*sei' nji' deh*) when his girlfriend's parents arranged for her marriage to another man. Maung Paw Tun stated: "She was Burmese and Buddhist, living in [location withheld]. Her parents got her married. I could forget about my disappointment when I was using drugs." Other patients give marital problems such as divorce and fiancées cancelling their engagement as reasons for turning to heroin once again. Patients tell stories of their friends who have left the Unit in previous weeks and have either suffered a fatal overdose or been rearrested. With no hope for a political solution and no chance of a lifestyle change once they leave the Unit, it is not surprising that heroin is an enticing alternative for the children of the Generals and their cronies.

Narcoarchitecture

The demolition of much of Rangoon paved the way for the creation of a modern city. The traditional building rule in Rangoon is that no buildings are to be taller than the centrally located Sule pagoda, from which all distances in Burma are measured (see Figure 4). The direct involvement of the military regime in the Burmese narcoeconomy has however resulted in a type of development that may be termed "narcoarchitecture," a collection of "joint enterprise" concrete skyscrapers and other buildings that have changed Rangoon and Mandalay skylines. Hotels such as the Trader's and Shangri-La Hotels, for which Lo Hsing-han contributed capital and laundered heroin profits (Bernstein and Kean 1997), are examples of the kind of development that has engulfed the capital cities in the 1990s frenzy of construction. This narcoarchitecture comprises a collection of grotesque parodies, such as monstrous concrete blocks of hotels containing hundreds of rooms that remain empty due to the dearth of tourists. These monstrosities are hastily constructed, employing hundreds of construction workers in place of automation, and are often made of flimsy materials.

In the not so distant past, important buildings were built on the buried remains of prisoners or slaves sacrificed for that purpose, and such modern buildings rest upon the weight of heroin addicts and the many

Figure 4. The modernization of Rangoon: high-rise buildings dwarf the Sule Pagoda. (author's photo)

families ravaged by this drug and its partner, methamphetamine. The Sule pagoda now stands dwarfed by such architecture.

Like narcoarchitecture, the Tooth Relic pagodas in Rangoon and Mandalay are typical of the conjunction of an economic with an incipient fascist agenda. The Tooth Relic pagodas were constructed with a significant proportion of forced labor to provide a venue in which the Chinese Tooth Relic could be viewed by Burmese as the Tooth Relic procession traveled around the country. The pagodas and their accompanying spectacles are used to signify to Burmese the successful way in which the military regime: (1) has become the main patron and defender of Buddhism and thus is the legitimate ruler of Burma; (2) has become accepted internationally, as evidenced by the Chinese government loaning Burma the Tooth Relic; and (3) has adopted the symbols and attributes of nationhood as established in the series of spectacles which accompany the Tooth Relic on its journeys around the country. These spectacles culminated in the permanent enshrinement of Tooth Relic replicas in the Tooth Relic pagodas (Schober 1995: 16). The Tooth Relic pagodas are quintessential symbols of the capitalist-authoritarian conjunction in Burma, spectacles created from concrete to immortalize the regime, to enforce labor and mass participation, and to draw political "support" for the State through fear of reprisals.

Burmese military bases both warehouse opium and heroin and provide distribution networks for the products. Burmese soldiers oversee the growing of opium (Levy and Scott-Clarke 1998), and military bases both protect the heroin and amphetamine refineries and coordinate the payment of government gem miners in heroin rather than cash. Bernstein and Kean reveal that

Managers of the SLORC-owned mines, some in joint ventures with Chinese businessmen, are giving their workers the option of receiving compensation in hard drugs rather than cash. Up to 200,000 miners, who travel from villages out of desperation for work can be found in one mine . . . two-thirds of the 100,000 workers at Hpakant Jade mine, owned entirely by the SLORC, have chosen to be paid by drugs rather than by cash. And the only way large shipments of illegal substances can find their way into Kachin State is through SLORC-controlled gates. (Bernstein and Kean 1996: 5)

On the one hand, then, heroin and smuggling revenues reach to the highest levels of State power and allow the regime to continually stave off bankruptcy. Through the use of joint-venture companies, in which capital is supplied by a foreign company, general, or drug lord, transnational capital buys for the regime the weapons of modern urban warfare, including the bulletproof vests, bayonets, and truncheons of the soldiers stationed throughout the cities. With the help of foreign governments and international telecommunications firms, and in return for rights on future infrastructure contracts, companies and governments have updated the surveillance abilities of the regime (Selth 1997; Ball 1998).

On the other hand, foreign companies, which have built airports, hotels, supermarkets, and department stores, give the regime a veneer of moral authority it would otherwise lack. In bringing modernity to Burma and conjoining it with the accouterments of repression, the Burmese Generals ensnare the populace in a network of repression. The more transnational capital flows into Burma, the more the trappings of modernity legitimate and enlarge the regime's capacity to launder money from its narcoeconomy and smuggling sectors and to purchase weapons to oppress the populace.

There is no doubt that urban residents deplore the effects of government corruption and the regime's alliance with the heroin trade upon the urban environment. A *Bangkok Post* article quoted a Mandalay resident as saying that "there are three lines of business here: the green line, the red line, and the white line. That's jade, rubies and heroin" (Mansfield 1998). It is perhaps only a coincidence that the word "line" in Burmese is used in the most common of Burmese phrases, "line money," to refer to official bribery which must be paid in order for almost any transaction or appointment to occur in Burma. I asked a former student, Ma Saw Shwe, if she thought most people understood that heroin profits were being used to build the new infrastructure of the cities? She replied:

People are aware that, for example, the Trader's Hotel was owned by Khun Sa, or was it Lo Hsing-han? People are aware of their activities and the majority of the people know it was black market money, laundered money. We all know that the banks, for example, are convenient money-laundering places and that the hotels are for the elite. We don't like it and we try to keep away from the banks, the hotels, and the tall buildings. As for us students, we are really happy to see how all these new things in the city are always empty, and how, during Visit Myanmar Year, hardly anyone came. We really like all these empty hotels!

Another example of the disgust urban Burmese have for the narcoeconomy is contained in Nyi Pu Lay's short story entitled "The Python."[3] Allott's analysis of the story gives an insight into the concerns of Mandalay residents about the changes that the regime's increasing alliance with the controllers of heroin production and other illegal activities have wrought. She writes:

The python of the title refers to the Chinese and Sino-Burmese businessmen, drug traffickers, and gem dealers, who are disliked by many Burmese, since they are perceived as moving into Mandalay, and squeezing out the Burmese: laundering their illegal profits by investing in property, they are seen as driving up house prices to a point where the Burmese . . . are forced to sell up and move out of their old family houses, in prime downtown sites, to the outer suburbs, the "new pastures" of the story, many of which have been newly built on former paddy fields. Since 1988, when Nyi Pu Lay wrote this story, the influx of Chinese has increased as a result of the SLORC's deals with the Wa and Kokang, who are ethnic Chinese from the Northeast Shan State, the main heroin producing area. Many Burmese resent that their city, the former royal capital and a symbol of Burmese independence, is becoming a satellite town of Yunnan Province in China . . . it is never explicitly mentioned in the story that U Myo Khin is Chinese. . . . His illegal business activities are indicated by the fact that none of his money bundles have been through the bank. (Allott 1994: 86–87)

In joint-venture narcoenterprises we see clear evidence of the incipient fascist vision of Burmese society where "disciplined democracy" is equated with the freedom to consume, even if the thing being consumed is heroin. It is of no more relevance to the Burmese junta than it was to the European governments of Benjamin's era that the working class has no money to spend in the newly created fairylands of consumerism.[4] As Max Horkheimer has remarked, "whoever doesn't want to talk about capitalism shouldn't talk about fascism" (Knödler-Bunte 1977). While this emergent heroin-funded, shoddily constructed, and mass-produced modernity is the veneer overlying the suffering of young heroin addicts and countless other urban dwellers, it is not false. It is the experience of the modern for Burmese people. The existence of wealthy, unemployed, recovering heroin addicts such as Maung Mhu Aung and Maing Paw Htun among those who suffer does not invalidate this experience of the modern as an authentic one. The golden façade is a mass-replicated process that inscribes individuals in modern collectivities. A façade is a veneer or covering over the part of an object that faces toward open space or the street. Burmese people must also adopt a façade that faces outward to the incipient fascist public sphere, a place of danger. In the following chapters I describe the process of creating this public façade and the dangers of holding on to an anomic sense of self for too long.

Chapter 6
The Veneer of Conformity

I'm on the top of the world, looking down on creation . . .
—Young, unemployed Burmese men singing karaoke
in "Fantasyland," 9.30 A.M. Monday morning

Repressed human beings are not the same as those who are free and
secure. Something happens to us when we are repressed, when we
are intimidated, when we have to worry every day about our security.
—Aung San Suu Kyi, "The Game Rules in Burma"

One of the most common propaganda signboards seen in urban areas
is the National Conference signboard. It depicts a procession of progress, a march of prosperity where a young Burmese man holds aloft the
Union flag, a beautiful young Burmese woman by his side (Figure 8).
They are followed by other heterosexual couples from the "National
Races." All members of the procession wear their designated "ethnic"
clothing. A superfluity of symbolism: the relationships that pertain
between genders, generations, tradition, and modernity, and between
model Burman citizens and the National Races, rise above the cracked
pavements of the cities, a pale, pastiched, and peeling vision of the dissemination of power through society under the military model.

The signboard is one of many attempts to create a feeling of participation by the masses in the public sphere. Theorists of European fascism
argued that fascism organizes and composes existing myths and stereotypes, such as the hope of unity and the hope of progress (Brückner et
al. 1977: 105). Fascist regimes most effectively mobilize these stereotypes
among the dispossessed, the demoralized, the unemployed, the returning war veterans, and so on (Negt 1976: 69–70). The National Conference signboard (Figure 5), like so many other forms of Burmese

Figure 5. March of Progress and National Unity signboard. (author's photo)

propaganda, plays upon old stereotypes of hierarchy, seeking legitimation from some gut feeling held by Burmese about their place in the
world; a deep tacit knowledge rarely questioned under the junta and
enshrined in the rewriting of history text books for school children.[1]

The creation of affect and of collective affect is part of how authoritarian regimes operate at the level of the "masses," a subject that has not
been well researched or theorized: "The investigation of fascism as a
mass movement has not gone beyond the initial attempts of ideology
criticism by Bloch and Benjamin and the social-psychology of Reich in
particular" (Knödler-Bunte 1977: 42). Knödler-Bunte argues that "Mass
movement means that interests and contents of consciousness are
moved on a mass level. Forms of expression are initiated in which the
masses recognize themselves" (43). Clearly the military junta wants the
Burmese populace to recognize and identify with the stereotypes portrayed in the signboard.

Some theorists question whether we need to investigate the state's
construction of collective affect, arguing, "the most important decisions
in fascism were, after all, made in private" (Negt in Brückner et al. 1977:
96). Others argue that there can never be a public sphere under fascism:
"'Shh . . . the enemy is listening, too' was a warning on signs over tables
in bars. The myths of the Nazis could not be understood at all. They
could at best be taken on faith. And even at that, the willingness to

believe was not great at all, otherwise so many methods of psychic terror would not have been needed" (Gottschalch in Brückner et al. 1977: 126).

It is certainly true, for example, that there was continual and significant resistance to fascism in Germany, Italy, and other fascist and incipient fascist states. But it is equally true that confusion, complicity, deliberate ignorance of the political situation, denial, opportunism, and tacit acceptance all comprise ways of experiencing repression. In addition, trust, truthfulness, and many other facets of meaningful relationships are abolished or suppressed in the Burmese public sphere. The junta is incapable of controlling purely by force and seeks to persuade through propaganda that, nevertheless, always contains the threat of violence. The nationwide incompetence and inefficiency of the armed forces and the bureaucracy, related to a lack of enthusiasm for the junta's ideology, is a key reason why the regime is not, and perhaps cannot ever evolve, into a fully actualized fascist state. There are myriad processes occurring in the public sphere, both in the creation of collective affect by the state and in a public spirit of defiance characterized by a hollow mimesis.

With regard to National Socialism in Germany, Brückner notes that

The participation of the populace was regulated through demonstrative, appellate public spheres: one only need remember the loud speakers which were everywhere, the ritualistic interruption of the work day, the school day and other normal everyday activities, the voice of Hitler, the demonstrations and ceremonies. Through these means a feeling of immediate participation "in the whole" was restored for the man on the street, for the people; a plebiscite, which, of course, cannot be described as (active) involvement. (1977: 97)

It is this nonactive, active involvement that is central to any analysis of contemporary Burma. The State's construction of collective affect is critical if we are to understand the ways in which Burmese people's lives have been shaped since the military coup of 1962. It is in the creation of model citizens through their forced participation in, and consumption of, state spectacles, that the State forces its captive population to recognize itself as a whole, a "Union" of Burmans and National Races, guided in perpetuity by its "father," the Tatmadaw. It is my argument in this chapter that common to such regimes of terror, the junta seeks to create a depoliticized society-wide mass movement, the objectification of Burmese people, who respond by presenting a mirror back to the regime. It is what I call the karaoke-like aspects of the population's relationship with, and outward response to, the imperfect forms of totalitarian control central to incipient fascist regimes. Burmese people consciously present a blank emotional tableau to the military regime at mass rallies and other state spectacles. This fixed form of social interaction with the Generals is, like the fixed form of karaoke, a collectivism in which the individual is safe in the anonymity of the group (Lum 1998: 174). The nationwide anesthetization of emotion in the public sphere is a process that has diverse negative effects upon the mental health of the population as they search for psychic sanctuary.

In this and the following chapter I take up this theme and show why "karaoke fascism" is the best term to describe the veneer of conformity adopted by much of the population. I begin with the experience of being a "mass," and the myths that are mobilized to create tacit, complicit, or demoralized participation in the State's project of social engineering. I move on to describe the ways in which Burmese people comport themselves at State spectacles, and then narrow the focus to one man, Ko Ma, the subject of a short story that allows us to understand the corporeal aspects of repression and the survival strategies devised by Burmese people which are the subject of the remaining chapters.

The Experience of the "Masses"

Mass organizations have existed in Burma since the AFPFL period in the run up to the granting of independence. These included the All Burma Peasants Organizations, the Trades Union Congress of Burma, and the Federation of Trades Organization. When Burma's first elected prime minister, U Nu, decided to temporarily hand power over to a caretaker military government under General Ne Win, it "began mass mobilization in a rather tentative manner. It set up a series of National Solidarity Associations" that "withered away following the end of direct military rule in 1960." A series of mass organizations were formed prior to the establishment of the Burma Socialist Programme Party (BSPP) as a mass organization. These were "people's worker and peasant councils called *asi-ayone*, or organizations. The workers councils started in 1964 and had a membership of 1.5 million by 1970, while the peasants councils, formed in 1969, had a membership of 7.6 million by 1980" (Steinberg 2001: 99–101).

GONGOs, or Government Organized Nongovernmental Organizations, are the government institutions that exist in the gaping hole left by the nationalization of almost all forms of civil society after 1962. During the BSPP period, the socialist Lanzin Youth Party was formed and my male Burmese age mates remember fondly their after-school marching exercises when they thought it was exciting to pretend to be a soldier and march around school playgrounds in formation. Burmese readily identify with GONGOs because of the prior existence of the Lanzin

Party and perhaps also the other anticolonial and workers' organizations of previous eras.

The GONGOs ostensibly have objectives concerning public health and development. They are in fact a ready way of mobilizing the population quickly. The most sinister of these organizations is the Union Solidarity and Development Association (USDA), created in September 1993 (Diller 1997: 39). It is no coincidence that the USDA was created two weeks after the SLORC decided to convene a National Convention, allegedly to draft a new constitution. Registered under the Home Affairs Ministry as a social organization, the USDA facilitates the mass mobilization of the population. With a membership by 1999 of more than 11 million people, it is the practical instrument for the dissemination of totalitarian ideology and practice throughout the populace (Steinberg 2001: 110–11).

Aung San Suu Kyi likened the USDA to the Brown Shirts, the Nazi youth movement, when its members were paid to assassinate (or perhaps only intimidate) her at the junction outside her home (NCGUB 1999). On another occasion, USDA members helped the military demolish houses in Kammayut Township when defiant residents refused to comply with a directive to pull down their homes immediately, and at their own expense. The area was earmarked for a commercial venture financed by a general on the ruling council. Aung San Suu Kyi has reported to journalists a number of occasions when USDA members were exhorted to use violence to break up congregations at religious ceremonies and NLD functions (Kean and Bernstein 1997).

In the most recent and most serious uses of this paramilitary organization, the USDA were mobilized to attack Aung San Suu Kyi's motorcade in May 2003, in what has become known as the Dipeyin Massacre. Aung San Suu Kyi and senior NLD members such as U Tin Oo were arrested after this violent incident and held at Insein Jail and other secret locations.

The USDA is the flagship GONGO, but it is the proliferation of GONGOs at the community level and the ambiguous nature of their many "duties" that confuse people. The Myanmar Maternal Child Welfare Association (MMCWA) is reported to have 1,100,000 ordinary members and 340,000 permanent members. In addition there are 104,000 members of the Myanmar Fire Brigade and 160,000 Myanmar Red Cross brigade members (Steinberg 2001: 115). All these GONGOS link health (or safety and well-being) with political violence, domination, and repression. Smith (1996: 55) noted as early as 1996 that "USDA representatives already sit in, as a matter of course, on planning meetings and health seminars in many townships."

In conjunction with local township health officials, GONGOs such as the Myanmar Red Cross (MRC) and the USDA explicitly link their two duties, which are "health promotion" and the crushing of "destructive elements." For example, a *New Light of Myanmar* editorial stated that "Red Cross executives [are] exhorted to drive for materialization of national policy, health planning" (NLM 1996e: 6). The editorial describes the mandate of the USDA as follows: "USDA members urged to ward off destructive elements in cooperation with the people" (NLM 1996h: 2). GONGOS such as the USDA, MRC, and MMCWA commonly enforce membership, although there are individuals who join voluntarily.

Members of GONGOs must appear at government events (such as mass rallies) a minimum of seven times per year. GONGOs function at a level below that of the military and the police, on a par with institutions such as public servants and teachers. Like public servants, members of GONGOs are used for forced labor such as the building of the Tooth Relic Pagodas, but their higher levels function as supervisors for forced labor both at government construction sites and in the townships. For example, a senior Red Cross leader told me that one of the jobs of the Red Cross members is to coordinate with the local LORCs to ensure that local communities conduct forced labor on a regular basis (usually weekly). He spoke proudly of his organizational capacities, and many public servants have told me of their happiness in adopting the role of forced labor supervisor so as to avoid participating in the forced labor.

Forced labor (see Figure 6) is, like everything else in Burma, optional if sufficient "line money" is paid to the relevant officials. A high ranking government health worker in Mandalay told me that another common way forced labor could be avoided by senior public servants was by conducting "telephone duty" once a week, where an employee remains at the government offices after hours answering the phone. This is, of course, forced labor, but it is preferable to carrying rocks and other tasks mandated at the construction sites. The other method this particular public servant uses to avoid doing the manual work usually involved in forced labor is to accept the position of supervisor of forced labor. This complicity is revealed by Daw Si Si Win:

There are "model" health workers, they are brought to Mandalay and put up in a camp. I think they're shown the sights. While they're there, they're sent to work on the Tooth Relic pagoda. They get a certificate as a "model worker" and have one up on the other VHW's [volunteer health workers]. It is a form of motivation in the townships. I was called to attend two opening day ceremonies . . . last month but I said I was sick. A lot of people don't have to do voluntary labor on the [Tooth Relic] pagoda because they do telephone duty.

Figure 6. Forced labor. (Dominic Faulder)

Executive members of GONGOs are used to coordinate groups of people for activities that span townships such as forced labor projects and for enforced performances. This is particularly evident in the marshaling of the population for the series of mass rallies conducted in 1996. The State media describe this process as follows:

> To organize all constructive forces the Government is encouraging social organizations including Myanmar Red Cross Society to enable them to further develop and actively participate in working in that direction. . . . Assistance of organizations or activities on self-reliance basis for social welfare and health and fitness of the people in border areas has helped consolidate national unity. . . . Other social, donor and wellwisher organizations declared at a recent mass rally that they are committed to safeguarding the stability of the State and further developing economic and social infrastructures. It is a national duty of all wellwishers and social organizations as well as the public to cooperate with the Government's nation-building endeavours. (NLM 1996f)

In the relocated townships USDA members provide a ready source of forced labor, and the State media are constantly lauding their "voluntary" efforts. An article in *New Light of Myanmar* in August 1996 details the USDA training of "volunteers" at a Tooth Relic Pagoda at which Secretary No. 1 officiates. It reports that Khin Nyunt "greets trainees of Basic Multiplier Course No 2/96 for Executives of Mon State USDA at the construction site of Tooth Relic Pagoda" (NLM 1996d). The general has stated that every citizen must be a part of such organizations (NLM 1996h: 2).

The GONGOs have become extremely influential within the relocated townships. Other more traditional organizations have been displaced, and township dwellers increasingly feel that they are dwarfed by the large number of GONGOs and the heavy influence they have over everyday life. Within an average peri-urban ward, the government presence is conveyed by the Yawata, the 100 House Leader, 10 House Leader, Street Leader, USDA, MMCWA, MRC, Fire Brigade, and Auxiliary Fire Brigade. These organizations go from house to house with monotonous regularity demanding "donations." One of the most distinctive aspects of the relocated townships is the loud disjunctive music from the competing fund raising drives along the main roads, which blares from mobile "voluntary contribution" vehicles. In order to stay in favor (and avoid the serious consequences that can come which refusal to cooperate), residents must give money on an almost daily basis to these parastatal organizations.

It is hard to penetrate the dense tangles by which Burmese participate in their own surveillance. The formation of GONGOs and the advantages of becoming plugged in to the system of hierarchy and patronage (and the consequences for not doing so) have led to most people in the capital cities living with members of government departments or organizations. The military council has, since 1993, inserted itself into almost every home. Performing politicized duties as a member of a governmental or quasi-governmental organization has become normalized. Belonging to one or more organizations does not engender feelings of betrayal in family members or colleagues; it is simply taken as a given like so many other elements in contemporary Burmese lives.

The prominence given to the GONGOs by the official media and their high visibility in the townships means that GONGOs are increasingly used at a local level for personal benefits. The Myanmar Red Cross, for example, is perceived by many young people in the relocated townships as a social club for unemployed youth. The Myanmar Maternal and Child Welfare Society (MMCWA), on the other hand, provides opportunities for women to become well known in their communities. A young female receptionist, Ma Swe, explains that

People join the MMCWA because it is seen as elite and signifies [that members have] money left over from buying necessities, as there is a membership fee and the cost of uniforms. They are very close to the LORC and it is one way of getting contacts and favors. Some people join because they want to, for these reasons, but others join because they are told they have an obligation to the TMOs [Township Medical Officers] and other government officials.

Complicity is impossible to define in this situation as advantages accrue to GONGO members (such as "getting close" to Yawata officials and therefore accessing systems of patronage). Disadvantages for not joining include being failed in school exams, losing jobs, denied access to certain black market avenues, lowered prestige and power within local communities, and an increased risk of political persecution. It is not unusual to meet families in Golden Valley who have a monk and a nun in the family, as well as a public servant, an NLD member, and a GONGO member. Such families do not see anything particularly unusual in this arrangement. Each family member is pursuing his or her own avenue for advancement and the goals may be religious, economic, or political. The enforced participation in so many parastatal groups means that these family members are never seen as traitorous or complicit, but rather as strategic, sensible, and altruistic.

Community Organizations

In the townships around Mandalay, existing villages were incorporated into new townships, and a significant degree of land speculation has occurred in the past few years as roads and bridges are built to connect these new townships to the city centers. Within these new townships there is no single pattern to the formation of civil society, except that residents of peri-urban areas conceive of community organizations as crowding around them, overlapping in their demands, and impinging on the local community. Some groups, most notably the Yawatas, while being perceived as the most powerful community organization, are placed spatially, in the minds of the community members, further away from the community than other institutions.

The government and individuals identified by community members as having influence over their daily lives include the following: the Myanmar Red Cross (MRC), the Union Solidarity and Development Association (USDA), the Ward Law and Order Restoration Council (LORC), the Head of the LORC, the Myanmar Maternal and Child Welfare Association (MMCWA), the Auxiliary Fire Brigade, the Fire Brigade, the Head of the Sub-Ward (100 House Leader), the 10 House Leader, the Government Midwives, the Primary Health Center Staff, the Police Sentry, and the Fire Watch.

The following nongovernmental organizations (NGOs) and individuals also have significant community influence: imams, priests, monks, private clinic health staff, elders, teachers, Indigenous Medicine Practitioners (IMP), community healers, astrologers, *Nat* spirit mediums, Buddhist groups, Dhammayoun leaders, single men's and women's associations, and social groups (*lumuye:apwe, thaye:naye:*).[2]

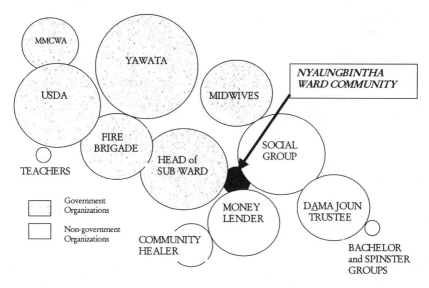

Figure 7. Community influence relationships.

Those who wield power through influence (*ana*) rather than authority (*awsa*) are of great importance at a local level. Wealthy businessmen, Yawata commanders who have democratic leanings, leaders of single men's associations, and charismatic religious leaders of all faiths were singled out as having much local influence. This is the same difference as that between headmen with *ana* and SPDC secretaries with *awsa* made by villagers in lower Burma. It is the same qualitative difference between ward officials and elders.

When asked to rate the importance of these groups and individuals, the Yawata was almost always considered the most powerful institution (see Figure 7). Monks were a distant second, followed by the MMCWA, the *lumuye: apwe* organizations, other religious practitioners, and primary health center staff. In one ward, the USDA was considered the primary powerful institution. When asked to represent the organizations spatially, the residents of the relocated townships unfailingly grouped the government and parastatal organizations on one side of the community and the NGOs on the other, suggesting that they perceive a definite separation between these two kinds of community structures and the two kinds of power that are wielded at the local level.

The wards that comprise mainly government workers and are well established have a higher proportion of GONGOs and fewer independent community organizations based on genuine voluntary participation and recruitment. These wards contain many government employees who have either chosen to relocate to the townships or been granted land in the townships. Conversely, the wards that are closer to a traditional village structure or have incorporated preexisting villages have a significantly higher number of NGOs structured around traditional Burmese patterns of authority and influence such as religion, elders, and organizations based upon gender segregation. In these wards there are large numbers of people who were farmers until their land was appropriated, as well as Nat spirit mediums and astrologers. Some GONGOs, such as the MMCWA and USDA, have only minimal influence in these wards.

To an extent, the GONGOs are recognizable as incarnations of political parties such as the Lanzin party. However, even though Burmese culture and social organizations have never been static, the formation of GONGOs is, in a very short period of time, significantly changing the community structure and forms of association that existed prior to their introduction. A clear pattern emerges here despite the diversity and character of individual wards within the relocated townships. As the townships become more established, nongovernmental community groups such as Buddhist organizations and community social groups are slowly losing influence as GONGOs aimed as specific demographics rise in prominence. Among the youth population, for example, the Myanmar Red Cross and the USDA are slowly supplanting their NGO counterparts as *awsa* (the power of authority) and *ana* (the power of charismatic leadership) begin to fuse through widespread community participation in the GONGOs. Joining the MMCWA, which recruits mature women in the townships, is thus a way of gaining local influence (*ana*), even though that influence is gained by purchasing power (*awsa*).

State Spectacles

The most sinister aspect of the creation of these parastatal organizations lies in the depoliticization of the masses as seen through the many reasons Burmese people give for participating in these organizations apart from their forcible recruitment. In the remainder of this chapter I describe the participation of Burmese people, through GONGOs, in the most ostentatious form of emergent modernism in Burma: the spectacle. Walter Benjamin viewed State spectacles, such as Armed Forces Day, as evidence of the conjunction of violence and modernity also embodied in mass consumption. The list of Burmese State spectacles is long, but the most common ones are the mass rallies held all over the country to denounce "internal and external traitorous elements" and the ubiquitous use of forced labor. In addition, there is a calendar of military

Figure 8. State spectacle opening ceremony. (Dominic Faulder)

celebrations and endless "opening ceremonies" of roads, bridges, hospitals, universities, and other monuments that immortalize the founding violence of the State. The images that appear daily in the State media consist of Generals cutting ribbons to the accompaniment of flags being waved by school children and beautiful young women in Court dress releasing hundreds of colored balloons (as in Figure 8).

Taussig argues that "occasionally these everyday productions, routinized as they are, have to blow up and achieve the scale of the spectacular so as to maintain the explosive promise" of [military dictatorship (1997: 149). The enforced participation of Burmese people in the never-ending cycle of "opening ceremonies" reached its culmination in the ultimate State spectacle to date, the opening ceremony for "Visit Myanmar Year" (Figure 9). Accompanied by the donation of robes and accessories for monks, public games of *chinlon*, and street festivals, Burmese were made to sit in sporting stadiums or participate in a choreographed singing, dancing, musical pageant that displayed all the familiar symbols of the new Union of Myanmar. The fat Burmese doll that was chosen as the official mascot of Visit Myanmar Year was replicated in a row of fat, bobbing children in costumes, who watched a float consisting of a replica of the royal barge move along an athletic track while the crowd, reminiscent of the audience at a World Cup football final, turned over cards en

Figure 9. Visit Myanmar Year opening ceremony. (Dominic Faulder)

masse revealing images of the "United" State. Patriotism itself, as Benjamin noted, becomes a commodity-on-display at such nation building moments (Buck Morse 1989: 89). State spectacles such as the Visit Myanmar Year opening ceremony and Armed Forces Day constitute a "promise lying dormant" regarding the violence that the State will use to ensure complicity with its ideology of "democracy as the freedom to consume" (Taussig 1997: 149).

Spectacles are enacted narratives of State power (and enforced participation and witnessing) that both naturalize and mythify State dominance through combining the fetishization of bodies-as-commodities with political ideology. This process has been occurring in Burma since the 1962 coup through the national cooperative movement. Steinberg (2001: 99) notes, "The leadership of the cooperatives has been coterminous with leadership of other, directly political, mass organizations in most of the military period, and with apparent design. The minister of cooperatives under the BSPP [Ne Win regime] was also head of the Lanzin (BSPP) Youth League, and under the SLORC/SPDC, head of the USDA."

It is the use of millions of Burmese bodies in orchestrated political events that shows most clearly how, as the state moves from pre-modern to modern, a new Burmese body (the body-as-commodity) is being constructed by the State. For Walter Benjamin, it was the Olympic Games that replaced World Expositions as the ultimate global spectacle. Benjamin had earlier written of the top floor of the Arcades, which he described as "fairy grottoes" in which "angels are nesting" (Benjamin 1983: 614, 700 quoted in Buck-Morss 1989: 83). Here Benjamin is referring to prostitutes who sat in the upstairs windows of the Arcades, their bodies transformed into commodities for sale. It was in the 1936 Olympic Games that Benjamin noted a further transformation of the human body into a "body-as-commodity" in which the body becomes the only commodity on display (Benjamin 1983: 256).

Benjamin's analysis of the relationships between Nazi patriotism and the modern body-as-commodity is useful for understanding the motivations behind, and the consequences of, the annual spectacles such as the National Trade Fairs and National Races Cultural Fairs in Rangoon, and the ongoing efforts to create "fit" Burmese bodies through international competition. At the cultural and trade fairs the new workhorses of the industrial age, including outboard motors, the latest surgical and medical equipment, and combine harvesters, are on display, but so too are pavilions of "authentic ethnic culture," transforming each of Burma's minority groups into a "commodity-on-display." A spectacle is only powerful when it is consumed by an audience, and State spectacles are solely intended for internal consumption (Allen Feldman, personal communication, 1997). In Burma the State uses the bodies of its model citizens to participate in its spectacles, which are then consumed by other Burmese who watch, read, and listen to the State media and the propaganda of the Information Ministry.

What are the consequences of this form of mass participation by individual Burmese? Is the State successful in its creation of bodies-as-commodities and a depoliticized mass movement of nationwide proportions? What kind of intellectual and internal life can be maintained by individual Burmese when reduced to the level of "mass ornaments"? It is to these questions that I now turn.

Burmese Automata

In the authoritarian vision of urban renewal pursued by the Nazis and the Italian Fascists, Benjamin and Baudrillard perceived a zealous celebration of the "acceptance of a culture of death" in the scant regard paid to the lives, traditions, and communities of displaced urban residents (Baudrillard 1993: 186). In this section I describe the ultimate form of deterritorialization, the remaking of the body as an "unsafe" zone and its reconstruction as an "automaton," or tool of the State. As Kafka (1948) reminds us, narratives of violence are often written or enacted upon the body. But how (and why) does the Burmese State produce what I call "Burmese automata"? The answer is deceptively simple: the enforced building of monuments that testify to State power (roads, railways, defense force monuments) and the enforced participation of Burmese bodies in mass spectacles (political rallies, "opening ceremonies," "ethnic trade fairs") are attempts by the regime to force Burmese to both acknowledge and accept their nation as a centralized military utopia of which the Tatmadaw is the progenitor and patriarch, and the pivot upon which Burmese life revolves.

In the production of Burmese automata, the regime reproduces itself and extends its celebration of the culture of death into the very bodies of its subject population. Of course the State does not consciously make Burmese automata; the regime requires Burmese to assent willingly to the rule of the Generals. The hollowness with which Burmese conduct themselves at the compulsory State spectacles and forced labor sites is, however, sometimes a conscious decision on the part of Burmese to give their bodies over to the State. Burmese will often allow their bodies to be made into automata as a deliberate survival strategy.

That is not to suggest that the regime's self-enriching economic policies have not resulted in Burmese having to participate as daily laborers under hazardous and very poor conditions simply for enough money to procure the necessities of survival. The following excerpt from a Burmese short story depicts the way the struggle for survival through continuous, repetitive, manual labor is strongly felt by Burmese to be responsible for their feelings of alienation and surrealism (I take up this theme of surrealism in the next chapter). This is a tale of a concrete salesman. He works from a warehouse where there are hundreds of laborers working for less than subsistence wages carrying cement, bricks, and other materials of "urban renewal" that will immortalize, in concrete, the conjunction of modernity and State power, and will thus cement the alliance that the Generals have made with the drug lords. As Taussig insists, "let us not forget that [the] most concrete of images in modernity, [is] concrete itself" (Taussig 1997: 149).

In the short story, "Ko Ma," written by a well-known and often imprisoned Burmese writer, a man buys and sells concrete and has a morbid fascination with it, a metaphor for the Burmese fascination with modernity and the West. Watching the Generals' narcoarchitecture arise almost overnight in Rangoon and Mandalay, it is difficult not to notice the concrete, mud, and plaster of paris that cover the bare-chested bodies of thousands of construction workers. The short story describes a magical transformation of human to material, of flesh to stone. But there is another miraculous transformation occurring here—the transformation of the white powder of heroin to the gray powder of concrete and of black money to white money.

One day Ko Ma suddenly becomes ill, and he begins to consult with a wide variety of doctors and is subjected to a barrage of biomedical tests. Over the following weeks his body slowly solidifies until, in the final section of the story, Ko Ma becomes imbued with the same properties as the substance he has sold. This story can be read as a metaphor for the changes occurring as the State moves from pre-modern to modern within the context of authoritarianism.

Each part of my body was X-rayed. My head, my chest, my ribs, my abdomen, my feet, my arms, my hands. After having examined the X-rays, the doctor who should have established a diagnosis, was not able to find a cause. Sweat beaded on his face and dropped onto the end of his fingertips: "Your body is in the strangest way. I have never seen anything like it. There is not a doctor in the world who would have studied this kind of anatomy."

"Please explain."

The doctor raised the X-rays to the light and examined them again. "First of all, your bones are not those of a normal man, they resemble welded iron bars rather than those of other people. Next, your body appears to be filled with fine particles, they are so numerous that it's alarming, and I cannot say what they consist of."

"Are you sure they are bars of iron?"

"Yes, look at the X-rays. They appear whiter than is normal, and the joints do not have articulations as normal bones do, they seem to be put end to end."

If I have come to be represented by iron bars, an inch in diameter, then as for the fine particles, are they cement powder? I knew that cement is composed of a powder of cooked lime and a little quartz powder, that the mixture obtained is extremely heavy, and that these particles could only be that. However, I was involved only with its sale, I thus had few occasions to breathe the cement dust. But its appearance in the X-rays is extremely strange. Is my body only an assembly of iron bars in a block of cement? Am I really only a concrete man? When had this started? Why did this thing happen now? And how is it that I am still alive? Am I still an ordinary man? I don't understand anything any more. The doctor picked up his bag and left, looking haggard.

Nine weeks later, I found myself at the hospital for good. I almost had to be transported there with a crane. The new X-rays showed that the particles were even more numerous, it seemed to me that my body was full of them. I could not move my feet any more, nor my ankles. That is why I was hospitalized. The chemical tests carried out on my muscular tissue at the department of medical research, revealed that it was composed of lime and quartz, that my body cells were gradually drying up, like all the other fluids in my body. I gave thanks that my brain had not hardened yet.

Four weeks later, my feet were crumbling, like cement dried between bricks. My heart, however, was still beating. My mouth continued to move but I did not breathe any more, I could not drink any more and my tears could not run any more. I no longer had any way of showing my emotions, as all of my body had hardened. My eyelids did not blink any more, and my eyes remained wide open until I was tired of the sight of the tiling that covered the walls of the hospital. I wanted to speak, but that was impossible for me . . . day after day, my mouth became frozen. My wife, my friends, and my children visited me, but I was unable to distinguish one from another.

In this story, little by little, the human is replaced with the artificial. Concrete powder invades the cells of the body and solidifies. The concrete salesman, Ko Ma, whose name is a play on the Burmese word for concrete, is a powerful metaphor for the ways in which Burmese are made over into Burmese automata: slowly suborned, slowly regulated and disciplined through both dehumanizing, repetitive labor under hazardous conditions and the never-ending repetition of State ideology at State spectacles.

In *Les fleurs du mal* (1857) Baudelaire transposes the machine over the human body. Benjamin has commented that "Machinery becomes in Baudelaire the sign of destructive powers. Not the least of such machinery is the human skeleton" (Benjamin 1985: 684). The French term "armature" can mean both skeleton and scaffold, and thus can signify the mechanistic dimensions of the modern Burmese body, dimensions that eventually overwhelm Ko Ma, until his corporeal body is transformed into iron bars embedded in a concrete block. It is a graphic depiction of a process of inscribing a new set of social relations upon the modern body.

Feldman has written about the way the seed of violent conflict has flourished in the wastelands of industrial culture in Northern Ireland. He looks back at the writers of the Frankfurt School such as Adorno to see how the commodity fetish merges with what he describes as a technology of death. The site of this merger is the body. He gives the example of a soldier holding a gun and argues that the Irish body becomes an instrument of violence, a "tool holding a tool," or a "political form" fusing with a "commodity form" (Feldman 1991: 234–35). In the surreal landscapes of urban Burma, power becomes spatialized through the body not just by regulating bodies in space during periods of urban warfare, but also in the treatment of real people as things, without the rights otherwise accorded to human beings. As Foucault has written, "in modernity, political power increasingly becomes a matter of regimenting the circulation of bodies in time and space in a matter analogous to things" (Feldman 1991: 8).

This inscription of power upon bodies is integral to the dissemination of Foucault's "Disciplines" throughout society. Ann Anagnost has addressed the manner in which bodies function as circulating systems of symbols of State power in China. She argues that although State power is undoubtedly inscribed upon Chinese bodies and that bodies "are now the vehicles for the circulation of signs in a play of representations that makes power visible" (Anagnost 1994: 138), nevertheless there is still a space between domination and the complete internalization of such domination. She argues:

In China we see many technologies of power that at first appear to be fully disciplinary in Foucault's sense of this term—placing persons on a grid that makes even intimate areas of practice visible to a panoptic gaze. . . . I suggest, however that . . . signs play on the surface of subjects, reordering their outward practice rather than their inner psyches. It is not that these techniques fail to affect one's sense of self, but they affect it more in terms of a submersion of the self into a moral category, a state of selflessness that merges into the collectivity, than by elaborating the self in all its particularity. (Anagnost 1994: 149–50)

Feldman's and Anagnost's analyses fit well the world's many amoral economic landscapes where the prostitute is emblematic of the body as commodity (Buck-Morss 1989: 183, 429). The amoral economic landscapes formed by the regime's narcoeconomy regiments the bodies of prostitutes, drug addicts, construction and other manual workers, and forced laborers and reifies these bodies to the level of consumer goods. This commodification of the body is integral to the junta's technologies of domination. As brutal and repressive as this system is, however, hegemony is never complete or total and, as Anagnost has noted for China, there is also a space in Burma where State domination and ideology are not completely internalized. This space is also represented in the story of Ko Ma. In the final section of the story, Ko Ma's solidified body enters a coma where his mind flies free from domination:

My condition is beyond the bounds of the end of twentieth century medicine's ability to identify. They say that I am frozen solid and hard like a rock. On the day of my funeral it is with amazement that people in my funeral procession pass by a crane instead of a casket. Despite being reduced to a solid state, I am still conscious, but only I know that I'm still conscious. Only I know that I am not dead, that although my body is inert, my spirit still lives. No one can understand my suffering. In scientific language, we can speak of a coma. And me, my name is Ko Ma, and we can speak of the coma of Ko Ma.

Mass Rallies and Other Enforced Performances

In response to the political rallies held by the NLD after the release of Aung San Suu Kyi from house arrest in May 1996, the military regime recreated a series of Socialist-style spectacles of enforced participation known as mass rallies (Figure 10). They were convened throughout the nation in any area that was sufficiently under the control of the government and that had a large enough population base. Organized through the GONGOs and other existing government-controlled groups such as the public service, one member of each family (unless they could afford

Figure 10. Mass rally. (author's photo)

the bribe) had to assemble at a certain point and march in formation to stadiums or sports grounds. If a family contained a member of a GONGO or a public servant, the family had to send that member plus an additional member. At the sports fields these captive audiences sat in silence for several hours, a mute witness to the fury of the Generals to opposition to their rule.

For several months the media were saturated by the vitriolic, xenophobic statements made at the mass rallies with their exhortation of the public to commit violence against foreign "interferers" and Burmese who support them. I was constantly struck by the way Burmese were made over into automata; only later did I discover that the process of becoming an automaton is often a conscious strategy of survival. After watching hours of television footage and newspaper photographs of millions of Burmese sitting as still as wooden puppets, I made the following field note:

On Myanmar TV every night at 7:55 p.m. the government objectives are shown and read out, as are the People's Desire Objectives. The news consisted of relaying the mass rally at a particular sports field in Rangoon. The crowds were solemn, statue-like, lips firm, many mouths down-turned, a dull, listless look in their eyes, dour, not a word muttered, expressionless like ranks of wooden dolls, eyes glued to the speaker. The only movement, a few women fanning themselves with whatever propaganda material was at hand. The rallies ended in slogan chanting: people limply raising their fists above their heads and repeating the necessary slogans. This was followed on the "News" by the opening of a bridge, yet another captive audience, expressionless, arms rigidly extended, hands on knees.

I compared these images with the animated faces of the people who listened to the NLD speeches outside Aung San Suu Kyi's home. Aung San Suu Kyi (1997b) has written that: "University Avenue became more lively after my release from house arrest, especially at weekends when our supporters gathered to hear U Kyi Maung, U Tin U and I speak about the political, economic, and social conditions within our country. But the authorities placed increasing restrictions on the activities of the NLD culminating in December 1996 with a blockade of the road to my house." The faces of the people listening to Aung San Suu Kyi telling her audience to "just say no" to the order to attend mass rallies shone with enthusiasm and a joy they found impossible to hide. Tears ran past their smiles as Military Intelligence snapped surveillance photographs of them and would later follow them home and intimidate their families.

Forced participation involves more than involuntary labor and mass rallies in Burma. It includes compulsory attendance at all the spectacles created by the regime. If one is unlucky enough to be deemed a "national race," this participation often involves "ethnic dancing" or the demonstration of other "ethnic" skills that become commodities exchanged with the regime. Burmese are thus mobilized, regimented, and circulated as mobile signs of State hegemony through various sites of military domination. This serves the dual function of promoting the myth of absolute State power and establishing control of urban space by controlling the movement of individuals through this reconfigured landscape of domination. The production of Burmese automata not only serves the purpose of providing a huge labor pool for the government, but, in conjunction with the executive levels of the GONGOs, it is able rapidly to mobilize a large proportion of the population in a structured formation. This "state of readiness" creates a heightened sense of tension in the capital and reinforces the everyday state of emergency. This process is not absolute, and small spaces continue to exist where State ideology is not completely internalized. The metaphor in Ko Ma used to represent this process is the comatose body with a form of consciousness free to depart the body. That such a severe process is necessary to escape the politicization and automation of everyday life indicates the smallness of this space of incomplete hegemony.

Mass Ornaments

Let us compare for a moment the psychology of the masses of European fascism with that of contemporary Burma. Stollman (1978: 42–43) has noted that "The aestheticization of political life in the Third Reich is first apparent in the permeation of daily life with celebrations, ceremonies, artificially created customs and staged folklore . . . in the Nationalist Socialist organizations and in professional life participation in these celebrations was by and large mandatory." Benjamin realized that "what is fully new in fascism [is] that the technical capabilities of the fascists make possible the actual participation of large masses of people in events, the object of which is their own aestheticization and objectification" (Rabinach 1977: 14). These technical capabilities relate to the modernization of Europe and in this sense it is impossible to separate out the mass rallies, the mass objectification of Burmese people, from the capitalist dimensions of the incipient fascist project. I see little difference between the creation of mass culture and "mass ornaments" in Burma and the way in which: "The Third Reich lowered over the entire public sphere an aesthetic, pseudo-socialistic veil behind which the capitalist-imperialist laws and interests asserted themselves unchecked" (Stollman 1978: 52).

An analysis of the fusion of the political with the capitalist agenda was attempted first by Kracauer and then later by Benjamin, through the concept of the mass ornament. Kracauer (1975) believed that fascism creates "mass ornaments deprived of meaning" through terror and propaganda. Benjamin uses this concept "to show how the aestheticization of political life occurs throughout the media and organized festivals in which aestheticization becomes a form of praxis, so that 'fascist propaganda must, moreover, infuse the whole of social life'" (Rabinach 1977: 14).

The phenomenon of the mass rallies, mass culture, and mass ornaments is described by Kracauer in, for example, *Triumph of the Will*, the official Nazi film of the 1934 Nuremburg Party Convention, where "The innumerable rows of the various Party formations composed tableaux vivants across the huge festival grounds. . . . They appeared as mass ornaments to Hitler and his staff, who must have appreciated them as configurations symbolizing the readiness of the masses to be shaped and used at will by their leaders" (Witte 1975: 61–62).[3]

The response of European citizens to the imposition of this combination of terror and propaganda upon their psyches was remarkably similar to that of Burmese individuals at mass rallies: "By an exodus of individuals into anonymity, through which their nature is deprived of its substance, the mass ornament presents itself as a cult of physical culture—mythological but devoid of meaning" (Kracauer 1975: 66). In the daily experience of individuals as part of the depoliticized masses, Burmese automata are in fact mass ornaments in a cult of physical culture, intentionally devoid of meaning.

The Body Silent

The silence emanating from the Burmese automata at the mass rallies is described by the State media as a resounding noise, a verification of the anger of the masses. The State media reported: "Mass Rallies to Support Constructive tasks and to denounce the destructionists were held throughout the length and breadth of the country and the reverberating sounds shattered the ears of Aung San Suu Kyi like the crack of thunder" (NLM 1996: 5). Silence is in fact a profound, torrential, deafening cacophony in Rangoon and Mandalay. Silent, alienated bodies sit in teashops where the tables are placed at a distance from each other so that the military intelligence and informers at neighboring tables cannot overhear conversations. Anna Allott writes that: "Since 1991, the tea shop owners have been told that they will be held personally responsible for anyone found discussing antigovernment politics on their premises, and the omnipresent informers have practically stifled discussions" (Allott 1994: 58).

A friend, U Kyauk Maung, led me to realize how long this kind of behavior has been the norm in Burma. He commented that: "the space between tables [in tea shops] is much further than in the West. In my father's day people wouldn't eat in restaurants if the tables were closely packed. They demanded privacy. These places are always, always packed with informers." Of course, it doesn't matter any more whether informants and intelligence personnel are actually monitoring conversations; Burmese have been conditioned for a generation now to be silent. They are aware of wiretaps on their phones and fax machines and silences are apparent in certain topics of conversation never uttered in front of strangers, in hotel rooms, or on public transportation. The only loud voices heard in public are calling for religious donations or parroting western pop songs in Burmese from the scripted safety of a karaoke machine.

Chapter 7
The Tension of Absurdity

There was a glass cabinet adrift in the foyer's center containing souvenirs which were, sadly, crappy rather than tacky—faded postcards, factory-woven "ethnic fabrics," and so on. I was hoping for a boxed set of miniature Burmese generals, or at the very least an I LOVE MYANMAR fridge magnet. Or perhaps a length of barbed wire, tastefully mounted, to commemorate the recent news, publicized without irony, that Burma now produced so much of the stuff it had begun exporting it

—Andrew Marshall, *The Trouser People*

Before we leave the city limits and witness the suffering and dissociative strategies of the peri-urban poor, let us indulge in some dark humor, some subversive sayings, and perhaps even a little karaoke with friends. In short, let us discover the limits of discourse as a survival strategy. As the city becomes a modern vista, unrecognizable to its inhabitants, these same inhabitants work assiduously with words to re-politicize their landscape and to recover the truth of their nation's recent history. Ernst Bloch slyly noted that although the fascist claims to a utopian worker's future are false, the myths (such as unity, progress, and fraternity) behind it are not exhausted by their use, and there is no reason why the populace may not use these same terms, reappropriated, in new ways to express alternate understandings of the past and visions of the future. In this chapter I present several furtive and only half-jocular ways in which the veneers of modernity and conformity in contemporary Burma may be punctured. I begin with the ever-present sense of absurdity and surrealism and move on to reportage of the urban war on semantics and a variety of tea shop pastimes such as lampooning and betting.

Artifice and Mimesis as Urban Reality

Walter Benjamin has advocated a radical view of history in which the concept of "order" is extraordinary and the potential for equality and revolutionary change is subsumed by a myth of prosperity. Benjamin's review of history convinced him that a particular political constellation of "national unity, patriotism, and consumerism" recurred throughout history and this formula "inevitably resulted in the betrayal of the working class" (Buck-Morss 1989:322). This circumstance constitutes, for Benjamin, a state of emergency.

In the work of Benjamin, the phenomenon of the Arcades, the center point of the "new urbanism," led to the reenchantment of post-industrial Europe with the range of new consumer goods encased in these glass fairylands. Kracauer (1975:64) described these "pleasure barracks" as well, using the "distraction factory" as a metaphor for the places where the middle class spends its leisure time. It was in the pleasure barracks and distraction factories equally as much as in the fascist propaganda and state spectacles, that Benjamin noted the changing perception of "people as producers" to "people as consumers." He adopts Marx's definition of "phantasmagoria" to describe this process of creating fetishes from commodities through their display rather than their exchange value (Buck-Morss 1989:81). The Arcades gave the impression of novelty through the sheer variety and number of material objects available for consumption. Rather than selecting a fabric for a milliner to make a hat, Arcades stocked an array of hats that could be visibly consumed even if the customer could not afford to purchase one. It was the beginning of the voyeurism that is "window shopping." The Arcades gave an allusion of plenty and wealth with large expanses of glass and bright lighting.

These emergent forms of modernism are painfully evident in the Union of Myanmar. In the past decade the junta has constructed its own "fairy grottoes." Burmese Fairylands include joint-venture Asian department stores, "duty-free" stores, and karaoke nightclubs. In the Sino-Burmese Department Stores, gaping Burmese ride up and down escalators, unable to afford the products well guarded by the staff. The escalators are free, however, and represent as great a spectacle as the rows of glittering Chinese cookware. The banks of television screens in these department stores are similarly the scenes of mass gatherings as scores of monks (from up-country, I was repeatedly told) come daily to watch Bon Jovi music videos on this latest miracle of technology.

Only in the latter part of the 1990s, however, has surrealism become an integral aspect of State-led modernity. Shopping, for example, has become an absurd juxtaposition of sweaty laborers bent double beneath the weight of charcoal and cement sacks and the whiteness of the marble foyers of department stores and luxury hotels. The elderly Daw Kay Thar commented to me that

It has become very common to see, for example, people selling iced-water next to these gaudy towers. Of course, some people are driving Mercedes and operating businesses, and people notice the gap between rich and poor. People have become really very worried, and that is another root of the problem, that Burmese people are beginning to think that there may be another uprising because the difference in the quality of life is becoming so great and the majority of the people are becoming poorer and poorer.

Then there is the ultimate in surreal phantasms, "Happyland" and "Fantasyland" amusement parks designed to lure young people with the novelty of "Western" amusements such as old pinball machines and "novelty-prize" games with robot arms that can be manipulated to win acrylic toys. Most young couples and groups of young men wander around these pleasure precincts eating "snacks." They cannot afford to sample the wonders of Fantasyland because they have spent all their money on the entrance fee. A few wealthy young men playing video games are thus the models on which the Fantasyland- or Happyland-goers base their experience of the Modern. Like the department stores, this is a voyeuristic experience.

Buck-Morss (1983: 213) argues that Benjamin

considered the new urban panorama, nowhere more dazzling than in Paris, as the extreme visual representation of what Marx called the fetishism of commodities, wherein "a particular social relationship between people takes on the phantasmagoric form of a relationship between things." One could say that the dynamics of industrialism had caused a curious reversal in which "reality" and "art" switched places. Reality had become artifice, a phantasmagoria of commodities and architectural construction made possible by new industrial processes. The modern city was nothing but the proliferation of such objects, the density of which created an artificial landscape of buildings and consumer items as totally encompassing as the earlier, natural one. In fact, for children (like Benjamin) born into an urban environment, they appeared to be nature itself. . . . This phantasmagoria of industrially-produced material objects—of books, boulevards, all sorts of commodities from tour-books to toilet articles—for Benjamin was mass culture.

The Arcades were Benjamin's "dream houses" of the middle-class imagination, a dream made concrete upon the urban landscape.[1] Yet these arcades deteriorated, and it was the Surrealists who recognized the power of these decaying street scenes: "Once the height of bourgeois luxury, the Paris arcades which survived in Benjamin's day had deteriorated, they had become a refuge for commodities now old-fashioned . . .

all this created a montage suggesting 'a world of secret affinities.' It was the Surrealists who originally recognized that the residues of past fashions in the present possessed a mythic power" (Buck-Morss 1983: 216).

The work of the Surrealists excited Benjamin who saw in their project, a similar aim to his new dialectic of history writing, that is, a further method for puncturing or dissolving the seductive conjunction of modernity and partriotism through a reappropriation of "the power bestowed on objects of mass culture as utopian dream symbols."[2] For Benjamin, this power lay precisely in the mimetic quality of industrial technology when applied to mass culture. He uses the example of film, where shutter speed is able to catch the increase in time and the fragmentation of space associated with industrialization and modernization, "not to duplicate illusion as real, but to interpret reality as itself illusion" (Buck-Morss 1983: 213–26).

Surrealism, a reevaluation of the kitsch of mass culture, and Benjamin's dialectic of history writing are analytical tools that enable us to fix a spotlight upon those fissures in both the veneer of modernity and the veneer of conformity that infuses authoritarian public spheres. Benjamin described this as a "profound illumination:" "a dialectic optic that perceives the everyday as impenetrable, the impenetrable as everyday" (Benjamin in Abbas 1989). Surrealism "discovered a method for reading and representing cultural forms which consists of highlighting the temporal gap, the hysteresis, between the wish symbols (of progress, Stability and so on) and the monuments that embodied them. The wish symbols have crumbled under the weight of history: the monuments still stand, but as the ruins of an intention, the 'residues of a dream world.' It is therefore the friction between images that wears down . . . and exposes . . . a façade" (Abbas 1989:48).

Surrealism is thus a mode of perception, a lens through which to examine anew the fetid downtown buildings with trees growing out of the walls and drainpipes, the plastic Chinese kitsch sold along the downtown streets under plastic sheets deluged by the monsoon rains, and the novel consumer goods whose layers of settled dust are industriously removed by young Burmese staff in department stores. Viewed through this lens, these "wish symbols" of a prosperous Asian tiger economy are the unmistakeable residues of an incipient fascist dream world, a world whose moldering marble monuments remain but whose ideology was worn down throughout the 1990s to expose, in the new millennium, a façade of morally bankrupt modernity and authoritarianism.

As a mode of urban archaeology (and activism), we can use Surrealism not only to unearth the ruins of the fascist and modernist intention, but also to magnify the precise interstices where the tension between the envisaged utopian state and the unemployment and hunger of the

Figure 11. "Karaoke discount"—Mac Burger, Rangoon. (Ron Gluckman)

masses is manifest. This tension is experienced in urban Burma as absurdity and expressed through its dark humor.

Buddhist Kitsch and the Absurdity of the State

Michael Taussig has defined kitsch as an "appropriate aesthetic for the magic of the state" (Taussig 1997:94). The absurdity of the "larger-than-life" aspects of State spectacles in Burma can be described as a kind of karaoke fascism, a vision of modernity dominated by karaoke nightclubs (with "private rooms" where prostitutes earn their living). Adams has commented upon the emergence of karaoke in Lhasa, Tibet, and its value as a metaphor for modernity. She argues that:

Karaoke is a spectacle of scripted simulation, and this phenomenon describes cultural performances of modernity emerging from particular constructions of cultural difference in Lhasa. . . . It is a simulation concealing not a more authentic or truthful act but the absence of a real act. Karaoke takes as its reality principle the idea of role-playing, but creates a site where role-playing is itself satirized, revealing the simulated character of acting . . . karaoke is thus not a representation but a simulacrum of fixed and singular authenticity. This does not mean the performance is not real. On the contrary, it means that the simulation is the reality. (Adams 1996: 510–11)

In the country's rush to modernize, parts of it now resemble a vast Burmese wonderland: a simulacrum of modernity cobbling together an array of consumerist-Buddhist kitsch, like the temples of Pagan lit up with fairy lights. The cities are dominated at night by garish flashing neon signs and lurid Chinese plasticware. It is not the case that an authentic Asian experience is being concealed, such as the Buddhist pagodas beneath the fairy lights; rather, this Buddhist kitsch is reality and the experience of the modern for many Burmese.

Benjamin commented that: "surrealism is the death of the last century through farce" (Buck-Morss 1989: 271) and it is true that humor, for the European surrealists of the early to mid-twentieth century, lay in the realization of the discontinuities and inconsistencies in the dominant ideology. Alfred Jarry, for example, believed that laughter "is born out of the discovery of the contradictory" (Shattuck 1965: 25). Burmese people are acutely aware of the marked disjunction between the Burmese fairyland created by the regime's "open market" policies and its alliance with the heroin trade, and the impoverished relocated townships it has simultaneously created. These discordances, inconsistencies, and juxtapositions are both noted and remembered using black humor, most especially through the notion of absurdity.

Emblematic of this sense of absurdity are the "Visit Myanmar Year" dolls, macabre parodies of a fat Burmese child (previously a popular cartoon figure) carrying a briefcase. Their grotesque and gargantuan proportions are captured in an essay posted anonymously on the BurmaNet: "In Rangoon, reminders that one is 'Visiting Myanmar' abound. Enormous, concrete 'Visit Myanmar Year' dolls leer at you from traffic islands. Mould is growing on their faces and their hair is missing in patches, causing them to resemble rancid cake decorations, or the sinister doll of a low budget horror flick. In one hand the doll is gripping a menacing black attaché case. What does it contain? Number 4 heroin according to Rangoon dwellers" (Anonymous 1997).

Absurdity abounds in Burma and is impossible to ignore. Even during my questioning at the Traditional Medicine Department about my possible political activities (which was a frightening experience for me), this sense of absurdity surfaced. Halfway through the interview, the Department was plunged into darkness and we sat, quietly, sipping coffee and eating cake, waiting to see if the power would return. On a previous visit the Director had informed me that there was not enough power to use the air-conditioner and the new photocopier that graced his office. Similarly, wandering lost through the labyrinthine Ministry of Health complex, one can come across great, decrepit ballrooms with enormous circular sweeping staircases. Peeling paint, hanging wires and mold now inhabit these British-made vestiges, and it is hard to imagine that an incipient fascist regime can inspire so much fear when its institutions are sheltered in such colonial relics waiting for the electricity to return.

The foot soldiers of this regime are just as absurd. During the militarization of Rangoon in December 1996 to March 1997 in response to the student demonstrations, child soldiers lined the roads, their hats falling over their faces, their uniforms rolled up at the ankles. At midday these fearsome soldiers crawled under bushes and crept behind trees to take a nap. I remember thinking that if another nation wanted to invade Burma, midday would be a good time. A diplomatic acquaintance had two soldiers appear in her garden where they took up residence for several days, ostensibly to survey the intersection in front of her house. The absurdity of having soldiers in one's garden (on diplomatic property) was made apparent when my acquaintance made them toast and tea for breakfast each morning and served it to them in the front yard.

Over the course of my field visits to Burma, I have noticed Military Intelligence using surveillance techniques that appear to be very stupid to the eyes of Burmese and foreigners alike. For example, during former Indonesian President Suharto's visit to Burma a strange sight could be witnessed on U Wizara Road. This road contains the Armed Forces Museum, Parade Ground, and other military structures. Daily throughout Suharto's visit there suddenly appeared on the grassy median strip of U Wizara Road approximately 100 men in small groups who appeared to be reading to each other, drinking tea, or relaxing under trees. This was suspicious not only since the regime heavily restricts pedestrian and motor transport in front of its compounds: these gentlemen of leisure were also wearing the pressed longyi and oversized aviation-style sunglasses that everyone in Burma knows are the trademark of Military Intelligence.

But while Burmese people poke fun at the ridiculous aspects of State power and the "kitschy-ness" of its vision of modernity, this laughter is fearful and hurried, often more ironic and sarcastic than humorous. Taussig (1997: 94–55) has noted that while the "art" of assuming power "seems to be second nature to the magicians and sorcerers who have peopled history, it is not at all easy for modern state machinery to pull this off without looking gauche or stupid. Given the power involved, however, nobody does dare laugh, not just for fear of reprisal, but precisely because of the power that arises from just this risk of absurdity."

The regime fears being parodied, not being taken seriously, not being feared enough. Thus Burmese clowns and comedians are imprisoned. One of the saddest aspects of the dictatorship is its attempt to gag all humor in Burma, a task that only an incipient fascist regime would set itself, being obsessed with its social engineering project. Two of Burma's most famous and loved clowns, Par Par Lay and Lu Zaw, popularly

known as the Moustache Brothers, are among the many clowns who
have been imprisoned by the regime. The ruling council explained the
consequences of voicing aloud the absurdities of the State in its official
media prior to arresting the clowns after their appearance at a festival
held in Aung San Suu Kyi's residence. As the State media (NLM 1996b)
reported: "Then came the turn of comedians Par Par Lay and Lu Zaw.
The two in synchrony attacked any undertakings of the Na Wa Ta Government [SLORC], disparaging its dignity, making it a laughing stock
and inciting riot and instability." Par Par Lay has since died in prison.
Although laughing at the absurdity of the State aids Burmese in understanding the discontinuities and contradictions in the regime's ideology
and practices, it remains a dangerous endeavor.

Notes from the War on Semantics

There is a pervasive sense of "wrongness" in urban Burma, a not quite
fully conscious feeling that some Burmese have described in various con-
texts as a Burmese "fairytale," a jarring juxtaposition of military and
civilian life that lends an air of surrealism to Burmese cities. This sense
of wrongness stems from the labeling of an object or ideology as "reality" and a truthful representation of the world, and then delivering this
message, at saturation levels, to the general public. George Orwell
described the 1984 version of propaganda, Newspeak, as the only language that gets shorter every year. Whilst the slogans recur in signboards, in television broadcasts and newspaper articles, and as part of
the repetition of speech making, this excess of noise and signification is
simultaneously an absence of diversity. It is a proliferation of discourse,
but an attempted silencing of all truths, all ways of knowing, that are not
sanctioned by the State.

The use of terms such as "unity" and "economic progress" are good
examples of what Lawrence Cohen (1998: 28) has described as an excess
of language "far exceeding the simple act of its signification." The Burmese cultural field is saturated with this excess of language embodied in
the propaganda created by the Department of Psychological Warfare
(see Comaroff and Comaroff 1991). This is of course a game that two
can play, and in this section I chart some of the major battles in the
course of a war of resignification played out between the Generals and
the urban population. The chief symbols or tropes include Aung San
Suu Kyi, ethnic identity, and the institutions of authoritarianism, including the military council itself.

The major sorties in this war seek to persuade through a cultural
logic, a kind of cultural flotsam that only thinly disguises the threats of
violence lurking beneath the rhetoric. In these psychological maneu-

vers, cultural symbols are given new meanings while the old meanings continue to have resonance. Mikhail Bakhtin glosses this subtle and effective strategy as "desemanticization," which is summarized by Feldman (1991: 12) as the situation "in which two or more conflictual . . . social codes are present in the same set of signifiers. These composite signs trace a history of desemanticization: their incomplete detachment from prior references and their realignment with new meanings and inferences." This ongoing process makes it easier for Burmese to transfer their acceptance or tacit assumptions about the objects previously designated by these symbols to the new objects designated by the signifiers: the regime, its monuments, spectacles, and boundaries.

All nations take symbols of office and of authority and the junta is no exception. An example of this shift in meaning concerns the mythical Chinthe (*chin dhei*), a winged lion of Buddhist legend that stands guard at the foot of pagodas throughout Burma. This symbol represents authority, ferocity, protection, and unremitting loyalty to Buddhism. It was coopted by the Chindits in the Second World War. The Chindit operation was an anti-Japanese operation led by the Allies during the Japanese invasion of Burma. The troops who fought behind enemy lines contributed to the enormous anti-Japanese sentiment within Burma at the time.

Most recently the Chinthe has been appropriated by the USDA. It is impossible to detach the strong religious force of the Chinthe-as-Buddhist and Chinthe-as-protector symbol from its new incarnation as a symbol of involuntary recruitment and political repression. The youths are encouraged to adopt the Chinthe's attributes and apply them as a ferocity and loyalty to the motherland and a willingness to defend it, even to their deaths, if necessary. This process has occurred a thousand-fold in Burma and threatens to trip up Burmese people in the confusion inserted into everyday lives.

Most particularly in its appropriation of Buddhism the junta has worked a wonder of propaganda, eliding veneration of the Buddha into an unspoken yet somehow tacit acknowledgment of the regime as the defender of Buddhism and as moral rulers. Through a process of desemanticization of Buddhist symbols, the dictatorship is carefully laying claim to what is known in Theravada countries as the role of *cakkavarti* or World Conqueror on the earthly plane, a leadership usually reserved for monarchs who establish order in the world so that Buddhist monks can get on with the process of showing, through example, the path to Enlightenment (Tambiah 1976).

Strong cultural symbols such as the Chinthe become part of what the Comaroffs (1991: 25, 31) have described as a symbolic struggle central to the process of producing hegemony. Through the application of Burmese and Buddhist symbols to the military regime and its organs of domination, and through the manipulation and politicization of Burmese social conventions and relations, the junta inculcates Burmese people with the dominant ideology of military rule: the politicization of everyday life and the central role of the Tatmadaw in Burmese society. As in other authoritarian states, the vision of a utopian society requires its own view of its place in the world and the cosmos. Much of the work of the Department of Psychological Warfare consists of devising appropriate symbols and spectacles of nationhood using disinformation, confusion, and techniques such as the naturalization of social inequalities.

Prior to 1989, the predominant Burmese origin myth cited by Rangoon residents consisted of two mythical birds, Hintha (*hin: tha*), that descended to earth in the middle of a lake at Pegu, not far from Rangoon, to create the land known as Burma and the people known as the Burmans. The dictatorship's origin myth situates the Tatmadaw (the military and hence the SLORC/SPDC) rising like a phoenix from the "hell fires" of the 1988 pro-democracy uprising to restore "law and order" (NLM 1996o: 5). Here we have rebirth of a nation through sacrifice and regeneration through death. The junta has appropriated through mimicry the origin myth of both the *Hintha* creating a new society, and the phoenix's rebirth, in order to naturalize the usurping of civilian power by the military (see Taussig 1997: 78). Continuous repetition of this violent origin myth is a strategy designed to take the 1962 coup out of the realm of contestation, and place it firmly in the "taken for granted" realm from which issues the assumptions that Burmese people make about their everyday world.

Desemanticization is a very subtle process whereas much of the regime's assertion of control over everyday ways of thinking is more consciously recognized and hence, contested. During the December 1996 student demonstrations, many people I spoke to were clearly fearful on a daily basis. But equally clearly, most people did not completely internalize the regime's threats of imminent violence, aware instead that the saber rattling of the military could be a psychological tactic to subdue the population. Similarly, the xenophobic statements promoted by the military government are not completely successful and there is enormous variation in the degree to which such ideology is internalized at the level of the individual.

I became aware of the degree of variation at a small gathering of my circle of friends when Ma Hla Hla returned from her eye-opening trip to Bangkok to visit her husband and take in the sights of Patpong Road's sex industry. The xenophobic statements about Burma's neighbors exhorted regularly in the State media over several decades had recently been replaced by an ideology of Asian brotherhood in preparation for

Burma's application for entry into the regional economic trading bloc, the Association of Southeast Asian Nations (ASEAN). In a very short space of time, Burmese people were presented with two contrasting views of Asian "Others" and, rather than internalizing this new rhetoric, some Rangoon and Mandalay residents began to question both sets of assertions.

I should probably not have laughed so much at Hla Hla's wide eyes and continuous head shaking, since the existence of the Thai sex industry, shocking to most Burmese, confirmed many of the prejudices she had learned about Thais over the course of her life. She asked me if it was true that Thais ate Burmese children because if so, why was the regime forming an economic union with Thailand? Our youngest friend, San San Pwint chimed in with her grandmother's teaching that the Thais use the heads of Burmese children as stones upon which to rest their cooking pots.

All of the women partaking in this discussion are young, university-educated women, and they took a variety of stances on the regime's latest pro-ASEAN discourse. Another friend, Yadana, repeated a common Rangoon rumor that Burma's entrance to ASEAN was part of a secret Muslim conspiracy that would result in the Buddhist architecture of Rangoon being replaced with Muslim mosque-style domes and minarets at the completion of (then Indonesian President) Suharto's visit to Rangoon. Yadana has internalized the much older anti-Muslim sentiment in Burma, including the propaganda concerning the need to be alert against the domination of South Asian entrepreneurs during the colonial era, and had rejected the recent pro-ASEAN rhetoric as too new to be credible in the face of much longer standing opposing views.

And finally, Nu Nu, confusing South Asian ethnicity with Islam, assumed that since Malaysia, Indonesia and India had large Muslim populations, India must be a member of ASEAN. San San Pwint asked me if it was true that all Indians are "mentally ill" (said in English) and if so, why should Burma form an alliance with them?

Clearly then there is a space in which new State rhetoric is compared with rumors, folk beliefs, and previous experiences. State ideology is accepted and internalized differentially even among a relatively homogeneous group of educated Burmese women of the same age group. Desemanticization works best when common and long cherished cultural tropes and tacit knowledge (such as the characteristics of the *Chinthe* and *Hintha*) are added as new and additional referents to State institutions, organizations, and ideologies. Propaganda works less well when it must work against these long standing forms of tacit cultural knowledge.

Puppets, Puppet Masters, and the Demonization of Aung San Suu Kyi

It is hardly a revelation to the members of the Department of Psychological Warfare that their rhetoric is most powerful when they play with long-established ideas. The critical importance of desemanticization for creating complicity, confusion, and the suborning of the population is nowhere more evident than in the demonization of Aung San Suu Kyi.[3]

The major political threat to the regime within the urban centers comes from the National League for Democracy (NLD). Universities can be closed and monasteries can be sealed off, but the NLD refuses to disband or cease speaking out against the regime. In particular, Nobel Peace Prize winner, Aung San Suu Kyi, poses a special risk because of her father's status as the most revered leader since the last Burmese monarch. A process of "Aung San Amnesia" has been inculcated in the populace, where the role of Aung San in Burmese political life is deliberately and quietly placed into the background of the achievements of the military regimes. It is a carefully managed process where one particular document written by Aung San, entitled *Blueprint for Burma*, is repeatedly used by the military as a rationale for their domination of everyday life. The remainder of Aung San's voluminous writings go unmentioned in the public domain because of the success of the 1988 pro-democracy movement in appropriating Aung San as a democracy hero (Houtman 1999).

Students carried Aung San photographs and emblems during the 1996 street demonstrations, and the image of Aung San hangs in many homes and businesses as a link with the democratic and independent moment that he worked to achieve. Although amnesia is the goal of the regime's propaganda, Aung San's image is the only visible marker that Burmese people can display that serves to guard against forgetting his legacies, and it is the only way they can publicly offer political legitimacy to his daughter. The potency of Aung San has been banished to the background, but remains foremost in the minds of a great many Burmese. Aung San amnesia has failed miserably and Aung San's daughter is careful to use her patrilineage to remind Burmese people of the continuation of democratic ideals in Burmese history and social life embodied in her person and party.

Aung San Suu Kyi's popularity is such that her death or extradition could cause rioting that may lead to revolution. The technique the junta has decided upon is to undermine NLD support through arrest and intimidation of its members and supporters, and through an intensive propaganda campaign in 1996–98, in which up to half the State newspapers on any one day were devoted to anti-Aung San Suu Kyi articles.[3]

Aung San Suu Kyi (1998) has commented: "It has been remarked by journalists that never elsewhere have they come across such vicious attacks carried out by the state media against a single individual as takes place in Burma. The newspapers controlled by the military regime (which calls our country Myanmar) regularly print articles vilifying me. There are times when such articles run daily for months without respite. Periodically, some of these articles are collected and brought out in book form. These books are, of course, widely advertised by the government-controlled press."

Arrest and intimidation is most difficult in Rangoon simply because of the number of people involved, and this is why the regime decided to have the USDA attack Aung San Suu Kyi and then arrest her in a rural area around Mandalay in May 2003. In the urban centers, sports stadiums and show grounds are initially used by the military as holding grounds for political prisoners because the jails and "guest houses" cannot accommodate up to 1,000 political prisoners at a time. An octogenarian NLD supporter described his frequent arrest and holding at what he calls the "O.K. Corral," drawing attention to the absurdity of trying to arrest such large numbers of the population. The anti-Aung San Suu Kyi propaganda campaign provides a warning to urban residents, just in case they are entertaining the notion of supporting the NLD.

The propaganda campaign demonizes Aung San Suu Kyi and represents her as the antithesis of the Generals. She is portrayed as politically inexperienced, non-human, and anti-Buddhist. The most common way in which Aung San Suu Kyi is portrayed as unfit to participate in the political process in Burma, however, is as a woman. Gender stereotypes are exaggerated in State propaganda to forever exclude women from Burmese political life.

This negative personality and motivation analysis of Aung San Suu Kyi was conducted by the Ministry of Information and appeared almost daily throughout 1996 and 1997. In addition to Aung San Suu Kyi, another female adversary of the military dictatorship is Maureen Aung Thwin, director of the New York based, Burma Project. The junta categorizes these women by their "feminine nature," which they imply is inherently duplicitous and untrustworthy. One newspaper article stated that her "feminist nature makes Aung San Suu Kyi unsuitable to rule" (NLM 1996c). The State media cites as evidence of the dangerous aspects of the "feminine nature," the use by Aung San Suu Kyi and Maureen Aung Thwin of their "womanly wiles" to gain their objectives, objectives driven by greed, lust, and pride. The following report of Maureen Aung Thwin's actions appeared in *New Light of Myanmar* in October 1996 (NLM 1996n): "She got married with an American citizen. . . . Such a one of marred genealogy has no right to say anything about Myanmar and there is no reason to believe what she says. . . . She has been able to take money out of the [Soros] foundation using her womanly wiles and guiles in addition to the pretext of democracy and human rights."

The marriages of Aung San Suu Kyi and Maureen Aung Thwin to non-Burmese citizens is a considerable source of anxiety to the regime, and the fear of miscegenation is apparent in discourse relating to these political foes.

The true place for the Burmese woman is, in fact, the home. Women have no place in politics in the "Union of Myanmar" and since all public life is politicized, they have no place in the entire public sphere. The State media (NLM 1996l) report, "there is no cause to care about and hold talks with an ordinary housewife [Aung San Suu Kyi], who had returned to the country just recently and had never even tasted pickled bamboo shoot curry, in the matter of emergence of a new State."

The most common reference to Aung San Suu Kyi's "feminine nature" is to her alleged prostitution. From July to October 1996 the State media published a series of linked articles suggesting that Aung San Suu Kyi engages in prostitution of both the body and the nation. Here we see the fusion of both a Buddhist (and older Hindu) notion of women as polluting and less spiritually pure (therefore, more corporeal) with the notion of male superiority and fitness to govern. Although these references may seem oblique or mild, there is no doubt in Burma as to the meaning behind the innuendoes. In September 1996, as part of a series of articles entitled *What is Aung San Suu Kyi? Whither goest she?*, the immorality of the Christian West is deplored and Aung San Suu Kyi is accused of adopting the loose values of the West. The article states that "When other cultures are sowing the seed of devoted affection, the west is just like getting married just for the sake of mere convenience. . . . As for the west they value their Christian culture only on paper" (NLM 1996j). This article was placed beside a piece chronicling bad queens and consorts in Burmese history, again suggesting that Aung San Suu Kyi should be included in their ranks: "The savior of the nation was assailed with insolence by Daw Suu verbally, and in deed, too, she tried to push it into the abyss. . . . If in such as [sic] situation she would persist in attempting to break up national solidarity and jeopardise national sovereignty . . . she would become a big, main culprit in Myanmar history. Narathu of Bagan Period, Nanmadaw Mai Nu of Konbaung Period and Supayalat of Yadanabon Period might possibly have some redeeming feature but Daw Suu has none."

In the following month articles appeared with continual references to Aung San Suu Kyi, prostitution, and "massage" which is often a pseudonym for prostitution in Southeast Asia. Prostitutes, those individuals masquerading as masseurs, and Aung San Suu Kyi, are all accused of breaking Burma's "good tradition[s]." One article (NLM 1996p:3) decries Burmese women engaged in prostitution in neighboring countries and says that what Aung San Suu Kyi is doing is worse. It states that the:

business of prostitution is no small one, that young Myanmar girls would be lured to go abroad as raw materials for it, and that those out to make dollars would pick selections of Myanmar belles to serve them up at sauna and massage parlours for the incessant influx of foreign tourists. . . . Whoa, Saya, whoa! My coming here is not about such lurid news that is painful to the ears. I have come with some news that is even more so. . . . Michael Aris is pulling the strings and his wife, Mrs. Michael Aris [Aung San Suu Kyi] is dancing accordingly, with proper time beat, to the dictates of the CIA [Central Intelligence Agency].

For Burmese, however, the most blatant propaganda involves the descriptions of Aung San Suu Kyi's *hta-mein* or *htami* (*htamein(mi)*) that the State media translates as "Myanmar woman's nether garments" (NLM 1996c). The regime implies that politics and sexual intercourse have become mixed for Aung San Suu Kyi, who pursues one in order to achieve the other. The State-sponsored media state that "in some townships [NLD members] . . . quit en masse group after group, having lost confidence in the political aims that had gotten near the hem of Mrs Michael Aris' *hta-mein*" (NLM 1996q). This propaganda peaked in July 1996, when the NLD attempted to hold an annual congress. At this time the regime accused various groups of grabbing Aung San Suu Kyi's "nether garments." The media reported that "In the 'Htami' grabbing contest between the BCP [Burma Communist Party] and the West bloc, the latter is the winner" (NLM 1996c).

The overarching logic tying together the articles which daily attack the character of Aung San Suu Kyi is explained to the populace through the metaphor of puppetry (see Figure 12). The weak will of Aung San Suu Kyi and her "feminine" and "animal-like nature" allow the regime to posit not only that she will prostitute herself but also that she will prostitute her nation to Britain and the United States. Thus in an article in June of 1995 entitled, "Let's Tell the Truth," it is reported that Aung San Suu Kyi's "htami dress moved from its nether garments every time the puppeteer [Michael Aris] pulled the strings" (NLM 1996a).

The regime has seized upon the familiar cultural idiom of puppetry as its model for explaining how it has come to be that some Burmese are acting in ways that oppose the State. "K" has written about Burma's showcase for its particular forms of theater and music, the *pwe* (*pwe:*), or festival. He describes how "the most famous of pwes are marionette *pwes*, or *yokethe pwes* which traditionally included 27 puppets, each up to a meter high. The cast includes . . . important figures in Burmese life. The

Figure 12. Aung San Suu Kyi puppet. (author's photo)

Burmese marionette tradition is thought to have emerged in the second half of the eighteenth century as a brainchild of the Minister for Royal Entertainment, U Thaw. Puppets could act in ways that the sexually modest Burmese would not be able repeat in public" (K 1981: 14).

Aung San Suu Kyi is continually portrayed as a female puppet whose strings were being held and pulled by her (now deceased) husband, Michael Aris. She is "a traitor puppet who is blatantly betraying the national cause and dancing to the delight of neo-colonialists Leik and Kan"(NLM 1996b: 5). The "Leik-Kan" alliance is a reference to the Chinese Opium Wars of the nineteenth century, when both Britain and the United States were breaking the Chinese law prohibiting the sale of opium to China. The regime alleges that Aung San Suu Kyi's husband acts as a messenger from the conspiratorial "Leik-Kan" alliance. That is, the junta portrays in the national media a conspiratorial, secret group comprised of representatives of both the British and United States governments, which funds and dictates to Aung San Suu Kyi methods for overthrowing the regime in order to recolonize Burma. Aung San Suu Kyi is portrayed as a witless, hapless stooge of her "neocolonial masters." She and her husband, Michael Aris, thus indulge in "pillow talk" wherein "instructions" are relayed to her. The "dance" of the puppet is sexually suggestive, implying that Aung San Suu Kyi prostitutes herself before the "Leik-Kan" secret alliance.

The exaggeration of gender stereotypes is just one of the many levels of "Otherness" that the regime attributes to Aung San Suu Kyi in order to disqualify her from the political arena. She is also portrayed as an Indian Other, a lower class Other, an uncivilized, savage Other, an evil non-Buddhist Other, as well as a non-human Other.

Her elite social status is called into question by the State media in order to suggest that only the highest social classes in Burma have the potential for leadership, and that she does not really belong to the Burmese upper class. The regime states that only social misfits and troublemakers attend her rallies. Derogatory cultural stereotypes of Burmese of South Asian origin are used to portray the democracy advocate as belonging to the very lowest social classes of Burma. She is called a *chetyar*, and those who attend her roadside speeches are labeled *awalas* and *jalebis*.[4] Her followers are further denigrated by their status being described as "not even that of the cleaners of the development committee"[5] (NLM 1996j).

In a discourse heavily influenced by Buddhism, her status is further downgraded by associating her with all things "uncivilized," savage, and wild. The primary thrust has been to represent Aung San Suu Kyi as a disciple of the animist *Nat* spirit cult and therefore un-Buddhist. She is also likened to other non-Buddhist elements in Burmese culture such as witches, sorcerers, and astrologers who divine the future. There is no place in this imagined Buddhist dystopian vision for non-Buddhists. She is depicted as an ogre and "worse than evil spirits and wild cats" (NLM 1996i). These life forms exist on a lower plane of existence than humans in the Theravada Buddhist cosmological hierarchy. The official media (NLM 1996p: 5) report that "Aung San Suu Kyi is a bad daughter who had not fulfilled her obligations toward her parents; Aung San Suu Kyi is a woman with an extreme pride much more than a true woman should possess and went after fame with a vain glory and is a selfish person. Aung San Suu Kyi is a person who fails to understand the gratitude she owed to the State and is evil educated [sic] person like an ogre. . . . Aung San Suu Kyi has chosen a foreigner who is not of own race and blood as her spouse and has given birth to two sons of mixed blood."

The inappropriateness of Aung San Suu Kyi as a political leader is explained in terms of her animal-like nature concerned only with survival and sexual intercourse. She is routinely portrayed as the antithesis of a good Buddhist for allegedly indulging in quackery, black magic, and sorcery. Such pronouncements include

Though the Sayamagyi employed black magician's means as in a saying "The more critical the patient's condition, the happier the quack doctor," things did not turn out as she expected. (NLM 1996m: 5)

Don't consult a fortune teller! It is certain that there will be traffic closure tomorrow due to the interference of the sorceress. (NLM 1996o: 3)

As they [Aung San Suu Kyi's supporters] were not those who came to watch the nat-pwe or the roadside magician's show. (NLM 1996o: 3)

The "traffic closure" refers to the blockading of streets around Aung San Suu Kyi's compound by the junta to restrict NLD political activities, including the weekend roadside speeches. The regime's propaganda portrays the longer commuting times for city workers resulting from these road closures as due to the selfish nature of the democracy advocate. The "roadside magician's show" also refers to the NLD's speeches on Saturday and Sunday afternoons. These political rallies are labeled *Nat pwe* (spirit festivals) and magical shows by the junta to stress the insignificance and fantasy-like nature of the NLD's aspirations to participate in the national political process. The regime also likens Aung San Suu Kyi to a Natkadaw, a female priestess of Nats. Former Prime Minister U Nu has written of the intense sexual appetites, polygamous natures, seductive beauty, and semen-less orgasms that characterize Nats, traits that place them firmly in contradiction with Buddhist morality (U Nu 1988: 4–9).

The writers of the Ministry of Information use the metaphor of puppets as a logical and culturally familiar means of tying these very different categorizations of Aung San Suu Kyi together. Puppetry is also emblematic of the broader program of the Generals to stop other sources of information reaching the population. Those who control the strings of the Burmese puppets control what constitutes "truth" in Burma and through their propaganda apparatus, the regime has a powerful tool of mass and continuous dissemination of its key messages.

The continual use of the puppet metaphor is also revealing of the junta's conception of their population as gullible children who are incapable of initiative.[6] This is a major flaw in their reasoning, however, because it drastically underestimates the intelligence and resourcefulness of the Burmese, many of whom are aware of the semantic deception promulgated in such propaganda and are quite capable of devising their own counteroffensives. The everyday battleground over which hegemony and ideology are fought is large and, as we shall see, the population have a series of adages that remind them in times of doubt of the duplicity of the regime's propaganda.

Counteroffensives

Although the Generals have effectively employed techniques such as desemanticization, they have underestimated the ability of many Burmese to also employ symbols and elements of Burmese cultural life to their advantage. The attempt to use gender inequality and Burmese stereotypes in nationalist discourse as justification for the military's fitness to rule the country has not yet succeeded in changing this ideology of male superiority into a hegemonic discourse.

Familiar religious and supernatural beliefs are used in the creation of counter-ideologies to the program of naturalizing gender inequalities evidenced in the State media. An example of such a counter ideology involves the glorification of Aung San Suu Kyi as "the Lady," whose gendered attributes are used in a positive way by the opposition movement to justify her fitness to rule. An "Aung San Suu Kyi cult" has recently arisen, part of the long tradition of "supernaturalizing" charismatic leaders in Burma (Pye 1963). Aung San Suu Kyi is also referred to as the "Goddess of University Avenue" (*te'kathou langa na'thami:*) and a "female bodhisattva," a female future Buddha who normally dwells in the Buddhist realm only one level below Nirvana. She is also referred to as the Angel and *Nat* of Democracy and "as a heroine like the mythical mother goddess of the earth who can free them from the enslavement of the evil military captors" (Mya Maung in Houtman 1999: 282). Houtman (1999: 282) notes the widespread reporting of a thickening or swelling of the left breast of certain Buddha images in Burma, and of blood seeping from the eyes of the statues. These occurrences are believed by many Burmese to be a good omen for the success of Aung San Suu Kyi as well as testifying to her spiritual strength. The popularity of the personality cult, Aung San Suu Kyi's imminent rise to political power, and the continual growth of her personal power, may have all been deciding factors in the appearance of monks on the streets in protest over the regime's refusal to hand over power to the NLD in the wake of the 1990 elections (Nemoto 1996: 26–27).

The ongoing censorship of both internal and international information regarding opposition to military rule necessitates alternative ways of accessing information, and for this the Burmese turn to culturally tested truths and to powers of authority higher than the regime. One of the most interesting ways of obtaining information in Burma is through the phenomenon of "no news." This means that when a significant political event is occurring, such as the March 1997 offensive against the Karen army in Mon State, there will be absolutely no news about it. This absence, or space of silence, alerts Burmese people to the fact that something is indeed happening and they tune in to illegal transmissions of the BBC and the VOA.

Linked to "no news" is "negative news." For example, if the United States government passes a resolution against Burma, the State media will carry news of HIV infection rates, drug addiction, and crime in American cities, again alerting Burmese people to the fact that the U.S. government is doing something the regime vehemently opposes. During the National League for Democracy arrests in June 1996, the official media carried stories about terrorism in the U.S and its embassies and military bases abroad, the Valujet plane crash, the prevalence of violent crime in the United States, and American interference in other country's affairs such as Cuba and Iraq (NLM 1996a).

"No news" time is also understood by Rangoon residents to be a time of marked and rapid increase in propaganda, such as the official newspapers reporting in one day up to fifty new buildings, organizations, or public works being opened by members of the ruling council. This nonsensical babble is supposed to stop Burmese people from thinking about issues such as the effects of American and European Union sanctions, the failure of the rice crop, and government offensives against minority groups. Even during the 1988 democracy uprising, the *Guardian* (then the official English newspaper) and its Burmese-language equivalent, the *Working People's Daily*, continued to print "nonsense" stories with no substantive content. This "news" breaks down meaning, leaving the never-ending propaganda buzzing in one's ears and creating the need to rely upon rumors, astrology, and Buddhist tenets, in order to predict a safe course of action.

Fortunately, Burma's complex and rich cultural storehouse of knowledge gives Burmese people a wide range of magical and religious means of discerning future portents and protecting themselves against negative consequences. Luck and coincidences are attributed to forces such as supernatural entities, Buddhist cosmology, astrology, and *dat* (*da'*). These are the systems of knowledge and power that Burmese people spend their time assiduously manipulating in order to reduce their fear and create "safe" strategies and personal good fortune.[7]

Burmese numerological practices include knowledge of *in:*. Maung Htin Aung describes *in:* as part of a "cult of the runes," consisting of "magical squares containing either letters of the Burmese alphabet or arithmetical figures, and it is believed that every potent rune is guarded by a guardian god" (Maung Htin Aung 1959: 54).[8] *In:* are employed therapeutically, as in exorcism and in the expression of illness or distress. In urban Burma, *in:* are most commonly used nowadays to avert problems of an economic nature as well as grave illness and marital problems, especially infidelity. The lack of adequate and affordable health care means that magical healers have proliferated in number throughout the country.[9]

Another important form of protection, especially in rural areas and amongst sailors, is tattooing.[10] Although less common now, tattooing is still a thriving business in Rangoon, with electrical implements used in favor of the previous wooden tools (Violaine Brisou, personal communication 1997). In rural villages, it is unusual not to see villagers with tattoos against snakebites and members of *gain:* (Buddhist sects) still have significant parts of their torso, back, and arms covered by *in:* tattoos. Armed insurgency groups and front line Tatmadaw troops use these tattoos to gain supernatural strength and protection in battle.

Astrology has been an extremely important means of predicting the future in Burma for over a millennium. A ninth century Chinese chronicle, the *Man-Shu,* mentions many Burmese astrologers and fortune tellers (Mi Mi Khaing 1962:20). Burmese monographs often emphasize the importance of astrology in Burmese daily life. Mi Mi Khaing (1962: 63–64) described the prominent role of the astrologer in predicting periods of illness, calculating karmic debt, and creating horoscopes of the life span in the first half of the twentieth century.

The military junta also depends upon these forms of knowledge, and during his lifetime Ne Win was famed for his gaggle of astrologers and his conversion of the currency to numbers divisible by Nine: his lucky number. However, astrologers also played an important subversive role during the Ne Win era by predicting the demise of the regime, something all paying clients desperately wanted to hear. In March 2002, Ne Win and his family were placed under house arrest as part of an alleged "foiled coup attempt" by the Ne Win family. During the ensuing court case, it was alleged that Ne Win's family sought to act with impunity in the economic sphere, and many urban residents were aware that one son led a gang called the Scorpions that made havoc in Rangoon by night. During the thwarting of the coup attempt, Ne Win's chief astrologer was arrested. The regime claims that the astrologer made a series of magical figurines that could inflict harm upon members of the ruling council via the same mechanism as voodoo dolls.

The junta has created a national Astrology Council that registers and controls the types of information that astrologers are legally allowed to give to the public, precisely for this reason of harnessing the significant power of astrologers in the political sphere. The fortune telling of military leaders is disallowed, but I have had Aung San Suu Kyi's future told to me by an astrologer who recounted the intimidatory visits of a military colonel to his office. The astrologer recounted the colonel's conversation: "You're getting old. You want a happy and safe old age, don't you? Well, don't make any political forecasts." The astrologer is terrified and states that all his fellow astrologers are similarly cowed. The regime is thus well aware of the power of astrological readings in Burma as bases for future action.

Astrology and numerology constitute readings of cosmological conjunctions of events, and a similar but less professionalized system of reading of portents involves commenting upon the significance of weather patterns. The last few years in Rangoon have been characterized by the rainy season beginning earlier than is "usual." It has, for example, rained in May on Armed Forces Day, the most important day in the military calendar, and it is with a deliberately malicious sense of glee that Rangoon residents watch the clouds building up in the weeks before the military celebration. Rain on such a day is seen as a fateful omen that spells the impending destruction of the fascist social order being commemorated.

Other weather omens include a small earthquake in Rangoon in February 2001. All Burmese know of the cautionary tale of King Mingun, who in his vanity began construction of an enormous pagoda across the river from Mandalay, only to have an earthquake split it in two. The pagoda remains in that state today, a testimony to the cosmological anger that can be wrought upon corrupt rulers. Similar rumors of bad futures abounded in Rangoon, rumors that only intensified in significance and in volume after General Tin Oo and several other members of the ruling council were killed a week or so following the earthquake in the helicopter crash over the Salween River. In these ways, Burmese people sit in tea shops in the cities, and tea circles in the villages, and systematically take everything out of the realm of the uncontested and the everyday, repoliticizing their world by refusing to think only about the coming modern and consumerist utopia promised by the Generals' propaganda.[11]

James Scott has commented that, "Fantasy life among dominated groups is also likely to take the form of schadenfreude: joy at the misfortunes of others," such as calling down curses (Scott 1992: 67). Burmese Buddhists often don't need to do this however. They know that on the scale of merit the Generals are doing particularly badly and will have a very unpleasant collective rebirth. This form of cultural knowledge has been around for a very long time, including during the other period of oppression remembered by Burmese people. George Orwell demonstrates his understanding of this cultural knowledge during British colonialism in his tale of the evil fat Burmese village headman in *Burmese Days* (1934). After years of raping young girls, lying, cheating, murdering, and other debaucheries, the headman had planned (as former dictator, Ne Win did) to build a huge pagoda to even out the merit debt he had accumulated throughout his life. Much to the reader's delight, however, Orwell's headman dies without being able to complete his pagoda, and his wife is often awakened at night from terrible scenarios of her husband's everlasting torment.

Betting and "Sayings"

In addition to the strategies mentioned above, Burmese people also devise a number of "street practices." These include gambling on political events, participating with fervor in illegal lotteries, and lampooning official slogans and titles. This moves further away from absurdity into cynicism and opportunism, and these street practices decrease sharply at times of increased urban militarization. Combining the need for money and a common hatred of the regime, gambling in Chinatown, for example, has an overt political element. During times of rapid currency devaluation, the junta arrests moneychangers and moneylenders, and closes gold and jewelry stores, many of which are owned by Chinese and by Burmese citizens of Chinese heritage. Rangoon residents love to quote the latest odds given by the Chinatown bookmakers as a form of conscious resistance to the regime. It makes them realize that, as the Buddhist doctrine of *annika* teaches, everything on this earth is temporary, and the regime cannot last forever. In this sense, such small everyday resistance practices also remind Burmese of their strong belief in the miraculous, and encourage them not to give up hope for change. Following the bookmakers' odds is thus a form of conscious resistance and a simultaneous investment in a more hopeful future. Such betting has become so well known that journalists from international media organizations have commented upon its subversive elements. For example, "For now most diplomats believe that the generals are firmly in control. But they may not be reading the same signs as the bookies in Rangoon's Chinatown. The betting line is 3–1 that SLORC will collapse by February" (Moreau 1996: 21).

An important aspect of the Chinese bookmakers' odds is that they remind Burmese people that there are two "sides" in Burma and that a war between these two sides is ongoing. In this respect, betting fulfills a similar function to that of certain Burmese sayings. Burmese is a highly idiomatic language with a large number of proverbs, and it is comprised of monosyllables that are joined together to form longer words and phrases. Burmese people love to play with their language, and one index of good poetry is the multiple ways a particular word interacts with other words in different lines and stanzas. This love of language play is used to remind themselves of what is "true" and which "side" is which in this ongoing war of the people versus the Generals. This word play is a key way in which Burmese people continually resist the making of an absurd modern dictatorship by ensuring that central cultural and Buddhist symbols and folk sayings remain in this contested area of public discourse and do not fade into the unconscious realm of hegemony.

There are many examples of this phenomenon such as the derogatory saying used to refer to the regime's mass political movement, the USDA. Burmese refer disdainfully to this organization as *kjaun ye gjou deh alou'*, which means "the cat washes itself." This refers to the way that cats wash themselves and therefore don't need to be washed by humans. The

USDA is said to involve itself in washing cats, a useless makework task of no value. The saying emphasizes the political nature of the USDA by deriding the tasks and duties of the organization.

Other sayings heard in urban areas include, "If they [the Generals] say it's black, then it's white," "the thief shouts 'thief' in the crowd," and "the man with wide eyes." These sayings refer to the way the regime accuses its enemies of treachery, murder, and violence, at the same time that it is itself perpetrating these offences. Such sayings are a comment on the continuous nature of the junta's propaganda. Aung Kin (1999: 4) believes that "Ne Win gained considerable advantage because of this massive propaganda as the people were unprepared for such a situation and did not know what to do." These sayings show how the urban populace has become more sophisticated since the Ne Win era in differentiating between the saturating propaganda and the shreds of truth that are occasionally printed in the official "news."

Burmese people also remind themselves of the propaganda component of the State media by playing on the name of the official English language newspaper, *New Light of Myanmar*. Early one evening I was sitting with my group of female friends when Nu Nu told me that she liked to rename the *New Light of Myanmar* as "the Dim Light of Myanmar."[12] I have never seen four grown women (not under the influence of drugs) roll about on the floor, as helpless as amoebae, but apparently "Dim Light of Myanmar" is *extraordinarily* funny to Burmese people. Nu Nu then reduced the others to a further twenty minutes of senseless hysteria by proclaiming that the propaganda signboards entitled "The People's Desire" should be renamed as the "No People's Desire."

Schoolchildren have a whole host of sayings that they pick up from their older siblings and make up in the school playground. One saying popular among schoolchildren is, "We're not going to support the bad guys" (*lu ma a:bei:*), which is used when referring to the many demands the State makes upon the time of schoolchildren. This includes their attendance at State spectacles as well as their active participation in the revision of Burmese history along the lines that the Tatmadaw is the foundation of Burmese society.[13] Schoolchildren are perhaps less subtle in their word play, but the same logic of separating an "us" from the military and the ruling council is apparent in children's sayings.

A "random utterance" (*abaun*) is a prophecy uttered by both madmen and children. It is based on the belief that spirits, gods, demons, and other supernatural beings can temporarily possess those not fully in control of their minds, and speak through them. One such random utterance (the author is anonymous) concerns the building of the Tooth Relic Pagodas in Rangoon and Mandalay: "Two tooth temples are similar, people beggared; army fissured" (*sawdaw hnit suu aywaetuu, pyi-*

thu lee mwe ta' lee kwa). This circumstance is presumed to have come to pass as the regime used forced labor to construct a Tooth Relic Pagoda in both Mandalay and Rangoon. The population is certainly impoverished, and in late 1997 the SLORC changed its name to the SPDC (State Peace and Development Council) and removed some of the more corrupt ministers. This prophecy predicts the imminent demise of the regime and can be voiced by those people not properly socialized, such as children and the mad. Burmese socialization, like the Burmese treatment of the mentally ill, uses a form of "moral treatment" where children are taught, through example and the telling of parables, appropriate forms of behavior."[14] Until children reach the age of twelve, they, like the insane, are not considered accountable for their actions or speech. But in Burma there is also the belief that madness is most often only temporary, and, as for many altered states of being, wisdom and truth can be imparted to the mad during dreams and through visions. Only children and madmen would dare to utter such a prophecy in public, but the regime is suspicious of mad people because of the potential of such utterances to be interpreted by the populace as received wisdom from a higher plane of reality, rather than the ramblings of the insane.

A popular saying attributed to a pair of comedians deals with the corruption of the regime: "Do you come, Yadana Tun Kyi?" The second comedian replies, "Yes I do, Pho Khin Nyunt." *Yadana* means jewel and *Pho* means heroin. The saying alludes to the involvement in the smuggling of gems of the former commerce minister, Tun Kyi, and to (now) Prime Minister Khin Nyunt's well-known alliances with drug lords such as Lo Hsing-han. This saying is a play upon the understandings of the depth of corruption in the "modernization" and "development" of the economy since 1995, and of the miring of members of the ruling council in graft and hypocrisy.

Other street sayings refer to the disbelief Burmese people have in the willingness of the regime to hand over power if a new constitution is ever drafted, and thus they refer to the now defunct (but soon to be reestablished) National Convention as the "timeless convention" (*amotha nyi la geh mahou', amyedan nyi la geh*), since the Convention Committee has been working on a constitution since 1994 with no end to the process in sight. Most urban Burmese have no doubt that the Convention Committee is a complete sham, and they are aware that the NLD were expelled from the Committee after boycotting it in 1995 (Steinberg 2001: 81). And finally, Sayagyi, an expatriate Burmese activist, notes that "The SLORC and SPDC transformed many villages into model villages throughout the country. Ministers visited there and the villagers have to entertain them with good food and dances. So the villagers are saying that their village is not a model village, but a model dining village: [*sanpya kyei ywa mahou', sanpya kjwe ywa*]" (personal communication 1998).

In the sayings given above, the Burmese use their love of language play and their sharp sense of humor to remind themselves of the corruption and brutality of the regime. Humor is a weapon of the weak (Scott 1985) that seeks out and derides the absurd dimensions of despotic rule, a process that is made easier by a regime that seems intent on parodying itself, much to the delight of the urban Burmese.

The Limits of Discourse

Burmese people chart changes in the tenor and volume of propaganda to discern changing military strategies and the possible negative effect of outside events upon the regime. Other, older sources of information are sought for "truth" however, such as the Dhamma, the words of the Buddha. Protection is sought from the regime and the everyday chaos it creates in urban Burma in the form of amulets, magical *in:*, and tattoos, to name but a fraction of Burma's rich cultural store of magic and symbolism. Action strategies are created on the basis of *dat* and astrology, with the movements of planets and the predictive power of numbers considered more reliable than government propaganda. These strategies demonstrate that actualized fascism will never eventuate because Burma continues to seethe with everyday defiance and myriad less conscious strategies of simply getting by, and making do. After more than four decades of dictatorial rule, one can still find enclaves of Burmese people who continue define an "us" radically opposed to the Generals.

Processes such as saturation propaganda and desemanticization work only at some levels, and convince only some of the population on any one issue. Burmese find a dark amusement in the absurdity of the State and use creativity to construct sayings and bets about the regime that puncture the veneers of conformity and modernity that overlay the city. It would be a mistake to end this chapter on a note about the triumph of discourse. In fact, this book will have failed if it should convince readers that the strategies that Burmese people enact to survive authoritarianism come primarily from speech acts. During the 1996 student demonstrations, students at the Rangoon Institute of Technology hurled abuse at the army stationed around the campus. They reappropriated the metaphor of puppetry, accusing the Minister of Education of being a mere puppet, pulled by the strings of the Generals. Some of these students were later arrested, some tortured, and some escaped across Burma's borders. Despite their brave resistance, the successful suppression of the student movement belies the usefulness of these techniques by a small minority against a state that brokers no opposition.

Burmese people play the roles of small time agitators and resistors, but even though it is the authentic and courageous expression of resistance, it nevertheless reveals the absence of physical acts of defiance by the majority of the population. Although Burmese people are wizards with words, sayings, and other cultural media, the realm of discourse and symbolism constitutes one of the only ways for an unarmed population to actively resist the Generals. But a military nation that imprisons all of its clowns sees little humor in these subversive acts and retribution is swift for those who are caught.

Chapter 8
Fragments of Misery: The People of the New Fields

Myanmar women are duty bound to protect their culture from the infiltration of alien culture and need to be more serious in nurturing the mass of women to cherish and preserve their culture and traditions, promote cultural heritage, strengthen nationalism and patriotism, and safeguard their originality.

—General Khin Nyunt

No need to pay the goldsmith! From the palm tree comes our gold! Rolled palm leaves are our earrings, chains of flowers are our necklaces.
Pleasant to look at are we- the well mannered rural folk
From the village of Aung Pin Lay near Golden Mandalay.

—Paddy Planting Song

Ruptured Lives

Soon after the failed democracy uprising in 1988, mysterious fires swept through neighborhoods in central Mandalay and Rangoon suspected to harbor people with democratic sympathies, as well as those townships abutting sites marked for tourist development. Shanty towns, those bamboo thatch settlements in the shadow of the regime's nation building endeavors, were not allowed to be rebuilt by their former residents. Instead, these urban dwellers were shipped, with their belongings and a few pieces of tin and sometimes other building materials, to rice fields on the outskirts of the major cities. Farmers were sometimes compensated for the loss of their acreage and given residential plots of land in what came to be known as the "New Fields" (Allot 1994).

It seems that the lives of almost everyone I meet in the cities touch upon the New Fields in some way. Nu Nu, for example, is twenty-nine years old and speaks English, and, like almost all the women in my circle of friends in Rangoon, this skill allowed her to cash in on the small tourist industry and economic liberalization program pursued by the junta in the early to mid-1990s. Nu Nu is part Chinese, round faced, with long jet-black straight hair that she leaves unbound. She is always dressed in the latest fashion in longyis and wears western-style blouses in coordinating fabrics. Nu Nu's family owned an apartment building with twenty apartments that they rented to tenants in a central Rangoon township. Until 1989, Nu Nu lived with her mother and her sister in a large family compound next to the apartment block. They had electricity for part of each day, a telephone that occasionally worked, piped water, and a garbage service. Nu Nu saw herself as an upwardly mobile young person, city smart and with much the same aspirations as other young people of the newly reemerging middle class. After the 1988 uprising, Nu Nu's mother was told by the ward LORC commander that the families in this ward were to be relocated to a township out of the city. The houses and apartment blocks were to be bulldozed to provide new modern amenities such as department stores, air-conditioned showrooms, and "modern accommodation." As compensation, the family was given two small concrete buildings in the New Fields. Her mother now lives in one, her sister lives in the other, and Nu Nu moves each year to a new rented apartment in the city. Rents continually rise, and she must either downsize or move a little farther out from the city center each time.

A second woman in my circle of friends, Ma San San Pwint, is twenty-seven years old and speaks English in a halting way, what the Burmese are fond of calling "Bunglish." Her family is based in Mon state, the name of the narrow isthmus of land shared with Thailand that juts into the Andaman Sea. Although she was born in Rangoon, her elderly parents and older brothers (one a rice seller, the other an engineer) have moved to Moulmein (Mawlamyine), the capital of the southern Mon state. She works as a receptionist for a small, struggling tourism company and desperately wants to become an official government tourist guide. Our relationship is not a happy one because of her need, due to her impoverished status, to use the reciprocal power of *anade* (*a: nade*) in order to make me adopt the role of her "patron." We met, soon after I arrived in Rangoon, through another friend, who suggested that San San Pwint would come to my apartment each afternoon and we would converse in Burmese, thus keeping me immersed in the language as much as possible. Because San San Pwint's English is rudimentary and she does not have the same educational background as the other friends in my circle, she has been lucky to find a job in the tourist industry.

It is only a matter of time, however, until the junta's promises of half a million tourists flocking to Burma for "Visit Myanmar Year" (which began in November 1996) are proven to be ludicrous, and many of the smaller tourist operators sink into debt and have to shut down. Until then, San San Pwint works all of her contacts as much as possible, desperate to find a job that will pay part of her salary in U.S. dollars. She lives with her older sister who is twenty-nine years old and a "cook by profession." San San Pwint and her sister have also been relocated to the outlying townships, and I have the impression that it is only San San Pwint's current tourist job that allows her family to survive. She never talks about her sister's current employment, but our common friends whisper that she may be engaged in prostitution.

Old Ule (Uncle) Soe's skin is stretched taught over his tall bony frame. He looks likes an ancient mummy, nut brown and wrinkled, with a faded red *longyi* slung low around his waist. His teeth, those that are left, are stained red like his gums and lips, from the betel juice he spits onto the pavement after every few sentences. He is a driver for an international aid organization. He is lucky to have the job. Uncle Soe lived in an area we might think of as the leafy suburbs between the townships and the city center.

Until their arrest and conviction for treason, the Ne Win family had a sizable investment portfolio of Rangoon real estate. One of Ne Win's daughter's entrepreneurial ventures included the construction of the Narawat hotel near Uncle Soe's modest home. It is no coincidence that a new highway has been constructed from the downtown area past the hotel. A broad strip of housing along the highway's route was torn down, and Ule Soe was relocated to a new township, the same township where Ma San San Pwint and her sister now live. Ule Soe's new home is made of bamboo and thatch. It has two rooms and a cooking pit outside the house, with a latrine at the boundary of his property, a few yards further away. There is no sewage system apart from the pit latrine, no running water, and no electricity. He runs his small television off a battery and listens to the radio.

Nu Nu, San San Pwint, and Uncle Soe's lives have been substantially altered in the new urbanization program initiated by the military junta. Comfortable lives have been ruptured in the "huts to high rise" scheme. The New Fields are not mentioned in tourist guidebooks and even though they are officially a "green" area for tourists, the roads and bridges circling these townships are guarded by a significant military presence. Military Intelligence and ward level security officials are very vigilant in the townships. It is not possible for anthropologists to live in the New Fields, but at various moments in the last decade, research could be conducted under the auspices of various government and NGO groups. This research window is narrow; since the end of 2001 all

foreigners working in Burma are required to be accompanied by government staff whenever they venture into these areas. In the meantime, I
buy a ticket on the Circle Line train and pretend to be a lost tourist who
speaks only English and has wandered too far from the city.

The Circle Line Train

Languidly winding its way through Rangoon's suburbs, the Circle Line
train takes more than two and a half hours to circumambulate Rangoon
and return to the cavernous central railway station. The fifty-year-old
coaches were for many years completely covered with advertising for
detergents. The train moves through the inner suburbs to Insein, the
township that harbors the tolerated Karen minority group and the
feared Insein prison. To residents of the forcibly relocated townships
that ring Rangoon, Insein is synonymous with the last chance for women
hemorrhaging to death from incomplete abortions. I have helped support the arms of women being ferried to Insein hospital and listened to
their anguished cries as the van or pick-up truck struggled to navigate
the ditches, potholes, and traffic on the way to the hospital.

Once the Circle Line train passed through fertile paddy fields adjoin-
ing small villages. The same was once true also for the outskirts of Mandalay, where villages such as Aung Pin Le entered the Burmese literature
as an idealized rural heartland where smiling peasants made merry
music in the monsoon, enamored of their place in the Burmese collective psyche. To the east lie the foothills of the Shan mountains, covered
in a blue haze, while to the west at night the Pagoda on Mandalay Hill
shines in the darkness.

Eventually the train slows to pass through a level crossing on the outskirts of Rangoon's established townships. I jump off, pick myself up,
and walk out to the dusty lanes of Nyaungbintha. Nyaungbintha is not a
real township. I have taken observations and data from a number of peri-
urban forcibly relocated townships around both Rangoon and Mandalay
and created a hybrid fictional township called Nyaungbintha, or "pleasant banyan tree village." It is no secret that these townships in Rangoon
include Shwe Pyi Tha, Dagon Myo Thit, and Hlaingthayar; in Mandalay
the townships include Chan Mya Tharzi and Aung Mya Ze. There are
distinctions between the two sets of townships. In Mandalay, women
have an average 1.6 children, but in Rangoon the figure is 2.6. In Mandalay, township residents must walk to the foothills of the Shan mountains looking for firewood, and there are no industrial zones, garment
factories, and other sweatshops to underemploy laborers as there are in
some of Rangoon's relocated townships.

As I traverse the long grass of the fields abutting the edges of the township, I can see several volleyball games underway. Moving into the first street, I count fourteen small children sitting in the road with stubs of cheroots. They have embedded them in the hard, dried dirt and are firing thin yellow elastic bands at then, knocking the cheroots into the air. Four children wear rubber sandals, the rest are barefoot. None of the children wear Burmese clothes. A little girl has a rope looped around her brother and they are running between houses, playing "horse." Four or five children have their faces covered in small red, white, and black streamers pretending, like generations of children before them, that they are participating in a Burmese festival. Other little boys ride tiny plastic bikes or push cars. These plastic toys speak of the relative lack of poverty of this section of the township, being the closest to transportation networks that allow adults to work in the cities.

A mother calls to two of the children. She is returning from the railway crossing where she works as a fruit seller. As she enters her small compound she removes a large, flat bamboo basket containing bananas from her head. I move near the entrance to her house and call across the drainage ditch:

"When did you move here?"

"After the fires," she replies.

"Did you work in the city before you came here?" I ask.

She nods and replies, "I worked as a secretary for an X-Ray clinic on Shwebontha Street."

"Why don't you catch the train into the city and continue to work there?"

"Who will look after the children?" she asks, as she turns and takes her banana tray into the house.

I can hear the train's horn from these nearby suburbs, but it may as well be a million miles away. Except for a minority of people like Ma San San Pwint, the Circle Line train does not represent transportation to Nyaungbintha residents. It is instead a mobile group of potential customers, a twice-daily marketplace that sounds its horn and slowly disappears back to the relative affluence of their former way of life.

Surrounded by Spirits

The lack of facilities and infrastructure that initially confronted the newly relocated residents of the New Fields meant that the toll on the physical and psychological health of the residents was significant. There were no bridges and insufficient roads connecting the townships to the cities from which they had been evicted. Residents speak of the sorrow and pain of loss of former neighborhoods, felt most acutely in the months and years following their sudden departure. Many of the residents of the poorest Mandalay townships lived their lives in the shadow of major Burmese Buddhist monuments, such as the Mandalay Hill Pagoda. They lived in streets full of relatives, and among long-established friendships and fictive kin relationships. Like almost all Mandalay residents and many people throughout Burma, the people of the New Fields count distances according to measurements of the old Mandalay Fort. Inside the Fort lie the ruins of the Mandalay Palace. The last Burmese monarch, King Thibaw, was removed from the ornate wooden palace by British imperial soldiers. The palace burned to the ground during fighting between the Japanese occupying force and Indian and British troops seeking to recapture the Fort in 1945. It is now the headquarters of the Burmese military in Mandalay and the beautiful entrances over the encircling moat are overshadowed by propaganda signboards extolling the virtues of the blood and sweat of Tatmadaw men that is sacrificed to the "unity" of the nation. The walls of the Fort are almost the only remaining structures. In the middle of the nineteenth century, King Mindon Min ordered the eight-meter-high walls to be built around the palace. Now that the palace has burned to the ground, it is only the walls that intimate the past wealth of the monarchy. The formidable fired brick walls are three meters wide at the bottom and narrow to one and a half meters at the top.

Five bridges and three gates provided entry through each of the four walls. The palace was a miniaturization of the Buddhist cosmology, where the gates symbolized the portals to the other three "countries" that exist in this *loki* (mundane world). Atop each of the original gates is an ornate wooden pavilion with a tiered roof called a *pyatthat*. Smaller versions of the pavilions adorn the corners of the wall and lie equally spaced between the main *pyattat*. Each wall is two kilometers long. The distance between large *pyattat*s is about 400 meters. This distance in Burmese is called a *pya* (or *da pya*), and it is the way in which Mandalay people have come to describe distances: "Is it a long way?" "No, just a *pya*." A *pya* means roughly the length of a street. It is a little longer than the most common distance in Burma, *da khaw deh*, or hailing distance, derived from the distance between which two people in the paddy fields can call to each other.

The harshness of relocation is expressed somatically by older residents as back and joint pain related to sleeping on wooden pallets or on the ground while weaving bamboo walls to construct a house. Any savings were quickly spent on creating the house and weatherproofing it for the coming monsoon season. Money for mattresses and other relative luxuries was spent instead on food now that families were not receiving incomes. Residents speak of mist falling in the paddy fields, and according to the humoral medical traditions of Southeast Asia, this cooling influence can cause weakness and sickness.

Residents felt as if they had been moved a great distance. The distance between the Mandalay walls is considered about as far as one would wish to walk. Any farther is a long way. A short distance is considered to be the same as a length of bamboo. To walk a long way would be to walk for as long as it takes a pot of rice to boil (about thirty minutes). Such distances require a bicycle or other form of transportation. Very few people could afford the transportation costs to continue to work in the city. The longer commuting time was also something people could ill afford, now that child minding could not be performed by members of the extended family who had previously lived together in the same compound.

The inhabitants of the New Fields conceptualize the Fort, its *pyattat*, and the towering form of the Mandalay Hill pagoda as the spatial, hierarchical, and cosmological dimensions of their worldview made manifest. Living in the shadow of Buddhist monuments, surrounded by more than half of all the monks who live in Burma, is exactly as a Buddhist should wish, with multiple opportunities for making merit ever present. All this changed when city dwellers became peri-urban shantytown inhabitants.

The geography of the townships is panoptic in that the central roads open out into the township square which is lined with official buildings, the preeminent one being that which houses the township peace and security office. In Rangoon there was no sacred geography outside of the suburbs immediately surrounding the Shwedagon Pagoda, but in Mandalay, the city was divided into quarters and a hierarchical system of Sayadaws, monks, local leaders, deputy leaders, and assistant leaders ruled the city and its surrounding districts from key political and strategic monasteries (Myo Myint 1987: 177–78). The Taikdaw monastery was one such Buddhist political stronghold, surrounded by 20 smaller monasteries and 33 resting buildings for Buddhist pilgrims (Chaturawong 2002: 25–28). In these ways, the structure of the Buddhist hierarchy mirrored the Palace hierarchy and the two forms of power were inscribed upon the landscape of central Burma from the epicenter of the royal palace and its monasteries outward to villages like Aung Pin Le (Lehman 1987).

At night, Mandalay Hill is illuminated by fairy lights. It can be seen for almost fifty kilometers on a clear evening, and it is a beacon on the hill for hundreds of thousands of Burmese who attend, until the early hours of the morning, the annual Taunbyon Nat pwe (festival). Taunbyon is a village about thirty kilometers from Mandalay and is located deep in the terrain of the *Nats*. Residents in the New Fields know that they are much farther away from the heart of Burmese Buddhism than their previous neighborhoods and they view the new landscape as in need of Buddhification. *Nat* spirits inhabit the area around Mandalay and reside in trees remaining in the paddy fields, and malevolent spirits also inhabit other features of the landscape such as canals.

Through the elaborate cycle of *Nat* festivals that occur throughout the cool and hot seasons, a series of negotiations of identity occur where village and peri-urban residents reposition their relationship with their local environment and with larger polities (Brac de la Perrière 1992b, 1998). This includes the relationships that residents of the New Fields have with their local *Nat*-infested environment, and the sundering of these Buddhists from their place in the sacred cosmography of Mandalay. Minor *Nats* are believed to be everywhere in the densely populated spiritual landscape of the New Fields. Certain routes must be avoided and at night residents wrap bright yellow fabric or plastic around themselves and their bicycles to ward off bad spirits. Pregnant women return to the safety of their homes as dusk falls.

During the decade of the 1990s, infrastructure such as roads was constructed largely from forced labor extracted from the residents.[1] In the first several years, this involved approximately four hours work on Saturdays or Sundays. Such labor was always given in addition to the labor required to build roads and other state public works programs (such as the dredging of the moat around the Mandalay Palace: one day per month per male), and to restore and build religious monuments such as the Tooth Relic Pagodas. GONGOs such as the Myanmar Red Cross and civil service workers supervised the forced labor and the signing of forced labor logs kept by the local security offices.

Those families unwilling to contribute a member for the forced labor gangs had to pay fines. Men in the townships became highly migratory, following seasonal work patterns involving the gem mines, agricultural laboring, and smuggling. The Mogok gem mine allowed seasonal workers to earn money as miners and then to smuggle some of the gems to towns bordering Thailand and China, where they could sell them to a variety of brokers who thrive in the lawless frontier areas. These men, trying to provide for themselves and their families, chased after fishing, logging, and a variety of forms of agricultural work. The burden of forced labor in the townships thus often fell to women, and even today Burma's roads are lined with women carrying children on their backs. They are accompanied by older children helping construct the road system by pounding large rocks into smaller rocks and pouring tar onto the new road base. One of the most common sights when driving through Burma are the road urchins, children of mothers conscripted to build and maintain roads. These children are covered in soot from the forty four-gallon drums of melting tar that the children stir over a large fire. Skinny bodies protrude from ragged shirts and shorts, and their black bodies contrast with their hair, covered in a gray coating of rock powder that comes from the labor of smashing rocks into ever smaller fragments.

Snapshots of Suffering

I walk further into the township, to an area that has a mixed composition and is not known for being one of the poorer wards. Ducks swim in the fetid green pools and in the drainage ditches beside and in front of the houses. Fire lookouts made from bamboo and thatch are common. Tiny bags, half-filled with water (and a little sand in the bottom) are suspended from long horizontal poles in all the front yards. This is the regime's answer to the dramatic loss of life that occurs when fire sweeps through the townships. These tiny bags of water will not put out a fire, but they do save residents from being fined by the fire brigade and the auxiliary fire brigade.

The better houses have front and side paling fences; some are made of wood (not bamboo) and even cement, brick, and tile. The houses are surrounded by dense foliage. Coconut palms, mango trees, breadfruit, mattress seed trees, and banana trees threaten to engulf the houses. The drainage ditches are clogged with weeds that grow over the banks and into the rubbish heaps at the front of the houses. Trees are chopped down and their trunks propped over the drainage ditches. Wooden slats form a crude walkway from the plank to the front entrance. Jute bags surround external latrines and serve as walls. Plastic sheeting makes the bamboo thatch and jute walls more rainproof. After a few feet, the woven thatch gives way to bamboo lattice that serves as windows.

Sitting on two bricks or on a small step of wooden planks before the entranceway, Burmese clay pots hold water for household cooking and washing. Sometimes a makeshift porch supports a hammock or baby swing. The bamboo lattice doubles as a clothesline. I stop to talk with a woman in her late thirties squatting on a wooden bridge that serves as the entrance to the family compound. This house is grander than the ones surrounding it, and on top of two bamboo poles about twenty feet high hangs a corroded signboard. The sign and the relative grandeur of the house mean that the family is connected to the regime in some way. The house may, for instance, have been a township health post at one stage. The woman, wearing a maroon and white cotton *longyi* and a faded green *eingyi*, squats, reaches to her right to dip a red plastic bowl into the water pitcher, and pours it onto a man's white shirt that she is hitting upon the small square of cement inside her compound.

I ask her where she gets her water. "From my neighbor, five houses away, but at least we don't have to pay for it." Behind her runs a short bricked path and a concrete slab that forms the entry porch to her house. The house itself is made of wood, painted a bright blue, and the roof and verandah are made of tin. It has two stories and shutters on the upper window. Double floor-to-ceiling window frames in the downstairs area are covered in a wire grill. Split bamboo fencing about six feet high surrounds the compound, and in front there is a pot of rice slowly cooking. The drainage ditch beside the rice pot is thickly flowing, and on the other side the household refuse has piled up. Plastic bags fall from the refuse pile into the river of effluent flowing past the house. Mothers in the townships draw a direct link between the environmental conditions in these slums and ill health. Alcohol shops, rubbish piles, stagnant water, and mud infused with untreated sewage surround most homes. Mosquito breeding sites such as polluted waterways and pools of stagnant water are facts of life, as are cholera, dengue, and malaria. The family in Figure 13 consists of five members; their living arrangements on a platform between two thatched huts with only a plastic sheet overhead are not uncommon. They cook and defecate in the mud in the foreground of the picture.

As infrastructure was slowly extended in Nyaungbintha, some of the relocated townships became sites for the relocation of industry and the creation of "industrial zones." The companies established in these areas have used the residents from the relocated townships as a source of very cheap labor, willing to work for less than subsistence wages. Children, for example, work unprotected in chili factories and weaving enterprises, and both men and women labor at construction sites to create private housing estates for wealthy urban residents. The people who live in this ward have jobs in the industrial zone; they constitute the "working poor" who are, in Nyaungbintha, looked upon with envy.

The development of roads, bridges, manufacturing industries, and government health services such as hospitals and township health posts resulted in land speculation, with urban residents buying land with the aim of eventual retirement to the townships, sometimes because of the increasing costs of urban living, and other times in anticipation of being forcibly relocated in the coming years. The junta, devoid of cash, often pays its employees in kind. This includes rice and oil but can also mean land in the relocated townships. This means that a group of "non-poor" residents exists, and that the townships have a mixed composition and services are unevenly distributed. In one such newly established household I saw a large old television and an electric fan. This is the only house I have seen with such luxuries, apart from brothels and the houses of women who own brothels.

Figure 13. Peri-urban poverty. (author's photo)

No statistics are available regarding the average income in Nyaungbin-tha because of the diverse socioeconomic groupings of different townships and wards within townships. For example, Mandalay's peri-urban townships contain both the most affluent and the most impoverished residents. Some sectors of the townships will have piped water and may have electricity, while others contain thatched huts or sleeping platforms with no facilities at all. A small group of people within the townships (primarily civil service workers, brothel owners and creditors) are thus not impoverished and this demographic continues to rise as more city residents seek cheaper land prices and as peri-urban infrastructure and small businesses become established. The townships have become the urban fringe.

In the more populous poorer wards, the houses have no wooden slats, planks, or walkways and residents squat in the mud with their rice pots. These houses are smaller, often consisting of just one room perhaps two meters across. Extending even farther into the paddy fields, a new generation of landless squatters live hand-to-mouth in straw and plastic makeshift huts.

The educational status of the population of Nyaungbintha is diverse. It is indicative of the variety of places from which the township residents have been drawn. Original inhabitants such as farmers have low education levels, while higher levels are seen in forcibly relocated settlers from other parts of Mandalay and Rangoon. Those residents at the higher end of the scale are most likely government employees given or offered land as well as wealthy Mandalay residents speculating upon future community growth and infrastructure development.

The most common employment skills possessed by the women of the New Fields are those traditionally associated with female cottage or domestic industries in Burma such as sewing, embroidery, and lace tatting, and service industry work such as cleaning, serving, and clothes washing. Vending, however, is the most common income-generating activity, along with manual labor, masonry, and cane and bamboo crafting. Other income-generating skills included driving pony carts, making brooms, traditional dancing, midwifery, working in beauty parlors, baking, farming, making bamboo thatch, teaching, rolling cheroots, making Burmese sandals, animal husbandry, weaving, collecting plastic bags for resale, and rolling charcoal into balls for resale. The husbands who are employed are engaged in activities such as unskilled manual labor, bus workers and drivers, carpenters and workshop employees, vendors, trishaw drivers, public service personnel, farming and animal husbandry, and brokering (acting as middlemen for almost any commodity). A number of trades are practiced by Nyaungbintha husbands, such as locksmithing, blacksmithing, and electrical and mechanical work.

Despite the diversity of these income-generating skills, most of the adult population of Nyaungbintha seem to be perpetually and chronically underemployed. The always jolly and often ribald Daw Ohn Myint tells me she sells vegetables in the market, but when we sit down and calculate the cost of getting the bus to a market in town where prices are lower, and combine it with her inability to sell all her vegetables several times per week, her balance sheet comes out 100 kyat up one week, and 100 in debt the next. Many semiskilled residents such as cheroot rollers and traditional dancers are vulnerable to fluctuations in the economic situation. The majority of women I interviewed said that they had a skill, such as rolling charcoal into balls for resale, but it is a strategy designed to earn any income at all; it is not a regular, full-time job.

The precariousness of the financial situation of Nyaungbintha families is manifest in the average family budget; in 1996–97 food accounted for 82 percent of family expenditure and more than 40 percent of families had fallen into debt because of their need to purchase food. Paying interest and capital on debts constituted a further 11 percent of family incomes. One-quarter of families regularly (an average of three times per week) drank the water in which the rice was cooked in order to quench feelings of hunger when adequate food was not available, and one-third of the 450 families interviewed stated that they did not have enough food to eat on a daily basis. In the New Fields surrounding Mandalay, 40 percent of the families had debts of more than 10,000 kyat (U.S. $61), with a further 14 percent having debts of more than 40,000 kyat (U.S. $244).[2] One-quarter of the families said that they were in debt because of their need to purchase medical care. The average cost of a caesarean birth, for example, was U.S. $72. The smaller family plots contain an average of six persons and each of these family units spend U.S. $45 per month on basic needs such as water, fuel for cooking, and food. Most families in the townships buy water for cooking from the few residents who can afford a bore; they use charcoal and wood for cooking and candles, batteries, and electricity (where available) for lighting.

The relocated townships are only a few kilometers from the main cities and better transportation links will continue to make them viable alternatives to the escalating costs of city living. The small group of voluntary residents contrasts markedly with the daily intake into the feeding centers of children dying from malnutrition, dehydration, and preventable diseases such as measles, and of women presenting to hospitals bleeding to death from incomplete abortions. The incongruity of these various groups of people living side by side can only be understood within the wider framework of a military dictatorship intent upon suppressing potential democratic neighborhoods, demolishing the inner city, and creating new urban centers that immortalize the principle of authoritarianism in Burmese society.

Structural Violence

Violence is a dimension of everyday life and not simply a technique brought out at times of group or personal conflict (Nordstrom and Robben 1995). Violence can be understood as being manifested along three social axes: (1) direct violence: state, torture, domestic; (2) indirect violence: fear and terror, surveillance, rumor, gossip, and suspicion; and (3) structural violence: poverty, gender, and ethnicity (Farmer 1992). Such structural violence is experienced disproportionately by the most vulnerable sectors of society: women and children. The following litany of suffering and misery emphasizes that violence against women occurs in every stratum of Burmese life. Although violence is most obvious in the torture of women by the military state, it is more common here amid the squalor, poverty, and hunger of the relocated townships. Gender-based violence has been called a "quiet violence" (Hartmann and Boyce 1983) and violence has been perpetrated against those urban residents forcibly located to Nyaungbintha. The dire socioeconomic conditions deliberately created by the military regime show complete disregard for the basic human rights of the Burmese populace.

Women as mothers are traditionally seen as the guardians of the domestic sphere, responsible for the safety of their children and for safeguarding the mental health of the entire family. Burdened with such stewardship, women and mothers experience this quiet violence of structural and institutionalized inequality differently from men. Gender is, of course, only one of many variables that distribute terror unevenly among the population. Young women who have been incarcerated and tortured have spoken of a heightened fear of rape when virginity is threatened during these torture sessions (ALTSEAN Burma 1998). Mothers fear for the safety of their sons and their husbands during times of mass arrests and student activism. Pregnant women and women with small children try desperately to remain in safe zones and to appear unimportant and docile. Women try to keep their teenage daughters at home so that they will not attract the eyes of the soldiers.

Women whose husbands and sons are involved in political opposition to the regime are verbally pressured and threatened by government officials and high ranking military officers to ensure their family remains safe by staying silent on political issues. Women, in short, strive to prevent children and other family members from interacting with the state. Women counsel their children into docility and teach them self-censorship. They tell their children about the dangers of informants and of the importance of never speaking out against the regime or trusting that anyone will keep such sentiments between friends.

Sexual Barter, Rape, and Despair

The small plots of land in Nyaungbintha cannot hold the extended families that seem to have evolved in the cities. Nuclear families and aged parents living alone are the most common living arrangements and this change in living arrangements has erased a number of checks and balances upon the behavior of some men within these families. While almost all women of reproductive age marry, these families are not necessarily stable. The highly mobile nature of the male work force in the relocated townships has caused an explosion of polygamy, and women are routinely abandoned for wives in different parts of the country.

It is hard to find unmarried women in the townships. Only 3 percent of households are female headed. All of the other women I have interviewed describe themselves as either married or remarried, sometimes as many as four times, a testimony to the depth of female unemployment and the need to engage in sexual barter to provide for children and other dependent family members. Sheer economic necessity requires women to remarry as quickly as possible after divorce, abandonment, or widowhood. It is not surprising in this economic nightmare to find women agonizing over unplanned pregnancies, unemployment, rising debt levels, and abandonment by their spouses. A further complication is the dramatic rise in alcohol consumption by unemployed men in Nyaungbintha. Women in these areas will sometimes divorce their husbands when the beatings and other forms of alcohol-induced abuse become too much.

This litany of divorce, abandonment, and remarriage has created great fear of rape and incest within families with stepbrothers, stepfathers, and step-uncles. This fear is sometimes well founded, but it is a subject of great shame about which Burmese people will rarely speak. Several women told me of their daughters being raped by their stepfathers as they all slept together on a long raised wooden pallet. Young girls spoke of their repeated rape over several years by step-uncles and stepfathers who returned to the house during the day while the mothers were working away from the home or at the market. These girls spoke of the fear of smelling alcohol on the breath of their male relatives, and some of these vulnerable young girls were subjected to repeated rapes from the age of nine.[3]

One of the best-known landmarks in the relocated townships of Rangoon is "looking for a husband hill." It is a small hillock just up the bank from the landing site of the boats that cross the river to Nyaungbintha.

It is a major site for prostitution because most boats are moored over-night while they are unloaded and reloaded and so young women come to the hillock from all over the surrounding township. Almost the only women profiting in the relocated townships are women working in pros-titution, women recruiting for prostitution rings, and women working as creditors, with lending rates of over 30 percent per month. In interviews with over fifty women working in prostitution in Rangoon's peri-urban townships, the general consensus was that, at any one time, one-third of all women of reproductive age in the peri-urban townships are engaged in prostitution. In the mid- to late 1990s, I found this figure to be credi-ble. A third of the girls and women had been raped by their boss or their relatives before deciding to enter the prostitution industry. They most often used the rationale that "My life is ruined now so I may as well make some money," or "I'm not good for anything else now."

The industry has grown so large that it has evolved a specific vocabu-lary that distinguishes types, duration, and frequency of sexual services. Powerful women known as "aunts," and former policemen, are notori-ous for their large brothels in the townships. Some brothels service only the police and military. Other women prostitute themselves aboard the government's ships and tankers, while others travel into the city centers each evening to work at the newly established nightclubs and at almost all of the international hotels.

Women in their twenties and thirties are driven into this industry largely because they have been abandoned or because they have initi-ated divorces (to escape from abusive relationships). These women, unskilled or uneducated, must continue to provide for their children. Unemployment and underemployment are high in the townships, and it is not possible to make a living from simply selling vegetables in the market. Women consistently told me they would immediately abandon prostitution if they could find the start-up funds for a self-employed ven-ding business. Often this amounts to about three U.S. dollars, but this work is seen as a remote possibility for these women.

Girls as young as fourteen may enter the prostitution industry for dif-ferent reasons. As mentioned above, young girls may be victims of incest, and this often leads to a belief that their life is ruined and they may as well make some money from their misfortune. Other reasons include an enormous debt of responsibility felt toward parents and younger family members. These girls and young women take it upon themselves to be the family provider. Mothers are usually aware of their daughters' occu-pation, and they collude to keep the knowledge from their husbands. Such women weep with shame when asked about their daughters, and many try to place their daughters with brothels, where they have more protection than they would if they were street workers.

A final explanation for the prostitution epidemic relates once more to the chronic poverty of the relocated townships. Trishaw drivers, taxi-drivers, market women, and other employed women engage in a lucrative and extensive recruitment process for the brothels and street pimps. Young women are targeted, often by their friends; the promise of a full stomach each day and a life devoid of the browned skin and calloused hands from farming or construction work is consistently held out to lure girls and young women into a life of sexual servitude. Like many poor nations, Burma is full of hungry people. Burmese people may not be dying of starvation, but many households in the relocated townships eat only two meals a day, consisting almost solely of rice. Food shortages have been documented across ten of Burma's fourteen divisions (People's Tribunal 1999).

Hepatitis, HIV, and other sexually transmitted diseases flourish for a variety of reasons. They include the number of men using prostitution, the practice of polygamy, the rate of heroin addiction in Burma (4 percent for men, 2 percent for women) and other unsafe practices such as reuse of syringes in medical clinics, and penis-enlarging procedures common in Burmese jails and among fishing communities. Carrying condoms is widely believed by the police and military forces to constitute evidence that a woman is engaged in prostitution, and has been legal only since 1993. In addition, men refuse to buy small or medium size condoms, and a majority of both wives and women working in the sex industry argue that they cannot make their sexual partners use condoms. Almost no mothers had ever seen a condom and had no idea how they are used. The first question I am often asked about condoms is, "can I eat it?" While injectable and oral contraceptives are perceived as "women's business," condoms are commonly seen as "men's business" or related to STDs and commercial sex workers. The women hold their two index fingers together saying, "we are like sister and brother." Most state that it is an inappropriate subject to discuss between the sexes.

The selling of sexual services also occurs within marriages, primarily through sexual bartering on the part of the wife. This is more common when women have alcoholic husbands or husbands with other drug abuse problems. Women admit using sexual intercourse to get enough money from their husbands to feed themselves and their children. Within such families, the toll on physical and psychological health is immense. In the most impoverished sectors of the townships, women spoke of the domestic violence meted out to them and their children. Several women related stories of regular (at least two or three times per week) bashings, and various accounts of torture were also given. These included being tied to poles and lashed, or left in a bound position for several hours.

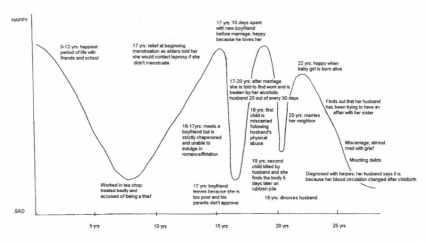

Figure 14. Ma Pyu's sexuality life line.

The greatest harvest of reports of misery was reaped from collaboration with women of reproductive age in the production of "sexuality life
lines," where women indicated on a chart their level of happiness or
sadness at events in their life that they took to be significant moments.
Of forty such recorded charts, almost all show childhood as the happiest
period in a woman's life, followed by a steady decrease into chronic sadness by middle age. Twenty-five-year-old Ma Pyu was one of the women
with whom I formed an instant rapport. I am not sure why I enjoyed her
company so much; certainly I have never been told such horrendous
things from such a young person outside the psychiatric hospital and
heroin rehabilitation unit. I think it was her defiant spirit: although several of the women told me that during periods of their lives they "acted
as robots," Ma Pyu never disengaged from her life, no matter how horrendous her personal circumstances. I have not been able to continue
my friendship with Ma Pyu as her economic situation was so precarious
that she continually moved farther out into the poorest wards, and eventually I couldn't find her at all.

Ma Pyu started out her chart at "happy" and drew a series of mountains and valleys, each time moving further into the depths of the "sadness" part of the chart (see Figure 14). Ma Pyu began by telling me that
the happiest time of her life was from when she was five until she was
twelve years old. At twelve she went to work in a tea shop and, even
though her life took many terrible turns, she marks this as equal to any
other sad period of her life because she was "treated very badly" and
finally was accused of being a thief before she was fired.

She was a small child, malnourished, who reached puberty late and had a boyfriend for a year when she was sixteen. She came from a very conservative Buddhist family and was at all times chaperoned by her family and there was never a chance "to say romantic things" to each other. At seventeen she finally menstruated; she was exceedingly relieved because the ward elders had convinced her that she would contract leprosy if she didn't menstruate. At the same time, her boyfriend left her because his parents didn't want their son to marry into such a poor family.

She then met another young man and knew him for ten days before they were married. She describes this period (lasting one month) as almost as happy as her childhood. Her life then took a series of downhill turns. Her husband immediately told her to leave the house and find work, an indicator of how far her family had fallen that they now needed to send their women into the workforce. Her husband, she soon realized, was an alcoholic and he beat her "twenty out of every thirty days," from the time she was seventeen until she was twenty.

Ma Pyu's husband became violent after drinking alcohol, and she miscarried with her first child because he repeatedly punched her in a drunken rage. A year later, when she was nineteen, her husband again beat her very severely and she was covered in dark bruises. Her son, a few months old, was gone in the morning and she searched the neighborhood frantically for him for five days before finding his body thrown onto a rubbish midden in front of her house.

In the silence surrounding her revelation, she quietly sniffles and then draws herself up and continues the narrative. She immediately separated from her husband and a few months later married her neighbor, just after her twentieth birthday. At twenty two she gave birth to a baby girl and she describes this as a happy period in her life. This happiness was short lived, however, as she discovered that her husband had been trying to have sex with her sister. She found herself pregnant again and again miscarried, and she tells me that she was "nearly mad because of grief." Now, as her twenty-fifth birthday approaches, she is deeply indebted and therefore cannot leave her husband. To make matters worse, she has been diagnosed with herpes. Her husband denies any responsibility, saying that instead it is because Ma Pyu's "blood circulation changed after childbirth."

The women's sexuality life lines and typical work day profiles reveal an alarming similarity to the lives of refugees; relocated townships are in fact internally displaced refugee communities. Their life stories constitute narratives of poverty, despair, domestic violence, child deaths, and the influence of alcohol on family relations and the safety of women and children. Secrecy and shame surround violence; one study showed that only 30 percent of women who had had abortions would later admit to them (Figa-Talamanca 1986). Violence is fundamentally un-Buddhist, and the many acts of direct, indirect, and structural violence against women are perpetrated behind bamboo fences; while they are often known to occur, they are almost never spoken of.

Abortion and Maternal Mortality

Nyaungbintha's women's life histories contain a number of common themes such as childbirth, weakness, and amenorrhea. Abortion figures often, and a great deal of cultural knowledge exists about varieties of abortion and miscarriages and ways to attempt to staunch hemorrhaging. Nyaungbintha mothers are adamant that their decision to attempt to abort pregnancies stems from their impoverished situation and their inability to look after and feed additional children. It is not a decision made lightly and they are aware of the danger of maternal death in their decision to seek illegal abortions. Many women initially deny knowledge of abortion because of its illegality but they have told me more than twenty ways in which they terminate their pregnancies, including jumping from heights, lifting heavy weights, putting pressure on the abdomen using a hot brick, and a variety of recipes that involve combinations of "hot foods." Before these methods are used, large amounts of the emmenogogue, *thwe-ze* (*thwei: zei:*), are ingested because of its "hotness" and ability to create a strong blood flow.

Following abortions or deliberate miscarriages, women attempt to stop the flow of blood, as too strong blood flow is believed to be as injurious as too little blood flow. Sometimes this becomes a life-threatening situation and women are admitted to local and city hospitals because of serious hemorrhaging. Several local hospitals are known as "green" hospitals because of the "green" or untimely, early deaths of so many patients. One particular hospital is greatly feared and people report seeing ghosts all around the hospital grounds. These ghosts are the souls of babies and mothers who have died in childbirth and as a consequence of illegal abortions.

The following two interview segments give an indication of the responses to questions about abortion:

I terminated my last pregnancy by using the *lethe* (*le'the*) [traditional birth attendant]. She used a stick in the vagina. After that, I didn't have any further problems. If I hadn't terminated the pregnancy, my smallest child wouldn't have had enough breast milk. Also, I thought the pregnancy was only two months old, but it was really three months old. I was very unhappy that I didn't have enough money to have the baby, so I had to do [abort] it.

During our worst economic times, I was one month pregnant and I wanted to end it. So I drank four packets of *Kathypan* [*thwei:-zei:*] but it didn't work, and when the child was born, his skin was yellow. At seven months of age he became worse and we took him to the hospital. The doctors suggested that we go to Rangoon because they'd never seen that kind of problem before. But the problem was that we didn't have enough money to go. The child died at the [local] hospital.

Unwanted pregnancies are but another aspect of a saga of poverty and gender-based violence, constituting further evidence of what Farmer (1996) calls "structural suffering." Women reported husbands who repeatedly punched them in the stomach if they refused to abort a fetus. Contraceptives are expensive and unreliable since they are often past their use-by date. Burmese women in the townships prefer injectable contraceptives, since this eliminates the need to try to remember to take pills on a daily basis. Women seldom record the date of their last contraceptive injection, however, and forget when the next one is due. Even more common is a lack of money to pay for regular injections. Intrauterine devices are popular because they also obviate the need to use regular contraception.

Abortion is illegal, and human rights groups have called for its legalization. Sterilization is performed in military and public hospitals and women are keen to avail themselves of this service. However, it is a costly and bureaucratically cumbersome process, and so relatively few go forward with the procedure. Sterilization is the main reason given for women choosing to have their second and successive children in a hospital (where sterilization can be performed after the birth). Approximately 3 percent of husbands have had vasectomies, but they are illegal except for military personnel. Menstrual regulation (of which abortion is one possible outcome) is the primary method of birth spacing. Menstrual regulation and other traditional practices of contraception and abortion are used in the estimated 40 percent of the country not covered by basic medical services, and in these areas, infant mortality rates are almost 400 percent higher than in areas where basic health services exist (UNICEF 1995).

The human cost of local abortion is immense. Maternal mortality is as high as 500 to 580 per 10,000 live births (WHO 1997), but while women are scared to induce abortions, they are even more terrified of having one more mouth to feed. Women present to regional hospitals on a daily basis with hemorrhage from incomplete abortions. Studies conducted throughout the country indicate somewhere between 33 percent and 60 percent of maternal mortality is directly attributed to abortions (Ministry of Health and UNFPA 1999; Ba Thike 1997; Khin Than Tin and Khin Saw Hla 1990). In some studies abortion has been found to be the leading cause of maternal mortality in Burma (Krasu 1992).

In a review of data about contraceptive practices in Burma, Caouette et al. (2000) conclude that the regime's birth spacing program focuses upon older married women, but a number of studies show that adolescents and younger women face more social stigma over pregnancies and are more likely to use contraceptives and to have higher risks for complications from unsafe abortions (Hla Pe et al. 1992; Bo Kywe and Maung Maung Lin 1993; Ba Thike et al. 1992; Ba Thike et al. 1993). Aye Aye Thein et al. (1995) report that the perinatal mortality rate among young women (46 to 67 per 1000 births) is double that of older women.

The large amount of knowledge about abortion methods and emergency situations resulting from abortion, coupled with the ease with which abortion is discussed in Nyaungbintha, suggests that the strong link between abortion, poverty, and maternal mortality continues to exist in the peri-urban townships. The women interviewed know that this link exists and that the "real" problem is not a medical one, but an economic one, and that economics is inextricably tied to the current political situation.

Childbirth

Childbirth has long been acknowledged as a dangerous time for women, not just because of the risk of maternal death, but also because of the postpartum period, *mi:dwin:* when special care must be taken. The body is cold from blood loss and must be slowly reheated. Because resistance to illness is lowered at this time, new mothers must be insulated from shock or sudden change. Women who have had complications in terminating pregnancies also follow the precautions taken in this period. They too seek to staunch the flow of blood and keep the body free from harm. Such postpartum beliefs and practices are common in Southeast Asia (Dixon 1993). Many Burmese women remain near a fire made from bamboo during the postpartum period. Washing the hair is unacceptable as it cools the body and heating, rather than cooling foods, are eaten at this time. In addition, foods that are thought to restrict blood flow (such as sour and bitter foods) are consumed.

A common illness thought to result from the body becoming too cold in the postpartum period is *mi:ja'chan*, a menstrual sickness whose main symptom is chills. Women include in this category illnesses in the postpartum period caused by giving birth at the beginning of the monsoon season when several months of heavy rain lead to an inability to stay dry and warm. This emphasis upon chills, the body being excessively cooled, and the difficulties of staying dry is an especially prominent concern in the many parts of Nyaungbintha that flood annually. Dirt roads become rivers of mud and earthen floors in many homes become quagmires. Several households I have visited have regular flooding of more than half a meter of water in their huts. They build their sleeping platforms as high as possible to remain above the water line during the monsoon period. The monsoon rains transform the relocated townships into a sea of mud, and diseases of poor sanitation are rife. Diarrhea, cholera, tuberculosis, polio, leprosy, and physical and intellectual disabilities are common.

Childbirth is thus a time when new mothers must take good care of themselves through observing postpartum taboos, diet changes, and "heating" practices. In the townships this postpartum period is made more dangerous because of the difficulties of staying dry and warm and because of the additional burden of worry placed upon mothers that results from the bleak economic prospects of relocated residents.

Lengthening Shadows

Unemployed and underemployed Nyaungbintha women believe that their life will be the same, day after day. They hold almost no hope that their lives will improve; they seem even to have given up hope on the miraculous. Their only remaining hopes are that their children may escape the relocated townships and find a life where a steady income leads to possibilities denied to the current generation. For many people this hope is tinged with the sadness of losing their sense of place and their separation from family members. For older people this can mean living alone without any means of financial income other than donations from neighbors and friends. For women with many children, smaller households mean less family support and childcare; the husband generally becomes the primary income earner. Domestic violence, sexual bartering, incest, and child abuse occur more frequently when the regular checks and balances of extended family living are no longer possible. These social problems are aggravated by the tensions of unemployment and underemployment.

Looking back through several hundred interviews, I am struck anew by the number of deaths or separations of parents when the women of Nyaungbintha were young children, the subsequent dividing up of their families, and the incorporation of these family fragments with step-relatives of newly married affines. There is a striking frequency of allusion to forms of abuse and usually alcoholism in some members of these new extended families. The young girls almost always are taken out of school and must work as unskilled laborers: as construction workers, in factories rolling cheroots, as vendors selling betel or spices. Marriage at a very early age, often to abusive young men, spontaneous miscarriages from the nature of their work, divorce and abandonment, and the deaths of parents, husbands, or children, are often the precursors for the spiral into misery that is Nyaungbintha. Like Ma Pyu, Ma Khin Khin Thaung is another archetypal Nyaungbintha resident. Only twenty five years old, but wise in the depth of misery achievable in the mundane world, she tells me her life story:

I will tell you the story of my short life. I live in an Industrial Zone. Before, my home was in a village in the Delta. I'm married and I have one child and I'm pregnant with another. My son is two-and-a-half years old. He had diarrhea and I sent him to the Children's Hospital. He was cured, but he had puffy swelling all over. I know that this kind of problem can cause death, but the Children's Hospital said it was all right, and they discharged my son. I was worried about him. I lived in [Nyaungbintha] at the time but I did not dare to go to the [Nyaungbintha] hospital because everyone here is so afraid of it, so I went to the Children's Hospital. A Clinic in [Nyaungbintha] later sent me to Insein General Hospital. After he got better, I brought him back here.

Before my son became sick, I worked at a government construction site carrying bricks and cement. I got 80 kyat each day [then U.S. 50c]. I have to work every day except if I get sick. My husband does the same work. We are very poor, but I want to be rich. I don't have a house yet, just a temporary hut at the construction site, in the paddy fields.

My life is the same every day. No one day is ever any different from the other. My life is miserable. I am so poor, and my husband is always drunk, so I feel very upset every day. I used to cry all the time, again and again, but now I try to relax, I try to exist just like this. I have no future and no future plans because I have no money. I don't think I can give a good education to my children, so I don't think anything different will ever happen.

Women such as Ma Khin Khin Thaung were driven, because of their inability to meet military rice quotas in their natal villages, into the industrial zones of the peri-urban areas. These young women would otherwise have been out in the fields. Their feet are splayed: wide and short, the tell tale signs of years spent in the water and mud of the paddy fields. It is the job of women to sort and then transplant the rice from the nursery fields to the main fields that have been prepared by the men. As the men would by that time have finished the bulk of their work for the time being, they regaled the women with paddy planting songs and infectious drum beats, like the song about the folk of Aung Pin Le. Instead, these women are sleeping, eating, resting, or carrying bricks, each seeking her own form of escape from the unchanging present of Nyaungbintha.

In her village, Ma Khin Khin Thaung may have been able to bear life's tragedies such as grief, loneliness, and the other vicissitudes of everyday life with community and family support. Buddhism, in particular, provides a framework for understanding suffering and sorrow and generalizing it to the world and to *samsara* (Obeyesekere 1985). There are many forms of traditional social organization and community support groups, both Buddhist and secular, that people can turn to in times of economic or other calamity. In the relocated townships, many of these structures have broken down, or have been suborned by the military government. More important, the socioeconomic situation of many of the peri-urban township residents is perilous and it is this combination of extreme economic vulnerability with the tribulations of quotidian life that allows the specter of despair to stalk the peri-urban townships.

My discussions with the women of Nyaungbintha have taken many full weeks of long days beginning before the heat starts and ending with the brief Burmese twilight. I put down my pen and glance out the open doorway. The women helping me have found a thin red cow and are paying the owner for some fresh milk that they take turns drinking from the bucket. My skin and clothes are coated with a fine layer of red dust. It looks like I have been doused with a packet of *thwe-ze*.

The women are beginning to disperse to their bamboo huts, calling to their children, some of whom are climbing nearby trees and tormenting small insects with broken-off branches. As the evening shadows lengthen I begin the journey back into town. I pass dusty laborers returning from construction sites. Most women begin cooking rice on an open fire. There is little entertainment in these peri-urban townships. The sound of guitars is not common here as it is in the more established townships.

The women have painted a bleak picture of their hopes and aspirations and have described days filled with the same constant frustrations and worries. The women of the New Fields link their reproductive health to their local environment, their socioeconomic situation, and the amoral economy of a military dictatorship that has created impoverished slums in which illegal abortions, hunger, and worry are everyday occurrences. Ma Khin Khin Thaung is subject to unceasing labor and to a health infrastructure that is inaccessible and in the case of Nyaungbintha's hospital, too frightening even to contemplate. Ma Pyu has no recourse to justice in the lawless world of domestic violence, where men act with impunity and the police are a threat rather than a solution.

Perhaps the legacy of such quiet violence and lack of recourse to justice will only become fully apparent in future generations of Burmese children. Will these children of dictatorship and civil war respect civil society, freedom of speech, and those basic human rights currently denied to their parents? Such a toll can best be gauged in the forcibly relocated townships where new spaces of suffering have been created as a result of the regime's infliction of direct and indirect violence upon much of the population. The Burmese military regime does not perform unsafe abortions, nor does it mandate sterilization, the prostitution epidemic, or that domestic violence should run rampant through cities and villages. However, through its systematic violation of the human rights of an entire nation, the military council sets the preconditions for the explosion in frequency and volume of systematic forms of violence that flourish in Nyaungbintha.

Chapter 9
The Forest of Time

The mind, the Buddha said, is like gold. A pure mind can pour
around the world without getting snagged and can roll all around
itself, like a bead of water on a lotus leaf. . . . In the same way, a pure
mind . . . can give results way in excess of its size. People who are
really intent on purifying the mind may even lift themselves over
and beyond the world.

—Phra Ajaan Lee Dhammadharo, namo tasso
bhagavato arahato samma-sambuddhass

Dreams preserved in the biographies of the Buddha provide a map
of the Buddhist dream world for those who would follow the same
path, such that all buddhas, whether past, present or future, have
the same life story and therefore the same dreams. . . . The common
dream world is available to striving Buddhists as a map of spiritual
progress.

—Serinity Young, *Dreaming in the Lotus*

I Resist in My Mind Only

Despite the "miasma of fear" that Aung San Suu Kyi has described
cloaking Burma, there is clearly both open and collective resistance to
the military regime. The continued existence of the National League for
Democracy, despite its dwindling ranks as members are imprisoned,
intimidated, and die in custody, is testimony to the enormous desire for
change in Burma in the face of overwhelming repression. Those who
braved the military roadblocks and military intelligence photographers
to attend the NLD roadside speeches give further evidence of the desire
for change. The will to resist is also evident in the number of people
arrested and later imprisoned for handing out leaflets at the roadside
talks. The large number of political prisoners in Burmese jails signifies

the open defiance that has persisted through four decades of military dictatorship.

Demonstrations by monks, students, and pro-democracy supporters, as well as sporadic workers' strikes (such as miners and garment factory workers) prove that the regime has not been completely successful in reconstructing Burmese as model citizens. The occasional bomb blast under symbols of repression such as the People's Desire signboards are enough to convince the regime of the need to keep increasing its control over the everyday lives of its subject population.

Collective resistance under the cover of anonymity is more common than open defiance in urban Burma, such as when the residents of Hledan Township opened their doors to the students who had staged a sit-down strike at their junction. United, they were able to deny individual acts of defiance. Attendance at state entertainment events is another example of the way in which collective resistance can emerge. Although Burmese would generally prefer not to patronize official sporting events, high unemployment and a lack of recreational facilities (together with a love of sport, gambling, and competition) combine to make some events too tempting to resist. Anonymity at sporting events allows hidden transcripts to be enacted publicly. George Orwell has written of the insults screamed by Burmese on the sidelines of a British football match during his time in Burma. Scott (1992: 77) notes that in Orwell's description "Burmans managed to insinuate almost routinely a contempt for the British, while being careful never to venture a more dangerous open defiance . . . taking advantage of a crowd or of an ambiguous accident, they manage in a thousand artful ways to imply that they are grudging conscripts to the performance. . . . Behind the "anti-European" acts that Orwell noted was undoubtedly a far more elaborate hidden transcript, an entire discourse, linked to Burman culture, religion, and the experience of colonial rule."

Upon reading this I was struck by how little the situation has changed. I recalled a friend's description of another football match seventy years later between the Army and the Customs Department, where the hidden transcript again breaks through under the cover of anonymity:

Everyone at the Sports Festival is against the Army. First the Army scored and everyone was quiet except the soldiers who were saluting. The people started shouting out *si'tha:ju:* [the word for soldier is attached to a derogatory term for madness]. They called out a lot of things. My son said that they shouted defence slogans, "*gagwe! gagwe!*" Then my son started shouting out "*lee, lee*" [slang for "penis, penis"]. Then everyone started chanting it. Louder, lots of dirty swear words. At one point the soldiers were so angry that they threw a bottle at the spectators. The people started throwing stones at the soldiers. The soldiers began arresting people, I saw one person who was arrested and dragged outside the stadium by the hair. Then the people cried, "Aren't you going to arrest the soldier who threw the bottle?" So they did, but everyone thinks he'll be released as soon as he gets out of sight. When Khin Nyunt gave out the prizes there was a lot of cheering for the first prize- [awarded to] Customs, but then no one cheered [for the army]. Then a voice said, "Hey, aren't you going to show sympathy for the soldiers and clap them?" The people responded by shouting, "Why should we?" No one cheered, then they started yelling, "We love Customs! We love Customs!"

Many urban residents also make a conscious decision to resist the renaming and reconstruction of the urban landscape, such as when Rangoon residents pointedly ignore "Ne Win's pagoda." I became aware of this type of resistance very early in my fieldwork when seeking directions to the Traditional Medicine Hospital. Burmese refuse to refer to this hospital by its name, preferring to direct me to "Daw Khin Kyi's hospital." Daw Khin Kyi is Aung San Suu Kyi's mother who was a nurse and later a politician. A hospital, her namesake, now stands abandoned beside the Traditional Medicine Hospital.

Resistance is also practiced by the wealthy urban elite who have enough money and influence to be able to perform token acts of resistance. The regime closely monitors such defiance. In a discussion about the construction of the Tooth Relic pagodas as part of a broader scheme to legitimate the rule of the military within a Buddhist paradigm, Schober argues that donations to the pagodas serve to make merit for the military leaders who inaugurated the projects. Some Burmese withhold donations or decline from attending donor ceremonies as a token resistance. Schober (1995: 28–29, n.53) describes the threat of menace with which the regime responds. She notes that

Absence from participation in State-sponsored merit making ritual is another common way to resist the state. . . . One such example is found in the daily lists of major donors published in the NLM [*New Light of Myanmar*] during the Sacred Tooth tour. A tabulation over the course of six weeks indicates that on any given day, nearly half of the donors chose to be absent from rituals acknowledging their donations and SLORC's patronage, despite their large contributions. . . . The paper's statistics on less than unanimous participation in the state's ritual patronage can also be seen as a veiled threat to those who stayed away from such ceremonies, while their names and actions were known to the authorities.

Some of these strategies carry more risk than others. With all the strategies, however, the hidden messenger delivers a public message.

Burmese make a large and fundamental distinction between those things done with their enduring consciousness (designated as "mind") and those actions carried out by the temporary, decaying, corporeal dimension of their person. Undoubtedly, the most common reply of

Burmese of all social classes and ages to the question of resistance is "I resist in my mind only." Such resistance is in fact extremely significant for Buddhists. Even seemingly inconsequential forms of resistance, such as refusing to be present at donor ceremonies, or refusing to allow the regime to remove previous elements of the landscape from public memory, require an enormous amount of courage because these acts constitute resistance of the most important kind: that of the mind. They entail a conscious decision not to accept a mandated form of the present and, more important, of the future. Resisting in the mind does not, however, mean that Burmese do not suffer distress at the fear and confusion that such strategies engender, which daily threaten to overturn stable assumptions and erase tacit knowledge. Most Burmese opt for strategies that minimize the burden of fear.

Water Flows, Fish Follow

My first few months in Burma were spent asking myself a variant on the old psychology and philosophy quandary, the "free rider problem." I was essentially asking myself, "Why don't Burmese revolt?" This is a stupid question, of the same genre of stupid questions asked by development agencies about what is to be done about all the poor people in the world. The answer, of course, is that "they are doing it" (Escobar 1994) and the same would apply to these kinds of questions being asked in Burma. The reason the "free rider problem" has not been solved is because it is not a question that has an answer. The question should be rephrased, "what is of significance to Burmese in their local worlds?" Burmese have a range of priorities different from those of people who live in comfortable democracies. There is, for example, very little familiarity with concepts such as democracy and freedom of speech for many people living in the New Fields, and therefore there are few expectations about them. Daw San San Pwint, who had spent time in Europe, brought this home to me, using my weakness for chocolate and the difficulty of finding chocolate in Burma. She is familiar with my research in the New Fields and commented that:

They are not interested in freedom, or whether Aung San Suu Kyi comes to govern or not. For them, their interests go to one level only. The only thing they [can] care about is their next meal. They are not aware of these rights. If a child had never known that chocolate had existed then he would never want to taste it. But I have tasted it, and I want my country to taste it too.

At the most fundamental level, the Burmese priority is for survival, and this often involves complicity and opportunistic collaboration with the regime and its organs of mass participation. The huge burden of fear placed upon the shoulders of Burmese by the military regime leads many of them to search for a piece of common ground with the Generals, to define a space that is, if not neutral, then at least not openly hostile. While still a rejection of the dominant ideology of authoritarianism, it is a compromise, and also a rejection of the more fundamental views of the expatriate Burmese community, who no longer have to live choked with fear for their own safety. It is primarily a strategy designed to minimize fear.

Opportunism is perhaps an outgrowth of this most common goal in Burma: physical survival. Simply finding enough money to allow one's family to eat regular meals and stave off the landlord or landlady's demands for rent is enough for the great majority of Burmese. Becoming voluntarily involved with the GONGOs is a luxury only those who live above subsistence can contemplate. Ma Kinmama Maw, a teenager working as a prostitute who lives in Nyaungbintha, told me that she had not earned any money for a week because the regime had closed the "People's Park." She stated that this was because "some big day is coming up." Ma Kinmama Maw was unaware of the rehearsals for Armed Forces Day and oblivious to the militarization of the city that had occurred. Her only concern was that the place where she earned her living was closed. Short of open revolution, political resistance (and even an awareness of the regime's goals and strategies) is itself a strategy that only the well fed can employ in Burma, and that population is very small. However, revolts have frequently been brought about not by the wealthy, educated middle and upper classes, but by the peasantry, whose severe financial situation threatens to rob them of the essentials for physical survival. The 1988 democracy uprising started in the countryside because of the threat of starvation. Lintner summarized this: "1988 started with demonetization and with Delta farmers who liberated the rice trucks: the situation was so much worse [in the countryside] than in urban areas" (Lintner, personal communication 1997). A university professor, U Ba Pe, summarized this poignant reality as, "When I'm starving, I'll fight."

Besides being strategies of survival, collaboration, complicity, and opportunism are also examples of a more general attitude in Burma promoting compromise, a formula often expressed as "water flows, fish follow." This emphasis upon compromise is attained through a focus on both collective values and on cognitive reframing. By this I mean that some Burmese continually strive to change their mode of thinking about the current political situation from one of rage, frustration, or despair (to mention but a few possible responses) to one of forgiveness. Public servants commonly use this saying when referring to the current political situation. U Ba Pe explained the proverb as: "It's a belief that somehow if you go along, there will come a point when you can change things." This proverb is being applied to the current situation because it is also illustrative of a very strong belief in the miraculous (Ferguson and Mendelson 1981). While many Burmese use this saying to explain working in the public service, they always imply that this is an unrealistic, naive strategy. Perhaps, then, it is more a form of "self talk" that Burmese use to rationalize to themselves the involvement of their friends in the public service, rather than a deeply held belief about the potential of effective subversion from within the ranks of government employees.

Going with the flow entails a conscious focus upon humane collective values. Ko Naing, for example, works with the Mandalay YMCA and he is proud of the charitable programs created by his institution, believing that by working for the betterment of impoverished Mandalay residents, he is in accord with certain aspects of the regime's ideology, namely a love of the motherland. He holds onto this belief as it serves to convince him that he has nothing to be fearful of on a daily basis because his job furthers the junta's goals for the nation. The danger in such a pragmatic strategy is that an overexaggerated sense of pride in Burma, its resources, people, and achievements, leads a great many Burmese to passively and tentatively accept the xenophobic and anti-Western rhetoric with which they are bombarded. In this sense, some Burmese stop resisting the tide of propaganda and are borne along with it, minimizing the need to struggle and contest the reality that the regime presents. A love of motherland is elided by the junta with a belief in a duty to the nation and this again makes it easier for Burmese to join the regime's organizations of mass participation. The State can be "helped," as long as individuals in the community are also benefiting from these activities.

Another method of going with the flow concerns the change to a market economy in the past few years. Some urban Burmese have inserted themselves into the liberalization of the economy and once inside, subvert its application. This method incorporates an element of resistance to the concept of an "open market" promulgated by the regime but which in reality only "opens" business opportunities for the Generals, their friends and relatives, and their allies in the drug trade. Even though foreign investment has had virtually no impact upon Burmese unconnected with the regime, it has led to a very small class of urban Burmese creating a small degree of wealth. To achieve this, however, this emergent bourgeois class must make economic deals with the military that serve ultimately to bolster the personal wealth of the Generals and their families. Burmese "aunts," wives of generals or high-ranking military officials, run a kind of mafia-style extortion operation at local Rangoon markets requiring all stall owners or lessees to have financial dealings with them. This kind of extortion is so thoroughly ingrained in transactions and commerce that it is difficult for Burmese to truly conceptualize a system in which corruption would not oil the machinery of government and the economy.

The blame for Burma's poverty and unemployment is placed squarely at the feet of the Generals. Burmese refuse to become involved in the charade of politics and instead invest their energies in resisting the enforced poverty that the regime has thrust upon them. But rather than using their wealth to reinvest in the regime's economy (and hence, the General's pockets), some Burmese use their new found wealth to buy a passport and leave the country for material and leisure pursuits (such as buying satellite dishes), and as leverage to buy personal influence and prestige at the community level. In this sense, some individuals use government organizations to further their own everyday strategies of economic survival. Resulting community influence also leads to prestige and status at the local level, factors that are very important to Burmese and have more to do with a desire for personal gain than with a desire to support the junta. Certainly other Burmese speak with disdain of such people who collude with the regime for personal power.

Despite the compromise of finding common ground with the regime, everyone must make a decision at some point as to his or her degree of collaboration. Unless they are active in the opposition, or have left the country, all Burmese collaborate to some degree. Joining the public service, for example, is an additional degree of collaboration, and it is a decision few Burmese make lightly. It involves swearing loyalty to the aims of the dictators, and it is difficult not to internalize some of the propaganda when working for the government. It must also be said that swimming against the current is tiring; many Burmese succumb to the despair of their situation, to hopelessness, and to a sense of betrayal that wider political organizations and foreign governments have not supported the population against the military. When friends become imprisoned, the desire to forget about the sociopolitical situation is great and this desire to forget tempts Burmese to choose strategies of escape rather than confrontation.

Rejecting Resistance

The attitude of compromise is reinforced by a strong Buddhist ethic pervasive in Burmese society. The older generations of ethnic Burmans are, in general, staunch Buddhists, for whom Buddhism is the central guiding focus of their lives, a filter through which events are understood and given meaning. It is therefore with a great sense of unease that older Burmese watch their children and grandchildren actively resisting the regime. Buddhist parents view the preaching of revolution as anti-Buddhist, potentially conflicting with the nonviolent tenets of Buddhism. They worry that their children and grandchildren will break central Buddhist rules such as the injunction against killing, and of course they live in fear for the safety of their loved ones should they be caught by Military Intelligence. Parents beseech their children to read Buddhist philosophy, and to actively strive, as they do, to forgive the regime, for this is the Path to Enlightenment. The following of the law of Dhamma in contrast to the laws of the Generals is of course a form of resistance, but it is not physical, armed, or open resistance and is evident only in physical acts such as patronizing "pure" monks, making merit, and obeying the Dhamma (Jordt 2001: 308), rather than through outward signs of disobeying the laws of the Generals. Fear for the safety of their parents, as well as a strong desire to please the older generation, leads many Burmese to adopt the strategy of "resisting in the mind only."

Public servants have often told me of their search for understanding. Many come to the conclusion that the Generals believe that they are making Burma a better place. A senior public servant told me quietly, one evening while walking at sunset in her garden, "I believe that the Generals honestly believe that they are doing the right thing for the people." Many public servants strive hard every day to continually forgive the regime for its repression. Standing on a Buddhist hilltop, overlooking the Irrawaddy, another senior government official murmured quietly to me, "Most foreigners don't understand how being Buddhist both makes us, and allows us, to put up with the government. We must find it in our hearts to forgive them again, everyday." The Burmese saying used over and over again is *gwin: loun: ta'de*, "We have to forgive them." Forgiveness is a crucial step on the path toward Enlightenment, a recognition of the temporality and, ultimately, the meaninglessness, of earthly concerns.

There are several other key reasons why Burmese "go with the flow" of domination. The Burmese emphasis upon collaboration is apparent at all levels of social life. Political collaboration is part of a broader theme of respect, conciliation, and reciprocity involved in the functioning of kinship obligations. Kinship and the hierarchy of respect is an important axis in Burmese culture, especially with regard to the respect due to parents and elders. Powerful fictive kin relations, for example, exist between young boys who feel immense pressure to use heroin or engage in other risk taking behavior so as to remain "brothers." A young woman entrepreneur, Ma Wa Wa, who is barely more than a teenager, told me of a female friend who had decided to marry a student known for his support of the NLD. While respecting the courage shown by the couple, Ma Wa Wa feared that the young woman had a "long life ahead of her and a hard road." She had made a decision that took her away from a peer group that relied upon powerful "aunts" (wives of high ranking military officers) to secure them employment and business opportunities. I have met Burmese who have become communists, prostitutes, civil servants, and heroin addicts because of the strength of their friendships with members of those groups. It is difficult to subscribe to ideologies and practices that conflict with the social obligation inherent in kin and fictive kin relations (see Mi Mi Khaing 1962; Spiro 1977; Nash 1966: 59–73).

While rejecting the domination of the regime, Burmese must often also reject the call for change because of both a lack of resources and a focus on different priorities, priorities that are also influenced by central themes and ethics in Burmese life including Buddhism and the strength of kin relations. The appropriate strategy for many Burmese incorporates gray areas of both confusion and complicity. The old question about why some people choose to take an action such as open resistance and others don't has no simple answer. The answer is in fact everywhere—in the cries of malnourished, dying babies; in the look of utter dread on faces of democracy supporters at the thought of being interrogated and tortured again; in the wrinkles that spread out from the worried eyes of the farmer living with his year-long fear that the fields will not produce enough rice to meet the military quota; and these answers are echoed and carried throughout the country in the disquieting cawing of the crows circling urban slums, rubbish middens, funeral processions, and other sites of Burmese misery. As Aung San Suu Kyi has commented, there is a Burmese saying so well known that it is not often heard voiced: "Morality (*sila*) can be upheld only when the stomach is full" (Aung San Suu Kyi 1993).

Trafficking in Possibilities: The Subjunctive Mode

The most prominent strategies that Burmese people adopt to survive the sheer brutality and ongoing fear associated with military rule are what may at the outset seem to be a pattern of conformity or passivity, but are in fact a kind of Cinderella complex. These strategies are close cousins to what anthropologists study under the rubric of millenarianism. They are based upon a number of strongly held long-standing cultural beliefs, most importantly, a belief in the miraculous. It is a belief that, at any moment, a miracle may occur and one's life may be completely transformed. Burmese people talk about a *Nat ye-gaun*, meaning a pond inhabited or presided over by a *Nat* spirit. Those who enter such ponds will be miraculously and immediately transformed from human beings to other kinds of entities. The hope of freedom and escape contained in the *Nat ye-gaun* belief makes waiting the number one positive strategy adopted in Burma.

Soteriology, literally defined, is the theological doctrine of salvation. In anthropology, soteriology is used more broadly to mean those times in one's life when everything is up for grabs. It refers to the processes that occur in the moments of clarity and suspended animation such as birth, death, grave illness, torture, unbearable pain, and other crises where the cut and thrust of daily life becomes suddenly suspended and ultimate matters of mortality and salvation totally erase a sense of daily routine.

Subjunctivization is one important way that we can describe how human beings understand this rupture of their sense of normalcy and the temporal progress of their life at such transformative moments. Victor Turner (1990: xx) has described the "subjunctive mood" in the following way: "I sometimes talk about the liminal phase being dominantly in the "subjunctive mood" of culture, the mood of maybe, might-be, as-if, hypothesis, fantasy, conjecture, desire . . . a storehouse of possibilities, not by any means a random assemblage but a striving after new forms and structure."

Through interviewing people with very serious or terminal illnesses, medical anthropologists have defined a number of significant subjunctive styles—a possibility of hope that the general situation in which individuals or groups are enmeshed may improve even in the face of what biomedical practitioners would regard as phenomenally small odds. But the potential for healing throughout an illness episode is much greater when the future is left open or unemplotted. For example, in a study of epileptics and their families in Turkey, Mary-Jo Delvecchio Good and Byron Good (1994) found that: "Most of the families we interviewed maintained a deep investment in the openness of the future, in its indeterminacy, in the presence of potent and mysterious dimensions of reality and the possibilities for healing." And as Edward Bruner (in Good and Delvecchio Good 1994) notes, "to be in the subjunctive mode is . . . trafficking in human possibilities rather than in settled certainties."

Within the illness narratives the Goods found blanks, negations, contradictions, and a rejection of the anticipated. They interpret this as a deliberate emphasizing of the unknowable dimensions of reality. By maintaining a space for the unexpected, both in narrative and in their lives, the narrators and their families hold hope for eventual healing. The most vivid way in which a space for the unexpected was present in the narratives was through "encounters with the mysterious." These parts of the narratives hinted at the ability of supernatural powers beyond the access of everyday experience to be brought to bear upon the illness.

Subjunctivization opens onto a larger discourse involving the simultaneous occupation by individuals or collectivities of various alternate realities, or alternate ways of knowing and experiencing daily life. Dreams, fantasy, and imagination can all be conceived of as spaces for subjunctivization. They are examples of what Sartre describes as the ability always to create a montage of the real and the unreal at any instant (Sartre 1972). Dreams, for example, transport a crucial part of the person to another reality, while the rest of the body remains anchored to the first reality. The subjunctive mood is the mood of Burma. To live with liminality, with the unexpected, and with possibility, is the normal *modus operandi* of the entire nation. It is only when one is "beyond fear," for example, in the darkest moments of terror or despair, that one can no longer exist in a subjunctive mode.

In Burma a strong belief in the miraculous provides an example of the subjunctive mode in which most Burmese exist. As the nation has become progressively impoverished, Burmese increasingly turn to the miraculous as a strategy for improving their daily lives. The construction of an ornate temple in Rangoon with its stress on supernatural imagery is evidence of this phenomenon (Bekker 1989). *Dagò*, the manipulation of sacred power through objects associated with the Buddha (Kumada 2002), is also evidenced in times of political and economic crisis, as are increased encounters with *Nat* spirit mediums (Brac de al Perrière 2002), and ornate funerary and other rituals associated with the movement from one world to another (Robinne 2002). The creation of new *Nat* spirits, the thickening of the right side of Buddha images (Houtman 1999), and the appearance of a poltergeist at the site of the origin of the 1998 uprising (Leehey 2000) are small, everyday occurrences that reveal the deep Burmese belief and investment in the miraculous as a source of potential political and religious salvation, their form of soteriology. Moving to meditation centers (Jordt 2001), monasteries and nunneries (Kawanami 2002), and autonomous Buddhist areas such as that overseen by the late Thamanya Sayadaw (Tosa 2002; Rozenberg 2002) are further examples of the increasing disengagement that Burmese have with the world of authoritarian power and their simultaneous engagement in realms where forms of supernatural authority and power hold the potential for changes in the material and psychological conditions of one's daily life.

But it is the existence of *gain:* in Burma that proves that "a pervasive and intense belief in the miraculous continues to underlie the world view of Burmese Buddhists" (Ferguson and Mendelson 1981: 74). The term *gain:* refers to any community group that shares "a common source of merit and power." Separate *gain:* are formed from followers who congregate around one particular mystic. Membership in these mystic *gain:* is based on occult law and practices and "most people involved with mystic practices live ordinary lives of householders and visit their mystic teachers only occasionally, anywhere from a few hours to a few days or weeks" (Schober 1988:16–19).

Many *gain:* are formed around *wei'za*. *Wei'za* are "conceived of as a human who has acquired supranormal powers through mastery of alchemy, astrology, spells, signs, meditation, or other occult arts" (Ferguson and Mendelson 1981: 63–68). *Wei'za* are always male, and once they have attained a certain level of mastery they are, for all intents and purposes, immortal. By remaining on earth until the coming of the final Buddha, they can instantaneously achieve Enlightenment. The most famous *wei'za* is Bo Bo Aung who is believed to have been whisked away by the last Burmese prince to the heavens, thus setting the stage for millenarian movements focusing upon the return of the monarchy (Ferguson and Mendelson 1981: 63–68).

The formation of groups of lay people around forest monks, hermits, and *wei'za* as *gain:* was a familiar theme in colonial Burma, often connected to a belief in the forthcoming restoration of the monarchy. Ferguson and Mendelson have argued that this is largely a nineteenth century phenomenon due almost exclusively to the tensions of colonialism and the killing of the last Burmese monarch (Ferguson and Mendelson 1981: 79). *Wei'za* and their *gain:*, however, continue to be relevant in Burma at the present time. Julianne Schober conducted research in the early 1980s into the *htwe'ja'pau' gain:* around Mandalay. The term refers to a specific kind of pathway of escape from suffering (*htwe'ja' lan:*). *Htwe'ja'pau'* means "a place through which one leaves" referring to the area in the Himalayas that members believe they go to after the death of their physical body, and before they either enter the cycle of rebirth again, or attain Enlightenment (Schober 1988: 14). These superhuman figures can retreat at will to this special realm and are safe from the current situation. They can also choose to provide aid to those remaining on the earth.

The *wei'za* thus remains a potent symbol of political protest because it presents an alternate view of Burma's future, one in which Buddhist and occult mastery empower a repressed population concerned with the achievement of Enlightenment. Other millenarian movements by such charismatic leaders as Saya San in the 1930s are reminders of the depth of faith and magnitude of support such leaders can generate. The Burmese military remain unconvinced that *wei'za* are not bent on political control and censor most *wei'za* material. *Gain:* members and "living *wei'za*" often audio record me as I audio record them. We are all scared; all engaged in something illegal; and all fascinated with the explosive potential of the *wei'za* phenomenon for the current political situation.

The subjunctive dimension of possibility thus has significant political import in Burma, as it has the potential to mobilize segments of the population into organized resistance groups. Subjunctivization is, however, just as important at a phenomenological level, because it is a core idiom with which Burmese experience their world and act upon it. A Swiss group of balloonists attempting to fly around the world recently landed in Burma. A Burmese farmer was reported by CNN to have described the balloon landing as: "I thought it was a Buddha flying through the sky." It is not difficult to understand how she thought the balloon more likely to be a Buddha than a mechanical device since her worldview incorporates the notion of Buddhas and of possibility, whereas she had had no experience of flying machines.

The lack of a category of coincidence is part of what gives omens, portents, and magical and Buddhist visions causal links with events in the mundane world. The frenzy of interest in lotteries in Burma is an example of subjunctivization providing such a model for action. Since there is always a possibility of the miraculous occurring, the lottery is a viable strategy for emerging from poverty. Ma Cho Cho, a woman in her twenties who lives in *Nyaungbintha,* recounted to me several recent occurrences that involved the miraculous:

CC: I saw a cobra snake that went up into the roof when I was changing the leaves at the shrine. It went into a large hole in the roof. I dropped the big pot but it didn't break, so I went and bought some lottery tickets. Last week I dreamed of a pagoda and Shin Upagote.

MS: What did you think it means?

CC: I think it means that I will receive some money.

MS: Did you get any?

CC: No, just my regular income.

Given the logic outlined above, it is not surprising that Burmese adopt waiting and a belief in the miraculous as strategies of survival. There is a long history of this strategy in Burma and other Southeast Asian nations. Smith (1999) notes that in Burma there are written records extending back more than 150 years describing millennial sects that combine elements of animism, Buddhism, and Christianity. Millennial cults that await the Buddha (or, more recently, Christ) are apparent throughout the history of Theravada Buddhist kingdoms and other Southeast Asian groups such as the Khmu and Hmong in Laos. Much of the millennial imagery and impetus derives from older Hindu and Mahayana Buddhist elements. This fits with the diffusion of millenarian thinking as a soteriological response to uncertainty and crisis throughout South and East Asia.

Burmese Cinderellas

Many Burmese have fled Burma in fear for their lives and, over time, some of their family members have joined them in the safety of other countries. The majority of urban Burmese, however, adopt a strategy in which their "minds" leave temporarily, while waiting for change. In the European fairy tale, Cinderella had to be back before midnight or her coach turned into a pumpkin. Burmese also amuse themselves temporarily with the equivalent of a medieval ball, but this strategy, like Cinderella's, is only a short respite from the drudgery of everyday life and from the never ending babble of nonsensical propaganda and threats of violence. Burmese continue to adopt a subjunctive mode of thinking where the possibility exists that their present reality, like that of Cinderella, may be transformed utterly by a miraculous event. The future remains open, but temporary strategies must be employed in the interim.

Burmese regularly turn to entertainment that allows their mind to wander from their present troubles. Outside the city centers, in the forcibly relocated townships and the countryside, Buddhist and *Nat* festivals, puppet shows, and other forms of street theater have traditionally been the main forms of leisure. These traditional forms of entertainment are periodic, whereas township and village residents can escape their lives on a daily basis via a form of escape manifested as the "video hut" phenomenon. Anna Allot (1994) notes that: "Since 1988, thousands of video parlors have sprung up in villages throughout Burma. Much of the machines run off batteries since the villages do not have electricity. The owner charges three to five kyat per person and an audience of a hundred or so cram into a small hut to watch. Hundreds of low-budget videos are shot in Burma each year."

In both the urban movie theaters and Nyaungbintha's video huts, there are several standard story lines around which endless permutations and inversions are created. Most frequent of all is the rags-to-riches, Cinderella-style story. Burmese women roll their eyes dramatically when discussing this theme and they invariably describe a wealthy young girl who falls in love with a "man from the wrong side of the tracks." The parents forbid the marriage, the young woman is heart-broken. Suddenly, consistent with a strong belief in the miraculous, an amazing event occurs such as the death of a rich aunt, or the purchase of a winning lottery ticket, and the young man is then free to marry his sweetheart. For the price of a few cents, Burmese can imagine themselves as Cinderellas. They are able to imagine that the endless waiting for their lives to be transformed has, for a few hours at least, finally occurred.

A young mother, Ma Nu Nu Swe, told me, "I don't go to the video shops in the rainy season, but in the summertime I go once or twice [per week] in the evenings. When I feel upset and I want to relax my mind, I go there." Her word for "upset" means not possessing the basic necessities of survival, translating literally as lacking adequate food, clothing, shelter, and water. Ma Nu Nu Swe is referring to her worries over her severe impoverishment; the video hut allows her to temporarily inhabit a world where she can forget about the continual struggle to afford the basic necessities of life. The poorest women in the townships cannot afford to leave their neighborhoods, and they spend their time resting and sleeping. Another acquaintance, Daw Khin Mya Kyu, commenting on her use of video huts, said, "It only makes me happy for a while. When I come back home, I feel unhappy again and just go to sleep," a strategy common to impoverished, miserable people all over the world. The strong belief in the miraculous allows Burmese to imagine that such a miraculous change in circumstances may also befall them. Until such time, they continue to pay a few pennies for the luxury of forgetting about the present.

The nature of the subjunctive mood that blankets Burma, with its chief characteristic of possibility and the potential for immediate transformation, makes waiting a positive strategy of both suffering and survival. The following poem, "Over the Mountain Ranges," was written by a prominent Burmese writer and translated by anthropologist Jennifer Leehey in Rangoon in 1995. The poem powerfully depicts this strategy as hopeful and active:

Over the Mountain Ranges
in the eyes there is a well
in the mouth there is a desert
in the ears a mad man with a broken leg is doing a jumping dance
in the stomach a complete poem
in the heart children are playing hide and seek
in the brain two rivals in love are fighting with swords
in the hand a flower which hasn't been presented
is starting to wither
I—
Sleepwalking over the mountain ranges
pressing and sharpening myself.

Leehey notes that "the overall image of the poem is of a body, with its various organs disassociated from internal experience: thoughts, emotions, aspirations. The poem evokes the experience of sleepwalking, moving through life without fully engaging in it." She argues that this is an accurate description of the way many people in Rangoon are living out their lives: "'Over the Mountain Ranges' suggests that a positive strategy of suffering, that of endurance training, has begun in Yangon. Individual defenses are honed like knives, and psychologically valued states such as hope and determinism are shored up. The threat of madness, of violence (dismembering), and of silencing are never far away in Myanmar" (Leehey 1995: 6–7, 11). Sleepwalking not only invokes disembodiment, but also the escape to more hopeful subjunctive realities. It is emblematic of a wider paradigm of escaping while waiting for the miraculous to occur.

Waiting can also be viewed in a less positive light, in which fear paralyzes Burmese into inactivity. Waiting becomes a timeless strategy trapping people in worlds whose boundaries are delimited by fear. Burmese make statements such as "Until my lucky stars come again," and "Now is not the time to become involved" to signal this period of withdrawal. They may become trapped between two impossible situations: the current sociopolitical situation, and the new society they wish to see emerge, but are too frightened to actively pursue. A professional man in his early-forties, U Tun Aung Chain, describes the situation in which many of his friends find themselves:

What I see is a lot of people, friends, who work for the military, who don't like this [situation]. But they don't see a better alternative. Especially us, [the younger generations] we have never known anything different. They're very familiar with the system here and they have climbed up the ladder to get power. And there are many people who hope that one day the government will change and start doing something to help the people. At the same time, they don't know Aung San Suu Kyi. A lot of people question what change they [the National League for Democracy] are going to bring in if they get into power.

While subjunctivization keeps alive the hope of escape and the possibility of an end to suffering, a fear of change represents a negative strategy of waiting. But regardless whether Burmese are adopting a positive and hopeful or a fearful strategy, waiting partially removes Burmese from the everyday world. The mundane world is deferred as Burmese sleepwalk through the forest of time into other subjunctive realities.

The Mind Wanders

Sleepwalking is a good way to describe a term that I hear over and over among psychiatric patients, heroin addicts, prostitutes, and people who are severely impoverished. The term is *sei' leide*, which means "the mind wanders or drifts." It is a cultural idiom used to express feelings which accompany, for example, high unemployment rates and the inward focus of many women in the forcibly relocated townships. This state is linked to another common idiom, *sei' makaun* "my mind is not good." It is conceived of as a temporary form of insanity caused by grief or strong negative emotions. These two idioms are linked by the assumption that Burmese are absolved of personal responsibility for their actions during this time. Thus common replies to "what do you do during the day?" Or, "what did you do between your last childbirth and your new marriage/job" include statements such as "my mind wandered" or "my mind was not good" or "I was mad at that time." Psychiatric patients, in particular, use these idioms to describe their states of mind immediately before they were brought to the psychiatric hospital. "Forensic" or criminal patients, especially men who have been convicted of multiple murders, talk about a numbness that can include up to a decade of time when they are unable to account for their actions other than to say that their mind was not good and they were mad at the time.

Outside the psychiatric hospital, to be in that state of "my mind wanders" involves an active, intentional ignorance of social conditions and events. It is a refusal to think about the sociopolitical situation or to psychologize one's feelings. Emotions are buried beneath this layer of "numbness," a term Burmese use in everyday conversation. Refusing to recall memories may be linked to refusing to remember certain affective states. Intentionally ignoring the political situation or engaging in social life by focusing upon minutiae, daydreaming, sleeping, watching videos, and so on, facilitates the ongoing process of actively forgetting events.

Miniature Worlds

Some of the worlds to which Burmese escape from the politicization of everyday life are miniature worlds of their everyday existence. Such worlds of absorption and withdrawal are created by a great many Burmese I have encountered. This phenomenon, which Geertz (1973) reminds us is common throughout Asia, is not entirely a trance state, rather it is most often described as a state of numbness, *sei' htounde*. These worlds exist in the here and now accompanied by the idiom "the mind wanders." They are characterized by miniature time which Stewart calls "deferred time." Referring to the labor involved in constructing miniature books, Stewart argues that: "From the beginning, the miniature book speaks of infinite time, of the time of labor, lost in its multiplicity, and of the time of the world, collapsed within a minimum of physical space" (Stewart 1984: 39). In the worlds of waiting that Burmese construct there is also the infinite time of unemployment, resting and sleeping, and time devoted to waiting, but here the mind is not engaged in pursuing more hopeful, subjunctive realities, it is instead wandering through an anesthetized miniature space. Burmese miniature worlds involve the numbness of thought and affect in conjunction with the focusing or absorbing of the mind in the minutiae of daily life.

My friend Shwe Shwe told me about her own miniature world that isolated her from the terror of being unable to focus on anything other than her husband's arrest and incarceration for his political views. We are collecting fruit and vegetables in her garden, a process of knocking the fruit off and then stooping down to collect them. It is a repetitive activity and it leads her to recall that

I learned to wash clothes when my husband was in jail. It was something I could do with my body and not think. Your mind is free; you don't have to put any thought into what you're doing. This is something you can do absent-mindedly. That was the first time I enjoyed washing clothes. It was so cool, you sit near the water, you put your feet in water, your hands in water, water splashes your face, your knees; you just think of something else, it's very nice.

In miniature Burmese worlds, processes such as reflection, memory, and emotion are shut out, and instead the minutiae of everyday life take on an exaggerated focus or absorption. Working with young unemployed women, I came to learn how circumscribed their lives are. A trip to the market is the highlight of a day, unless one can afford to go to the video hut and lose oneself among the Burmese Cinderellas. Such women often go through the labor-intensive chore of starting a fire and watching a large pot of rice slowly cook, up to three times a day. Although this could have been done once in the morning, these women have nothing else to do. Several hours each day are spent sleeping, resting or daydreaming.

Ma May Khine Zaw is typical of the women who provided me with profiles of their daily lives. She is twenty-seven years old and has two children, seven and nine years of age. Her husband works as a "spare," collecting fares from passengers on overcrowded pickup trucks that transport commuters from Nyaungbintha to the city. Ma May Khine Zaw recounts her average day as follows:

MKZ: I get up at 4 a.m. in the morning and I cook breakfast at 6 a.m. From seven to 8:30 I collect water from the houses of my neighbours on either side of me. They have tube wells. From 8:30 until twelve I have free time and then I eat lunch. I have to stay at home all day because there are a lot of thieves around here.

MS: Have you ever been burgled or know of anyone who has had something stolen?

MKZ: No.

MS: What do you do in the afternoons and evenings?

MKZ: After my lunch, at one o'clock, I take a bath and I grind up *thanakha* and put the paste on my face and body. From two until four I have free time at home, and sometimes I do some housework. At 5 p.m. I have free time and I watch my children doing their homework and then we eat dinner at eight. I watch the children doing their homework until nine and then I prepare the beds and go to bed at ten.

I collected a further forty profiles of women in Nyaungbintha but they are all very similar. Ma May Khine Zaw's neighbor, twenty-one-year-old Ma Swe Swe Soe, gave me the following typical day in her life:

I get up at five in the morning. I cook breakfast at six and I go to the market at eight. I come home at nine and wash the clothes and the dishes. I eat lunch at twelve. I go to the video shop from one until three and then I go home and cook rice until five. I do the ironing at five and then at six I go to the video shop. I come back at eight and eat dinner. I go to sleep at ten.

I thought it odd that she made no mention of the child dangling from one nipple. She didn't want to talk about her husband either, and by then I had learned not to open up another window of misery.

Perhaps the most startling aspect of these women's lives is the lack of communication between neighbors like May Khine Zaw and Swe Swe Soe. The only conversation the two women have is a one-minute exchange of pleasantries as Ma May Khine Zaw draws water from Ma Swe Swe Soe's tube well. Like the wooden persona of Burmese marionettes, miniature worlds are characterized by silence: the verbal equivalent of numbness. Although Burmese will keep a close eye on their neighbors (bamboo fences seem especially suited to this occupation), when Burmese converse with their neighbors it is most often about the minutiae of daily life: the need for a child to have new sandals; the leak in the roof, queries about rice, salted fish, and beans. Fears, reflections, and comments on the political situation go unvoiced. In general, there is no concept of trust and no need for such trust as thought-feelings are firmly swallowed and held down, away from the humor and surface banter of everyday conversations with self, family, and friends.

In the miniature world of Burmese everyday existence, essential chores to do with the basic necessities of life become an almost exclusive focus and loom large in everyday thoughts and conversations. This absorbed focus of the mind is starkly juxtaposed with the rigid wooden bodies that Burmese present to the State for use at its mandatory mass rallies, state spectacles, opening ceremonies, and other enforced performances.

Worlds of Ignorance

Ma Si Si Win, the oldest woman among my group of sex worker informants, was willing to talk about the "physical" act of sexual intercourse,
but "not the mind." She told me that she numbs her mind and body
(*sei' htounde*) with alcohol to survive the ordeal. Like many commercial
sex workers around the world, Burmese prostitutes construct a wall
around themselves so that when they are told that AIDS is incurable and
that they will likely die if they contract it, they answer: "Yes, yes, if I get
it, I'll die," and quickly change the conversation back to the present
rather than a future that is impossible to contemplate. Another woman
working as a prostitute, Ma Khin Yi, told me in response to a question
about AIDS: "I don't want to know because I'm scared to find out."
These women cannot think about the future but they also cannot think
about what may be happening to their bodies as they earn their living.
They remain in a timeless world where information about themselves,
AIDS, and the current sociopolitical situation threatens to take them out
of their state of ignorance, a psychological status quo that allows them
to survive.

They are not alone. Urban residents deliberately refuse to think and
to psychologize about the current situation. That is why a great many
Burmese made a physical choking sound when my questions forced
them to dive into the thought-feelings which they normally skim across:
A lump deep in their chest that welled up through their throat and
became verbalized as huge shuddering sobs, as though tears had been
held back for years. It is difficult to explain the level of intimate contact
made at these moments as psychological barriers are allowed to come
crashing down. There is a good reason for these barriers: how can individuals remain continually conscious of disappointment in their lives,
and of their fear for their children's future? How can they dwell on the
disappearance or torture of friends and relatives, or on the children who
fled the regime to Thailand, and from whom they have heard nothing
in over a decade? It must be remembered that in Burma, strong negative
emotions such as grief and anger threaten to bring madness. Forgetting
becomes an active, ongoing process necessary for psychological coher-
ence, sometimes conscious, and other times as a barely discerned mental habit.

Burmese find ways to make life go on as if there were no military dictatorship. At a bodily level, this active, intentional ignorance of the everyday state of emergency is characterized by inertia. If an individual does
nothing, it is more difficult to accuse that person of doing something
wrong. Burmese thus consciously ignore and avoid politics. Most deliberately stay away from "flash points" of confrontation. This is why, as

one woman noted, the "threshold of fear" can continue to rise in Burma. It is also why urban Burmese will state that they are not afraid on a daily basis. They attempt to chart sanctuary spaces and believe that they need not be constantly afraid if they stay within these boundaries.

Finally, a refusal to think is also useful as a form of immunity from propaganda. Refusing to read newspapers or watch Myanmar Television programming creates even more isolation from the world as a small amount of international news is also broadcast. The advantages of such a strategy far outweigh the disadvantages, however, as Burmese can ignore the daily onslaught of propaganda. In a similar way, urban Burmese simply refrain from focusing on the junta's propaganda signboards. Merleau Ponty (1962) has argued that objects in one's field of view have no solidity, no identity, until we focus on them. He gives the example of a boulder, which is nameless, formless in our perception until such time as it becomes an object to be surmounted. Rangoon and Mandalay residents slide their eyes over the billboards, refusing to focus on them, thus denying them reality in their social field.

Eschatology: Mimicking Death

I turn now to a more serious form of wandering, namely that of bodily dissociation and the withdrawal of attention from all but the most necessary daily chores. The psychological and ethnopsychiatric literature contains a large number of studies of patients who have withdrawn into an inner realm, and the anthropological literature is replete with examples of soul loss or soul flight, such as the butterfly fairy in Burma. In Cambodia, psychiatrists have considered this phenomenon among survivors of the Khmer Rouge era genocide. Hiegel and Landrac (1993), for example, found that some individuals created an inner psychological space characterized by numbness of the senses and thought processes in order to survive the atrocities they witnessed and the pain they suffered. "Inner psychocultural process[es] of absorption" have also been documented within the realms of illness and performance. In severely traumatic or dangerous circumstances, dissociation is a mechanism by which attention is withdrawn from the situation and located in a safer domain. The Burmese term for this phenomenon is *ajoun pjaun,* meaning the transference of attention from one object to another, or the diversion of attention away from something. The prerequisite for dissociation is a threat to the integrity of the self, which can be an individual, intersubjective, or collective phenomenon. The self may be safely relocated in "one's imaginings, [as] an alternative self, or [via] concentration on a highly focused part of the social field. Perception, imagination, and memory are absorbed into that particular focus" (Kleinman and Kleinman 1994: 717–18).

Dissociation is most often categorized by psychiatrists as pathological. At the Rangoon Psychiatric Hospital there are a great many chronic patients who have repeated admissions over more than a decade and who clearly fall into this category. Such patients, many of whom if diagnosed in North America would be categorized as having Dissociative Identity Disorder (DID) (formerly called multiple personality disorder), form one extreme pole of the dissociative spectrum. At this end of the spectrum, trance behavior is interpreted by psychiatrists as causing serious ruptures to the integrity of the self and to an individual's ability to function in everyday social life. Aligned along the dissociative spectrum are possession cults, shamanistic or spiritual healing, "the posttraumatic stress disorder (PTSD) patient reliving his or her trauma . . . the DID patient tracing his or her amnesias . . . or any hypnotic subject engaged in a simple task like arm levitation." At the opposite end of the spectrum to DID are semi-conscious processes such as daydreaming, reverie, and automated tasks that are often culturally discouraged in Western societies. This includes the type of daydreaming or imaginative worlds entered by children but considered unproductive in late capitalism. Laurence Kirmayer argues that individuals shift rapidly along this spectrum, from self-consciousness to a variety of dissociative states, and that some psychiatrists may view "shifts away from self consciousness to absorption through externally focused attention or reverie" as dissociative experiences (Kirmayer 1994: 96–103). Kirmayer is drawing attention to the Western cultural values inherent in such psychiatric diagnoses. It is clear that in Burma inner mindfulness and the withdrawal of consciousness from the external world is the basis of Burmese Buddhist meditation and a first essential step along the Path to Enlightenment.

In previous chapters I have described the enforced participation of Burmese in a never-ending cycle of State spectacles and forced labor. I have also suggested that Burmese who are employed as manual laborers in the rapidly developing downtown area and in the regime's Industrial Zones must work for less than subsistence wages doing back-breaking repetitive work, often under hazardous conditions. I cited the short story of the concrete salesman who feels his body turning to concrete, the substance that construction workers inhale, and carry, and that cakes their bodies each day, as emblematic of the alienation Burmese feel towards their bodies in this peculiar conjunction of modernity and fascism. Burmese attend State spectacles as rigid, silent masses that I liken to wooden Burmese puppets. The regime appropriates the bodies of Burmese for its nation building endeavors, but there is much more occurring in these processes than is apparent in the State media's carefully constructed images.

Burmese are using old cultural strategies of dissociation (such as *Nat* spirit possession) at the same time as the State is consuming Burmese bodies for labor and for the reproduction of State ideology. Feldman has stated that: "Multiple and antagonistic counter discourses and acts can be attached to the same performance, thereby transforming its semantic efficacy" (Feldman 1991: 15). This is a sophisticated concept of resistance, one that fractures the notion of the body only, or even primarily, as a site of centralizing authority. In these public performances there is an identifiable Nietzschean "multiplicity-of-being," a sometimes conscious decentering and fracturing by Burmese of the notion of both bodies and States as nuclei of authority. Burmese are engaged in a variety of strategies that involve different degrees of dissociation, from possession to automation. Waiting is one such strategy in which attention is withdrawn (*ajoun pjaun*) from the social field. Mimicking death via the adoption of the automaton role, the wooden puppet, is another dissociation strategy. Several authors have written of the positive and negative implications that such strategies might have.

Allen Feldman, for example, describes how atrocities were committed in Northern Ireland through a conscious process of mutilating bodies in order to separate a sense of self and identity from a cadaver; the products of such torture become a detached self and a politically reconfigured body, an automaton (Feldman 1991: 64). There is a double meaning here. On one hand, the perpetrators of violence mimic automata in detaching their sense of self from the violence they inflict. On the other hand, the victims of torture sometimes become corpses as a result of the torture, and at others they may also mimic corpses as a way of resisting and surviving violence and domination. The latter insight is applicable on a national scale in Burma. Feldman argues that, "the experienced captive exchanges his body for silence. He mimics his death and transforms himself into a cipher. . . . In this process, the prisoner literally autonomizes the body and sends it out . . . as a detachable part of his political agency. . . . Was this exchange what Adorno was searching for in the mimesis of reification-the extraction of a modicum of resistance in the death-like parody of domination?" (138, 144).

Adorno writes of the mimesis of reification where mimesis involves "making oneself similar to the environment" (Cahn 1984: 31), an argument derived from biology where an animal being hunted survives by playing dead. It is an almost absolute identification "with dead, lifeless material." Mimesis is more than imitation, it is an active adaptive strategy of "identifying with" the regime. "Literally, it is an 'identification with the aggressor' according to the principle that 'becoming one with the enemy immunizes you'" (Cahn 1984: 32–33). But there is no clear delineation between "subject and object or inner and outer" in the mimetic attitude, and Adorno concludes that ultimately this strategy of survival is a "triumphant failure." He believes that in most cases individuals lose something integral to the integrity of the self when such a strategy is adopted. Unless a fragmentation of the individual through a process of "self-alienation" occurs, Adorno believes that mimetic strategies do not result in freedom from oppression, but instead, result in complicity (Cahn 1984: 33–35).

Other writers also warn of the danger of identification with the enemy entailed in such a desperate strategy for surviving atrocity and authoritarianism. Taussig, for example, perceives the mimicking of death as a disfiguring of the integrity of the self. He recalls the fear that both residents and visitors to military-ruled nations encounter when they pass the barricades and checkpoints manned by armed guards. He asks: "As you pass through in your car at a snail's pace, coiling like a spring, awaiting the policeman, arm at the ready, to nod you on, does not your all too studied casualness, your studied disconcern, resemble the zombie-faces of the entranced. . . . Do you not for ever so prolonged a brief moment of tensedness become possessed by the spirit-the spirit of the state? We would do well to remember that" (Taussig 1997: 148).

In such militarized states, Taussig notes the decompression of time, and in Burma this decompression of time occurs when the transformed automata of the mass rallies and forced labor sites enter a miniature world of watching and waiting. He argues that the individual "becomes corpse-like which is something more and less than death, the corpse being but the beginning, the materialization of death . . . charged like a spring compressed in the utter stillness of this corpse-performance collapsing giant rhythms of quietude and decay into staged proportion of telescoped time" (1997: 166–67). The Generals have created a voyeuristic culture of watching and its implied flip side of waiting. No one is actively creating the regime's envisioned fascist utopia. Rather, Burmese play dead. They adopt silence as their corporeal engagement with the world and they identify with culturally familiar lifeless manikins.

Once automatized, Burmese begin a process of exchanging production for repetition, thus not actually accomplishing anything on behalf of the regime (Baudrillard 1993: 29–30). This is an illusion of production since there is no use-value in the repetitive and absurd work of the government machinery such as sitting for hours listening to the speeches of the regime. Baudrillard falls into a different camp of theorists who offer hope for the subversive project of the willing automaton. He writes, "As long as we can still discover a 'production' corresponding (even if this is only in the imagination) to individual or social needs . . .

the worst individual or historical situations are bearable" (Baudrillard 1993: 30). Baudrillard is suggesting that productive work is still being accomplished in the form of the creation of a survival ethic and thus conscious, positive resistance to the regime is occurring. He sees a situation where the mimesis of death will eventually "wear out" the aggressors (Baudrillard 1993: 38).

Baudrillard is not alone in his belief that the appropriation of the automaton body can be an empowering strategy for dominated people. Feldman (1991: 178), for example, asserts that "this construction of the Other (by the state) is a transfer of force, an empowering investiture of alterity that can be played back against the state, so that the 'copy' can affect the 'model'. . . . The prisoner's capacity to resist exploits the principle of auto-domination and auto-punition that Foucault identifies with panoptic penal regimes. In assuming 'responsibility for the constraints of power' and 'making' them play spontaneously upon himself, he inscribes in himself the power relation." This more hopeful model suggests that in the appropriation of the automated body, Burmese become voyeurs, viewing the actions of their bodies from a safe and distant realm. This method of detachment from the body is taught as basic to the meditation process in Burmese Buddhism.

There are, then, two distinct strands of thought as to the efficacy of disembodiment and the parodying of death as a strategy of survival in the face of violence and domination. One is that it is entirely destructive and leads to complicity and a form of identification with the aggressors, while the other suggests that it can be mobilized to create power, however marginalized. In the following section I map some of the landscapes accessed by disembodied Burmese selves while their corporeal components wait in silence and rigidity at State spectacles and as mechanical laborers on State projects. I then return to the strategy of dissociation and the possibility of reanimating automata when the danger has finally passed.

My Mind Flies to Freedom

The bleakness of these terrible strategies of automatization is matched only by the shame, despair, and defiance in the eyes of sixteen-year-old girls prostituting themselves in bamboo thatched brothels above the pestilent flood waters of Nyaungbintha. When I realized that Burmese women engaged in prostitution were consistently describing a pattern of dissociation characterized by "flying," I began to ask the women, "How do you feel when you are having sex?" Examples of some of the replies appear below. "Flying" involves a deeper state of trance than the confused drifting implied by the term *sei' leide.* All the girls and women were interviewed in Nyaungbintha, and it is a testament to the horror of contemporary Burma that they are more fortunate than other prostitutes I have interviewed, in the sense that they do not have to prostitute themselves in the mud under bridges, or on the floor of Rangoon and Mandalay markets, or on the regime's boats and tankers. Most of these informants are based in brothels. I interviewed them in a neutral location away from pimps and family members. Each woman or girl has between three and eleven "clients" during the day. These are known as "shorts" or "hits" as opposed to a "long" or "night-order" that involves between one and twelve men. Long orders generally average around three men, but there is no limit to the number of times each man will require intercourse.

The first vignette comes from a twenty-nine-year-old woman with six siblings, Ma Khin Me Si, who lives in the urban area but works as a prostitute in Nyaungbintha. The daughter of an army officer, at seventeen her parents arranged her marriage to a man who physically abused her after drinking alcohol. On average, Ma Khin Me Si was beaten once every three or four days. Upon divorcing her husband when she was twenty-four, she tried a variety of jobs but was eventually lured into prostitution by the extremely active recruitment network that exists in Nyaungbintha. When asked how she feels about having sex for money, Ma Khin Me Si replies:

KMS: [I feel] Nothing. I am earning money, that's all. I feel pain, that's all.

MS: And your mind?

KMS: My mind is not here. My mind flies to my parents because I am . . . [breaks off, tears stream down her face].

Twenty-year-old Ma Aye Aye describes her experience of working as a prostitute in one of Rangoon's recently opened nightclubs, where she is paired with Thai, French, Malaysian, and Chinese customers who pay her between 40 and 100 U.S. dollars as a tip, on top of the 2,000 kyat (approximately $12 U.S. in 1997) she was paid by the pimp. This job is a new one for her, as until a few months ago she was supporting her child by having intercourse with ten to twelve men every day in Nyaungbintha. Ma Aye Aye is listless but willing to talk of the improvement in her personal life, and she is proud of her ability to now send her child to school. She remarks that: "When I am having sex, I take my mind far away from my present situation."

In the next statement, the crucial importance of the mother-daughter bond is apparent (see Nash 1966). Ma Shwe Shwe, a twenty one-year-old woman, cried throughout the interview. She stated: "My father has already died and my nieces and nephews were starving at home. I didn't know what to do. That's why I've sacrificed my own life. . . . After I became sick, my mother begged me not to do it again. I've given my mother so much trouble throughout my life. Only now am I aware of my actions and I've stopped giving her trouble." Ma Shwe Shwe and her mother lied to their neighbors about Ma Shwe Shwe staying with her uncle during the week so that they wouldn't know she was working in a brothel. Ma Shwe Shwe cried, "I can't stay apart from my mother, that's why I didn't go to Mandalay." In this respect she is different from many women working as prostitutes in Burma who follow a route around the country that coincides with harvests, pagoda festivals, and other cycles of income generation and spending.

Sixteen-year-old Ma Nge tells of her experience of having sex with four to five men each night. Ma Nge has recently become pregnant and been beaten by her family, who now realize that she is engaged in the prostitution industry. However, since her family in southern Burma is desperately poor and her father is unemployed, Ma Nge's mother has decided to continue to accept the money that her daughter brings home without telling her husband of its source: "Actually, I'm not fond of sex but I have to do it because they pay me. I put my mind somewhere else when I have to sleep with clients, like the places I've visited such as my school which I like the most." At this point Ma Nge begins to cry as she explains that she misses going to school, but that her parents can't afford to pay the fees.

Another young woman, Ma U Gon, stated: "when I am having sex, my mind flies to my mother. My mind is always inside my mother."

The final vignette is given by Ma Nyun Nyun Me, a twenty-one-year-old woman who has never been to school, and again the strength of the mother-daughter bond is apparent. Mothers are the only refuge for the minds of these girls and young adult women. She began to cry as soon as she mentioned her family. Ma Nyun Nyun Me is recovering from an illness (most likely typhoid or hepatitis) and states that by working as a prostitute she has "sacrificed my life for my family. I will do anything to stop them from starving . . . my life is ruined, spoiled, I don't even have any money for myself." When asked about the experience of working as a prostitute, Ma Nyun Nyun Me said:

NNM: My mind flies during sex.

MS: Where does your mind go to?

NNM: To my home.

MS: Where?

NNM: To my mother. In my mother's heart.

As terrible as these stories are, I am just as saddened by the opposite cohort of my informants, the boys and young men arrested and forcibly detoxified of the heroin running through their veins. These young and often wealthy youth turned to heroin as a form of escape and they are aware of the loneliness of the strategy of flying solo through the Burmese landscape, unable to engage with other people or everyday life. Most of these young men became addicted as adolescents and had no one to turn to as the purest heroin available in the world birthed an all-consuming addiction within their skinny bodies. A dying body, but a free mind, is the trade-off that many Burmese heroin addicts unwittingly make when they become addicted, as eighteen-year-old Maung Aye So describes:

I studied until ninth standard then I worked digging gemstones. I could get heroin there but I didn't do it. I was afraid I'd die. I was chasing after money and I wasn't interested in drugs. Drugs are very common there. Once you start, you'll continue to use it, 90 percent of users can die. When I started using heroin I didn't know anything [about it] on the first day but I was addicted a week later. I couldn't stand to be without it after that. Tears were rolling down my face, and then I was yawning, vomiting, and having a runny nose. Muscles like my heart and lungs gave me great problems. The feeling at that time was bad. Even while I was using, it was good only at the time of injecting. It was not good when the effectiveness began declining after five hours. I felt as if my body was floating and I was interested in nothing but heroin. My mind would fly away.

Young men like Maung Aye So explain their suffering using a cultural script common to many parts of Asia where spirit possession and the ability of parts of consciousness to leave the body and travel to other locations or dimensions is well documented. The powerful male shamans of the Himalayas for example, whose spirit selves travel as birds seeking knowledge of their patients' afflictions, are well known (Kalweit 1992: 11). In other Buddhist cultures such as in Nepal, the heart-mind can fly to other dimensions (Desjarlais 1992: 2003). In Theravada Buddhist Sri Lanka, Bruce Kapferer argues that during demonic possession an individual becomes more "demon" than "I" or "self" for a period of time. Exorcism is required to reincorporate the self and pull together the fragmented body. Kapferer concludes that the psychological reintegration of self into body is indeed possible and that the expulsion of the demon from Buddhist society continues to be played out at a national level (Kapferer 1988: 101). The experience of suffering given by Burmese heroin addicts, of a flexible body with detachable agency, is thus common throughout the Asian region.

The porous nature of the Burmese body is documented in the literature pertaining to *Nat* spirit possession. *Nat* are the spirits of Burmese royalty who have died violent deaths and each year, in the "*Nat* belt" of

Figure 15. "*Nat*-scape."

central Burma, the deaths of individual *Nat* are celebrated in a calendar
of *Nat pwe* fixed around the lunar cycle (Nash 1966). Taunbyon, the site
of celebration of the Taunbyon sibling *Nats*, attracts hundreds of thousands of people each year (Brac de la Perrière 1992). New *Nat* can
appear in different parts of the country, and the various *Nat pwe* involve
multiple forms of the negotiation of contemporary identities between
individuals, families, ethnic and religious groupings, and between local
communities and the State (Brac de la Perrière 1998). Possession of *Natkadaw* (*Nat* spirit wives) by the *Nat* is central to the cult. Figure 15 depicts
a "*Nat* landscape."

There are many other accounts of the fluidity of the Burmese body
which demonstrate how "mind flight" or "soul flight" (in the earlier
English literature) is a culturally familiar theme. The most prominent
involves the *lei'pja*, which is variously translated as butterfly fairy, butterfly soul, or Burmese soul. Urban residents told Spiro the *lei'pja* was the
basis for their belief in spirits: "A Nat or a ghost, they explain, is the
reborn lei'pja of the deceased" (Spiro 1967: 70). A great many Burmese
beings such as *Nat* and *wei'za* linger on the earthly plane long after their
physical bodies have died (Ferguson and Mendelson 1981: 64). Ortho-
dox Buddhists insist that the *lei'pja* is really *jiva*, the life principle, similar
to the Hindu notion of the soul being able to leave the body when the
individual is sleeping (Ba Han 1968: 6–8). The boundaries between the

many planes and levels of reality are extremely porous in Burma, and this is another reason why miraculous events can easily occur. A recently widowed woman in Nyaungbintha, Daw Yin Nu, who has turned to prostitution to support her family, related to me the story of her husband's ghost:

I grieve for my husband. Whenever I look around my house there is something that he made, I feel it even when looking at the children. Now he is a ghost, haunting us every night. I must help him release his soul. He is so worried about me, and that's why his ghost can't be freed.

Witch doctors and *Natkadaw* believe that an absence of an individual's *lei'pja* is a cause of sickness remedied by compelling the wandering butterfly fairy to return to the body. But butterfly spirits can become intertwined with other butterfly spirits. Ba Han (1968: 7) explains: "When two persons are wrapped up in each other, as in the case of a child and its mother or of a husband and his wife, their butterfly fairies are closely knit together. On the death of one, it is feared that the butterfly fairy of the other will follow that of the departed. To prevent this calamity a witch-doctor is asked to perform the leikpya-kwe ceremony (Separation of the butterfly fairies)."

As in other parts of Southeast Asia, there is in Burma a folkloric literature about the fleeing of humans, both literally and metaphorically, to the realm of nature (the wild forests and jungles) in times of crisis. Eggar (1957: 420) published a short folk-tale from Amarapura, near Mandalay, about a young Burmese girl whose *lei'pja* leaves her body and is exchanged permanently with the *lei'pja* of a pig: "Win-laik-pya means 'the inner thing' (Win) and 'butterfly' (leippya). When anyone is sound asleep, the soul-butterfly escapes and flits far and wide, going wherever it wills. It meets the soul-butterflies of other persons, or of animals, and disports with then, returning in a flash when the sleeper awakes. If the awakening is too sudden, there is a risk that the soul-butterfly will not be able to return to its rightful body." In "Over the Mountain Ranges" we learn of Burmese walking over the mountainous jungles. The sparsely inhabited regions of the country (often the home of the many minority groups) occupy a special place in the majority Burman collective psyche. Since the Burmese body is not a rigidly bound entity, as evidenced by the *lei'pja*, elements of consciousness can flee, during times of crisis, to the culturally constructed "natural" sanctuaries.

A recurrent myth-theme in Burmese literature is the refuge of the Himalayas, in particular Himawuntha, "the Himalayan forest where Queen Maya conceived Gautama the Buddha" (Ferguson and Mendelson 1981: 73). This primordial forest is similar to the "*Nat*-scape," a forest growing on the top of Mount Popa, and populated with even more mythical beings. Himawuntha is an earthly realm to which beings about to attain Enlightenment can go "out" to so that they will not accumulate any further karmic death in this rebirth. *Wei'za* such as Bo Bo Aung and Bo Min Gaung are in this category (Schober 1988: 19). In contemporary *gain:*, *Nat* troupes, and other occult institutions, especially in lower Burma, it is common to hear all of these escape realities used interchangeably. The Himalayas, the farthest reaches of the Burmese imagination, embody many of these alternative realities. *Htwe'ja'pau'* mystics and all the other varieties of mystics who practice the *wei'za* path to alternative forms of this-worldly power, believe that *htwe'ja'pau'* is a place in the Himalayas where they will, like the *wei'za* before them, await their "final going out" (Schober 1988: 19).

In urban Burma, young Burmese have not been taught much of this cultural knowledge. When they need to send their minds flying to safety, they often travel to places within the urban landscape that they have visited before, such as school, theaters, and parks. The *Nat* spirit tradition is strongest in the areas around Mandalay and Mt. Popa; most long-time Rangoon residents have less familiarity with the rich cultural store of escape routes than those who live "up-country." There are clear and strong Buddhist elements in the creation of, and flight to, other dimensions, not only through practice of the *wei'za* path and the use of *samatha* meditative techniques, but also in the Buddhist philosophy of the space-time reality of *samsara* that is the anchoring framework in which these alternate worlds exist.

The concept of Buddhist refuge is another example of the creation of alternate worlds. Burmese people undoubtedly have a rich variety of pre-Buddhist, Buddhist, and contemporary cultural themes from which to derive escape routes from the everyday state of emergency. The enormous rise in mysticism in the past several years parallels the emergence of a rash of millenarial figures under British colonization. Aung San Suu Kyi describes the fight for democracy as the second struggle for Independence; at both times of acute political and economic crisis, Burmese people have used their cultural and religious heritage to create survival strategies that involve removing their minds to alternate planes of reality.

Burmese Wizardry

Is the inscription of silence and the rigid configuration of the corpse onto the body the beginning of the death of coherent concepts of self and society, or is it reversible? Can Burmese people eventually emerge from the worlds to which they have escaped? Can viable notions of civil society, community, and trust reemerge in Burma in the absence of a culture of terror? Is it possible that the memory and images of Burmese supernaturalism allow for a recovery of self and society?

In earlier chapters I suggested that two theories exist regarding the mimesis of death. The rigid wooden puppets the State constructs as model workers are appropriated by Burmese as a survival strategy that involves dissociating the body from the mind. Some theorists see such a strategy as ultimately doomed to fail, while others point out empowering aspects of the strategy. As Feldman and Orwell have noted, violence becomes an enclosed sphere, a shared culture of enslavement. Its long term effects consist of replicating this shared environment of alienation and both politicizing and disabling structures such as "civil society," "community," and "association." In light of these differing emphases on the results of the process of automatization, it is useful to reflect upon a theme seldom elaborated in contemporary Burmese culture but which is well known, and which provides a link with the strong belief in the miraculous. This theme is Burmese wizardry, embodied in the figure of the *zo gji*.

A *zo gji* is an alchemist who possesses supernatural powers. To become a *zo gji*, a Burmese man uses alchemy to create a philosopher's stone (*da loun*) that is then eaten. The alchemical process is long, expensive, and dangerous, not just because substances such as burning quartz and red hot fire pits coexist uneasily with bamboo thatched outbuildings, but also because powerful supernatural forces are harnessed under the cover of darkness. That is why the alchemically-produced *nawarat* ring is so special: producing this ring requires the correct alignment of spiritual forces, the appropriately auspicious astrological conditions, and the precise following of the ritual words and actions in order to inculcate the ring with a power that is more than the sum of its constituent parts. Alchemical practices are highly secret and much derided by the military government officials who see them as *prima facie* evidence of the lack of modernness that besets Burma, while at the same time never taking off their own *narawat* rings.

Despite its anti-modern associations, this occult, alchemical, and experimental knowledge was, until the last decade or two, an unquestioned part of the heritage of Burman men of advanced age and social standing. Many of these men spent their evening hours in an outbuilding behind or beside the main house, experimenting with metals and precious stones in an attempt to transmute base metals into gold and create a philosopher's stone (Mi Mi Khaing 1962). I know a great many gentlemen alchemists, and they are all at least seventy five years of age. One man in particular works feverishly most days in his workshop, trying to create a philosopher's stone powerful enough to cure AIDS. Another acquaintance, an old astrologer living in a village a few hours from Rangoon, learned alchemy while studying as a monk in his village when he was a young man. The astrologer and his male companion chuckle through their few remaining teeth as betel juice drips from their mouth onto the teak floor, burnished to a bright shine from fifty years of clients coming and going. They are bent over on their sides on the floor, convulsing and cackling as he describes the amount of time and money that he spent searching for the perfect alchemical technique for creating a philosopher's stone. Finally he gave up, penniless and luckless, and resigned himself to telling fortunes as a more useful way of making a living.

For those few Burmese men who achieve the feat of creating a philosopher's stone, it must immediately be eaten. The alchemist promptly dies and the body is buried for seven days. This part of the process requires a very trustworthy assistant, because it is the job of the assistant to watch over the corpse and, after a week, to dig it up. At the end of seven days, the alchemist emerges, reborn as an immortal wizard. The *zo gji* possesses a number of startling properties including the ability to fly through the air. The abode of the *zo gji* is the kingdom of Himawuntha (Maung Htin Aung 1959: 45).

The temporary nature of the body and its continual decay even during life is reflected on at length during Theravada Buddhist meditations on the corpse (Klima 2002). The life of the monk and nun, particularly those who live in forests and caves as hermits, is austere and mindful of the body as the source of craving, desire, and hence, of all suffering (Tambiah 1984). The rigid bodies so easily adopted by Burmese people at State spectacles, and the repetitive labor carried out by both forced and manual laborers at the regime's urban construction sites, are made possible, in part, by the conditioning of meditative techniques from an early age. This in no way lessens the suffering of Burmese people, but it does provide a framework for their experience of authoritarianism and for constructing and enacting strategies of survival, such as dissociation. The reversibility of such strategies is unknown and dependent upon individual psychologies and many other factors. The recent experience of other Theravada Buddhist nations such as Cambodia (Ebihara et al. 1994) and Sri Lanka (Tambiah 1992) suggest, however, that violence inscribes deep scars upon individuals and communities.

The *zo gji* provides a useful tool for thinking about Burmese conceptions of death and the possibilities for reanimation. A belief not only in the miraculous, but also in the positive attributes of waiting as embodied in both *htwe'ja'pau'* mysticism and the figure of the *zo gji* has significant cultural and psychological strength in Burma. It makes strategies such as compromising and collaborating with the military dictatorship easier to understand. Not only are Burmese people seeking to reduce their

Figure 16. Paw Oo Thet, *Zo gji* flying, from Khin Myo Chit, *A Wonderland of Burmese Legends*. (Bangkok: Tamarind Press, 1984, copyright © Orchid Press)

crippling burden of fear, they are also practicing the maxim, "Water flows, fish follow," safe in the knowledge that they exist in a subjunctive world where the possibility of miraculous change exists. The model of the *zo gji* also makes more comprehensible the strategy of the dissociation and fragmentation of the body as a sometimes deliberate and, again, subjunctive strategy. Perhaps the mimesis of death by Burmese puppets or automata can be viewed in this light, as part of a road map through various Burmese dimensions of reality (see for example, Figure 16), rather than as an eschatological process. Burmese myths and cosmology contain many examples of Burmese who have, through death and subsequent reanimation, become immortal and now wait in other dimensions for the coming of the ultimate arbiter of power in Burma, the fifth and final Buddha, Arimettaya.

Chapter 10
Going to Sleep with Karaoke Culture

"Letters to the editor" columns in Myanmar-language newspapers often include complaints about noisy karaoke lounges and video booths. . . . Members of the public lodged 50 complaints last year . . . especially those regarded as undermining the morals of young people. . . . An example was the jail terms of up to 9 years and three months imposed on 14 people for video piracy last month. "Those who break laws protecting intellectual property rights or who show videotapes which have not been passed by the censor can expect firm punishment," said U Thein Tun Aung [Ministry of Information]. "We will protect national culture," he said.

—Nwe Nwe Yin, *Myanmar Times*

The top of a pinnacle now; firewood soon.

—Burmese proverb

A Return Journey

It is late 2001, the rains have stopped and the cool season has begun. I board the Circle Line train, its detergent advertising obscured by a shiny new coat of paint, already peeling in the tropical humidity. I jump off at the level crossing near Nyaungbintha and begin the trek out to the townships. What a difference four years has made. Looking-for-a-husband-hill is no more. The new bridges carry cars and trucks high above the riverbank. The small hillock, the site of so much painted cheer and private despair, has been graded to a uniform slope and planted with fast growing saplings. The makeshift houses of jute rice bags and thatch have been torn down, replaced by a golf course. Mist and haze cover the township in the early morning, and women walk beside the eight feet high chain link fences that separate Nyaungbintha from the Generals playing golf on the verdant greens of the course. The frenzy of condominium construction has ended. I buy photographic film at a new supermarket constructed where a shantytown stood only a few years before. In the supermarket I meet a Burmese movie director making a soap opera about the turbulent lives of the wealthy, young elite of Rangoon. This section of Nyaungbintha has become a model of modernity, but where have the residents gone?

I walk away from the main roads and into the "real" township, as I think of it. At the entrance to the residential part of the township a pagoda festival is being readied for the evening. Thirty-foot high bamboo frames are being erected and fabric is draped over them, like elliptical circus tents. There are many severely impoverished households here at the fringe of the township, but there are also many houses that appear to be prospering. The video hut is still here but it is expanding to include Karaoke DVD. Tiny, one-room huts on stilts, not much more than 1.5 meters square, with names like "Bravo DVD" are everywhere. I give up counting at twenty. For the equivalent of fifteen American pennies, one can sing along, in air-conditioned isolation, to a four-minute western pop song before emerging again into the sweaty reality of Nyaungbintha. I look for the old Globe Video hut and find that it has thrived in my absence. It is reached by a bamboo mat over the drainage ditch and has two blackboards at the front of the windowless thatched shack advertising the current love story that is showing. A water jug sits to one side and two bicycles are abandoned under the blackboards. The shack abuts the owner's house, a two-story wooden structure.

There are more schools here now. Long wooden fences enclose the yellow concrete schoolrooms with their white square wooden windows and tin roofs. The roads are still one-lane dirt that falls away precariously into the drainage ditches. The market has quadrupled in size and there are more plastic toys and a wider range of vegetables. Tea shops have sprung up, elevated high over the drainage ditches that swell with the June rains. As the frenetic construction of condominiums for the wealthy city residents ended, a new class of people moved into the apartment buildings that line the entrances to the townships. Yet another class of people is also apparent. Far out from Nyaungbintha, in the paddy fields on the other side of the industrial zones and golf courses, are the people who are too poor to live in Nyaungbintha. Squatting in the rice fields, in one-room huts made with a bamboo frame and jute bags, these newest residents push the urban fringe ever outward into the countryside. Nyaungbintha is becoming just another suburb, the stories of misery graded over, the desperation moved further out for a new generation to experience.

Beyond even this emerging area of suffering and misery are the now defunct joint-venture garment factories and the technical institutions that have replaced the universities. These sites draw students from the city and until the U.S. sanctions in May 2003, they also drew villagers from Rangoon, Ayerwaddy, and Bago provinces, away from their rice fields and home industries, into the clutches of the neoliberal model of young, docile female workers in what was the latest cheap labor global hotspot.

Later I find a taxi and travel back into the city to have dinner with Daw Shwe Shwe, the oldest woman among my circle of friends. We catch up on the news. My life has moved on, a marriage, a child, a return to my home country, a new job, a house and mortgage. In some ways, the lives of my friends have not moved on at all. They still speak of waiting for change. Time is still pooling all around them, and for a short while I am again in this puddle of time, wading through contradictory thoughts and confused emotions.

But in other ways, everything has changed. That is the paradox of Burmese conceptions and experiences of memory. Time is simply not a linear dimension in Burma. Time is experienced in an ongoing sense of moving through successive rebirths and moving between levels of existence. This is most commonly understood within a Buddhist cosmological framework. Time is also conceived as moving in fits and bursts. While time is clearly in a "pooling" mode, with waiting being the strategy of choice since 1962, events can change suddenly, in an explosive burst. Like winning a lottery, change can be immediate and profound. But unlike Western understandings of sudden change, in Burma the changed situation is not a leap further along a life continuum. Rather, the sudden change can just as easily be reversed, as when a person becomes suddenly mad with grief, and just as suddenly, is no longer mad.

The following day is Saturday, and my friend spends her day shopping at the markets. Her son and husband help her to prepare a meal for me for Sunday lunch. Her kitchen hands and maids have been sent back to their village and food must now be prepared by the members of the family. When it is ready, the son and husband disappear. This is extremely courteous behavior in Burma, and although I express delight with the preparation of my favorite Burmese meal, chicken and noodles in a spicy coconut soup, we do not talk during this meal as this shows disrespect for the chef.

We eat the meal in her new kitchen. When my friend and her husband first married, his political and moral beliefs about the need to be engaged only in "white" business (that did not draw upon military contacts) meant that money was always scarce. They moved into her mother's compound but built an oddly shaped little house because the dowager insisted upon retaining the coconut grove to the side of the main house. The house needed to be built around the coconut grove, but also around a large old tree that grew not far from the coconuts. The new kitchen stands where this old tree recently grew; it was chopped down to make way for the extension. This extension became necessary because three brothers and sisters (and their large families) had also returned to the parental home when their businesses failed in the ever worsening economic climate. Shwe Shwe leads me to a steep staircase next to the kitchen. We climb up to a new room added to the house, a meditation room where my friend's husband spends all his time. Shwe Shwe is leaving the country to earn hard currency to send her children to university outside Burma. Her husband retreats into meditation. They have left behind the world that we shared when I was first in Burma, and they have steered a course that removes them from the day-to-day control of the military.

After the tour of the extensions, we sit in the comfortable old lounge room and eat watermelon from my friend's childhood village. I say to my friend, "Do you remember, when I was here last time, you told me about what it was like to be afraid. Do you still feel like that now?" She was shocked that I would remember specific details from our conversations, a reaction common among all the friends and acquaintances I visit during my return field trips. I quote her parts of my field transcripts. "Really?" she said, "What else did I say?"

After a while we get back to the subject of the current political climate. No one wants to talk about it. Everyone is talking about the economic situation. Fuel prices have increased 600 percent in a year, and the value of the local currency, the kyat, has dropped as inflation passes 50 percent. My friends have moved to smaller apartments, they have put plans to move or to extend or to start new ventures on hold. They are waiting for the economic situation to change.

Iron Butterflies

These return visits reinforced for me the rate of change of Asian cities. In the last decade, Rangoon and Mandalay have changed more than they had in the preceding century. Burmese people do not choose to retain memories in the same way that I do. No Burmese person could ever, for example, be accused of "living in the past." I had remained in the militarized city of 1996–97, with its forcibly relocated townships and its topography of fear courtesy of the continual writing of grant applications, conference papers, publications, and other ways in which anthropologists profit through the suffering of others. But my Burmese friends had lived an entirely different life, made up of present moments. Burmese people live always in the present. The present is a subjunctive space of possibility where change happens immediately, rather than incrementally. This understanding of the past and the present can teach us much about peace and conflict resolution because it challenges understandings of accountability for the past that we enshrine as "international law" in our human rights courts and international justice system. Members of the National League for Democracy consistently include in their public speeches the old Burmese Buddhist adage that "no one remains an enemy forever." Forever is a Buddhist age in Burma, precisely 5,000 years, and reincarnation ensures that one is around to witness it.

The Burmese *zo gji*, or wizard, is a model we can use to understand how individual Burmese may perceive reanimation after the mimicked death of the body. The butterfly spirit, the detachable part of the body, is of much greater value than the temporary and decaying physical body. The butterfly spirit can be tied down only through the great love it bears for a kindred butterfly spirit. That is why the Generals know that ultimately they have failed. They have lost their bid to be recognized by their captive population as the legitimate bearers of Buddhist nationhood because Burmese people, in what will perhaps eventually prove to be a great risk to their integrity, have escaped the regime. Their minds fly to safety while they await eventual or miraculous change in Burma.

The despair and rage of the Generals and their belief that they have been betrayed from within can be heard in the State media pronouncement that the Burmese population has "gone to sleep with karaoke culture" (NLM 1996k). Since a form of karaoke fascism was introduced that links patriotism and State power with rapid unbridled modernization (including the laundering of profits from the heroin trade), the population has seized upon these kitsch spectacles as forums of temporary escape. "Kara" in the word "karaoke" means a void (Mitsui 1998: 40), and it is into this void in the script of authoritarianism that Burmese people have sent their butterfly spirits. Karaoke is emblematic for the military regime of the population's ability to escape their constant barrage of nonsensical propaganda and to successfully resist the complete internalization of such propaganda. Burmese people have chosen a scripted performance other than that pressed upon them by the regime.

The death of Ne Win in December 2002 allowed Burmese people to feel that a great evil had been removed from the world and to reflect again upon the impermanence of all worldly things. Similarly, with the overthrow of the Suharto dictatorship, the people of Indonesia have given an enormous psychological lift to those who fight, or who secretly wish, for democracy and human rights in Southeast Asia. Perhaps it is just a matter of time until Burmese people judge the confluence of events and signs sufficiently auspicious to arise from their "miasma of fear" to confront the dictators.

On an individual, psychological level, one can only wonder if the forms of internal fragmentation that have been the subject of this book can be sufficiently patched together to form healed and whole persons. Rereading the statements of the sex workers of Nyaungbintha, I realize that one particular image recurs. It is an image of crows circling overhead which breaks into the miniature worlds, worlds of denial, and worlds of ignorance created by these women. The caws of the crows signify the nagging worries: "When will I become infected?" When will I be arrested?" Wheeling through the sky, the black harbingers break the concentration and internal focus of these women, proof that such retreats from the world can never be completely successful.

Both George Orwell and his main character in *Burmese Days*, Flory, found the tension involved in holding onto very different public and private transcripts in Burma too difficult in the end. The Forest of Time is an alienating and lonely place, and Burmese strategies of temporary escape require great courage and hope. It is salient to recall Orwell's reflections upon his British colonial character, Flory, in the moments before he committed suicide in the jungles of Burma. Flory "had learned to live inwardly, secretly, in books and secret thoughts that could not be uttered. . . . But it is a corrupting thing to live one's life in secret" (quoted in Sheldon 1991: 92).

Notes

Preface

1. It has not been possible to include images of the military confrontations with student demonstrators in late 1996 and early 1997. Video images of the violent clashes can be viewed at http://edition.cnn.com/WORLD/9612/03/; http://www.journeyman.tv and http://www.ibiblio.org/freeburma/

Chapter 1. Rangoon: End of Strife

1. Throughout this book I use the term "General" to mean a member of the ruling military council and "general" to refer to the particular army rank. "U" is a male honorific similar to "mister" or "sir," and "Daw" is the female equivalent. Usage of kin terms depends upon the relative age of the two conversants. I address men older than myself as "U," "Ko" (older brother), or "Ule" (uncle), and men or boys equal or younger in age as "Maung" (younger brother). I refer to older women as "Daw," or occasionally "Aunty," and younger women as "Ma," often depending upon the degree of familiarity between us and the level of respect I wish to convey. Burmese people use these titles or kin terms in referring to themselves depending upon the public persona they wish to portray, their age, the age of their conversants or readers, and so on. Other titles are used for children, monks, and people of high status. Burmese names may often include the name of another family member, such as the inclusion of Aung San's name in the name of democracy leader, Aung San Suu Kyi. Burmese people feel free to change their names at any time if the name is considered inauspicious, if another name is suggested to them as being more auspicious, and according to a folk system that connects the days of the week with the day of a person's birth and the eight-day Burmese calendar. Although initially confusing, this system is fluid and flexible, responsive to changes in circumstance and social situation, and indicative of the relative lack of emphasis upon property transmission and family lineage, and is consistent with the ease of marriage and divorce in Burma.

2. *Nat* (na') is the name given to a particular kind of spirit venerated in certain parts of the country. The pantheon of the 33 *Nat* and its changes and relationships to Buddhism over the past few centuries have been extensively documented by Bénédicte Brac de la Perrière (e.g., 1989, 1992a, b, 1998). Unfortunately it has not been possible to include a Burmese font in the printing process. Instead, Burmese terms are romanized in the script and accompanied

by their pronunciation according to the "Myanmar-English Dictionary" produced by the Department of the Myanmar Language Commission, Ministry of Education, Union of Myanmar (1994). I have used this system for consistency and because of the many different ways of spelling the English equivalent terms that exist among the international Burmese scholarly community. It is my hope that any romanizations that are unrecognizable to Burmese speakers will become clear when the accompanying pronunciation guide is read.

3. Throughout this book I follow Michael Taussig's (1997) use of the term "State" to emphasize the larger-than-life fearful aspects of governments that use terror, violence, and symbolic violence to maintain their grip on power.

Chapter 2. Bombs, Barricades, and the Urban Battlefield

1. Sasana "refers to the teachings of the Buddha, the practice of the teachings, and the fruits of the practice" (Lottermoser 1991).

2. Further evidence of military fear in Rangoon is believed to be the wearing of the *narawat* ring by the highest members of the regime. The *narawat* (*nawara'*), when made by traditional methods, involves a process of binding powerful and auspicious forces into the setting of nine precious stones. The particular conjunction of stones, when properly aligned and magically created, results in a flow of powerful energy that repels most accidents (mundane and supernatural) and malevolent forces and beings.

Finally, in their over-the-top public patronage of Buddhism, the hasty and shabby restoration of pagodas, the fervent new public Buddhist Works program (Brac de la Perrière 1995), and the sponsoring of suborned monks and monasteries, the members of the military council try to protect themselves against the potential effects of their actions in both this and future lives.

3. A Dhammayoun (*dama joun*) is a building (*joun*) for Dhamma (*dama*) (the word of the Buddha). It is a building located near a monastery or pagoda in which pilgrims can rest or sleep when on pilgrimage, and where monks come to give sermons to the faithful on full moon days and other religious occasions. Some Dhammayoun have become makeshift tea shops and restaurants, equipped with billiard tables, refrigerators, and karaoke machines.

4. A *tou'* (*dou'*) is a truncheon or baton and is the least frightening of the standard issue equipment of the Lon Htein (riot police); a variety of other security forces also carry rubber tou'.

Chapter 3. Darker Than Midnight: Fear, Vulnerability, and Terror-Making

1. Robben and Nordstrom argue that fieldwork under such conditions "involves a number of responsibilities above and beyond those associated with more traditional ethnography: responsibilities to the fieldworker's safety, to the safety of his or her informants, and to the theories that help to forge attitudes toward the reality of violence" (1995: 4). It is important therefore to acknowledge the debt I owe to the outstanding work conducted by anthropologists over the last two decades on the state construction of affect and the embodiment of violence in the routines of everyday life. Looming large in this research is Michael Taussig (1987, 1992, 1997), who, as Green (1995: 107) correctly notes, captures more closely than any other anthropologist the nuances of terror. On

the subject of fear, Delvecchio Good and Good (1988), Green (1999), Jenkins (1991), and Leehey (1995, 1997) have structured my understandings of dimensions of affect, including my understanding that intuitions of an "eerie calm" or a "deafening silence" can be profitably analyzed using anthropological tools. Several Burmese authors, most recently Aung San Suu Kyi (1990), Burma's Nobel Peace Laureate and the public face of opposition to repression, have written eloquently on the nature of fear in Burma. The routinization of fear and violence in everyday lives has been the subject of several volumes and articles in anthropology (e.g., Daniel 1996; Das 1990, 2000; Feldman 1991; Green 1999; Kapferer 1988; Nordstrom and Martin 1992; Nordstrom and Robben 1995; Scheper-Hughes 1992; Sluka 2000; Suárez-Orozco 1990; Warren 1993). I have also found the work of Baudrillard, Benjamin, Foucault, the Frankfurt School, Orwell, and the Surrealists to be of great use in understanding the conjunctions among power, patriotism, modernity, and hegemony. These issues are central to an understanding of contemporary Burma.

2. Emotion has been a fruitful area of anthropological interest in recent years, with a number of monographs and edited volumes that explore the cultural and political construction of psychological worlds and of affect (Levy 1973; Rosaldo 1980; Shweder and LeVine 1984; Lutz 1988; Lutz and Abu-Lughod 1990; White and Kirkpatrick 1985; Schwartz, White, and Lutz 1992; Wikan 1990; Desjarlais 1992; Russell 1995).

3. Jenkins distinguishes between the state construction of affect and the phenomenology of affect by "degree and self-reference." The state construction of affect is a "relatively enduring situation" as opposed to "relatively discrete traumatic events." She contends that the Salvadoran state constructed affect by what Marx termed the "transforming of quantity into quality" (Jenkins 1991: 153). The collective experience of state-induced terror, paranoia, anxiety, (including the feeling of unreality that accompanies psychological warfare) is, according to Martin-Baró, a global phenomenon. It is the "dominant process that subordinates all other social, economic, political and cultural processes" (Jenkins 1991: 153).

4. Related to the ethical gathering of fieldwork narratives are the responsibilities that the ethnographer holds toward his or her informants with respect to their positioning in ethnographic texts. This issue is obviously pertinent in a situation such as contemporary Burma, but it is also important when communities are small or when the groups of people interviewed have high public profiles. Not many people in Rangoon hold high-ranking civil service positions, or are university lecturers or known democracy activists. Before working with such informants, I explain to them that their identity will not simply be withheld in published accounts of the research, but will be deliberately disguised. Together, these informants and I have chosen pen names and deliberately altered gender and age descriptions, but always within the parameters of a self that is recognizable to each informant. The ethnographic account may seem like a partial work of fiction for these reasons, but the informants are able to identify the statements they have made and also to identify with the chief (but not always *all* of the) characteristics of the described narrator. This brings a measured sense of relief on the part of the informants, because in choosing the ways in which to disguise their identity, they are reassured of their anonymity in the text.

5. The amount was equivalent to U.S. $170 in late 1996 and U.S. $60 by May 2003. By the end of the student demonstrations the students who were not arrested had been given around 400,000 kyat which they used to form a number

of literary circles throughout the country and to acquire political and historical texts for these groups.

6. Expatriate groups called for an uprising in Burma on September 9, 1999.

7. "Crushing" is the regime's favorite term for the infliction of political violence.

Chapter 4. Sometimes a Cigar Is Just a Cigar

1. In many countries, fascism failed to become actualized because other solutions to the crisis of developing national capitalist societies emerged. Often this is because of a lack of any fascist support base (for example, one-third of Germans, and a smaller figure in Italy in the run-up to World War II).

2. Moe Aye (1998) further reports the following vignette: "To be frank with you," said one elderly man who had to live under both rulers, "the Japanese troops seemed to understand only killing, torture, and rape. I am not confused about why the junta is trying to hide the history of Japanese occupation. It holds the same attitude to its ethnic minority people at the borderline. And remember that after Daw Aung San Suu Kyi criticized the junta as fascist, the Generals were so angry that they put her under house arrest for six years."

3. The following statements, made by Aung San Suu Kyi or issued by the National League for Democracy, show how the events of the past are understood to have occurred and to have salience in the present:

After becoming President of the All Burma Students' Union, my father graduated to the activism of the Dohbama Asiayone, an organization of young men more aggressively nationalist than earlier generations of Burmese politicians. However its members, the thakins, worked closely with some older counterparts in established parties. Through these contacts, my father left Burma clandestinely in 1940 to seek help. (Aung San Suu Kyi 1998)

General Aung San in his writings recounted that before this resistance to the Japanese Fascists, he and his political colleagues resolved that to overthrow the British colonial government they needed to take up arms. Therefore the decision to form the armed forces was made. . . . This was why General Aung San and the "thirty comrades" (the youths of Burma) secretly went to Japan to train and equip themselves with the skills of warfare. After that they spearheaded the fight for Burma's independence in collaboration with the Japanese armed forces from Bangkok in Thailand. The Burma Independence Army (BIA) was formed on the 26 December 1941, by General Aung San and his thirty comrades with him as their leader. . . . General Aung San's BIA fought alongside the Japanese forces and caused the retreat of the British army from Burma. General Aung San acted as General of the Burma Defence Army (BDA) which replaced the BIA on July 27, 1942. (NLD 1999)

The National League for Democracy (NLD) commemorated Fascist Resistance Day this year [1996] with a lecture at which several people spoke of their personal experiences during the resistance movement. The first speaker was Bohmu Aung, a hale octogenarian who had been one the Thirty Comrades, a group of young men led by my father who received military training from the Japanese army on Hainan Island in 1941. Then U Tin U and U Maung Maung Gyi, another member of the NLD, spoke of events during the early months of 1945 from the point of view of those who were at the time merely junior officers in the Burmese armed forces. The last two speakers were a widely respected literary couple, U Khin Maung Latt and Daw Khin Myo Chit. Their modest and witty recollections of the part they as civilians had played in the resistance movement were particularly valuable. It reminded us of the crucial contribution made by the ordinary citizens of Burma toward the success of the struggle to free our country from both fascist domination and colonial rule. There are some things that we should not forget. (Aung San Suu Kyi 1996)

4. In late 1997 the regime reincarnated itself as the State Peace and Development Council. The older term for Yawata still pertains in the townships, but the newer term is beginning to be used.

5. Ardeth Maung Thawnghmung (2001) details interactions between farmers and local officials and representatives of various government programs and departments. In her study, farmers make decisions about individuals and personal characteristics and ethics of those individuals, dissociating them from more coercive power structures if their interests are more closely aligned along other axes, such as age, socioeconomic class, similar occupation and background, and so on. In this sense, her study shows no difference from the way in which Burmese people interact with local officials, representatives of the State, and bureaucrats in most urban and peri-urban wards. The situation changes only when the officials are highly placed within the regime, and this occurs most often in urban areas of Rangoon, and to a lesser extent, Mandalay. At such times, individuals are so subdued by the degree of power attached to the official, that doing nothing wrong becomes the overriding aim of all interactions with such powerful figures.

6. Local leaders are not necessarily employed as government officials. In Burma, villages are grouped together in village tracts. The number of villages grouped together to form a tract depends upon the geography of the area. Most village tracts seem to comprise between five and seven villages. In each tract there will be both a headman and a State Peace and Development Council (SPDC) Secretary. Both of these people will command respect from the villagers, but often in very different ways. In one village I asked a middle-aged woman what she thought of the SPDC secretary: "He has a government boat. Every full moon day he takes the Sayadaw from the monastery around to the other village," she replied, throwing a stick at a pig trying to get into the door of her house. "Is that all?" I asked. "Yes, that's all." No one else ventured to say anything about him, even his sons-in-law. The headman, though, that was another story. Women would stop hanging out washing or taking their children to school to tell me about his long history in the neighboring village and the many public works he had donated to, and in general felt free to gossip about a man clearly held in high esteem in the community.

7. Burma has learned much of its intelligence and propaganda techniques from China but the comparatively docile propaganda seen in Chinese cities takes on a sinister and overtly violent aspect in Burma. For example, Chinese "Model Towns" such as Zhangiagong have their own "Booklet of Rules," "Neighborhood Committees," numerous signboards exhorting citizens to be clean, and so on. There is the continual celebration of "Spiritual Civilization" with its attendant songs, videos, and dances. As in Burma, Model Villages have awards for "Model Citizens." In Burma however, "Model Citizens" are rewarded

by being put to work (without pay) on Government edifices such as the Tooth Relic pagodas.

Rather than exhorting the population be clean, Burmese signs and other forms of mass propaganda exhort violence, extreme nationalism, and unremitting loyalty. Examples include:

Only when there is discipline will there be progress
Down with the minions of colonialism
Crush all destructive elements
Beware of aboveground and underground destructive elements
Observance of discipline leads to safety
Anyone who is riotous, destructive and unruly is our enemy

These mobile threats of violence spring up at intersections, outside tourist accommodations and attractions, and in front of foreign institutions such as the United States Embassy.

Taussig has remarked that such propaganda is a "political art-form par excellence" which he describes as "mimesis unto death," the perpetual replication of the ideology of the State. The violence with which the regime routinely threatens Burmese and expatriates serves to remind residents of the original violence that birthed the SLORC (in this case, the deaths of pro-democracy supporters in the 1988 democracy uprising). Salient to the modern character of violence in Burma are Taussig's comments on the changing methods of propaganda that track the changes of an increasingly mobile population. Like monuments, he argues that this mobile form of propaganda reminds us of the founding violence of the regime and commemorates both this violence and the power that it confers upon the State (Taussig 1997: 78, 113).

Chapter 5. The Veneer of Modernity

1. Burmese make an exaggerated and very deliberate effort to pretend that "Ne Win's" pagoda does not exist. It is very poorly patronized and spoken of only with disdain. Most Rangoon residents seem to be making a conscious effort not to include any reference to the pagoda in their conversations. When I asked a good friend about this phenomenon she told me that, although Buddhism theoretically allows one to build a pagoda to increase one's merit store and thereby ensure a better rebirth, she was of the opinion that only those with a "pure heart" and "good intentions" would in fact be granted a better rebirth.

2. Burma's population is estimated to be 42,510,537, of which 11,932,188 are aged fourteen or under (CIA 2002). That is, around 12 million people have been born since the 1988 uprising.

3. When Anna Allott published "The Python," Nyi Pu Lay had already been imprisoned for fourteen years. He comes from a family of powerful writers and political activists, a dangerous combination in a military state. "The Python" was first published in 1988. Allott (1994: 61) notes that "it is a bitter irony that an author who voices the anxieties of so many of his fellow countrymen concerning the undesirable results of failing to control the production and trade opium should be locked up in prison."

4. Benjamin's chief concern was with the body not as a market commodity, but as a commodity-on-display. The organizers of the 1867 World Fair gave free entrance tickets to 400,000 French workers. They were encouraged to "make

the 'pilgrimage' to these shrines of industry, to view on display the wonders that their own class had produced but could not afford to own, or to marvel at machines that would displace them" (Buck-Morss 1989: 88). Benjamin argues that the value of the items on display becomes irrelevant except in so far as they can increase the symbolic value of a commodity. This symbolic value is a "purely representational value" (Buck-Morss 1989: 79–80). What is of import to the State is the changing image of the body to one of consumption rather than production, even if that consumption is primarily a voyeuristic process for Burmese, because, in formulating this new notion of the consumer, the route is paved for bodies to become commodities and for a new system of relations between individuals, and between individuals and the State, to be established. In creating a Burmese body that is simultaneously a producer and a consumer, the State inscribes docility upon the Burmese population, a "Burmese Daze" (Albright 1995: 18).

Chapter 6. The Veneer of Conformity

1. There is no false consciousness here; Ardeth Maung Thawhmung (2001) demonstrates that many of the lowland rural population of agriculturalists identify with the socialist revolutionary themes in such propaganda and are willing to tacitly accept the regime as a pragmatic strategy of protection from local and regional officials.

2. In addition, the impoverished nature of the new townships is reflected in the various creditors who command local influence, including money lenders, video hut owners, "business men," rice shop owners, grocery shop owners, general store owners, pawn shop owners, and "hawkers" (*gaun: jwe' zei: dhe*). These people are considered to have only a small amount of local prestige, yet they are common fixtures in the poorer wards and consistently appear in the narratives that people give about the constraints of their everyday lives.

3. Kracauer notes the application of the following techniques to achieve the hypostatization of the masses through the manipulation of propaganda: (a) The masses are forced to see themselves everywhere (mass gatherings, mass pageants, etc.); thus, they are always aware of themselves, often in the aesthetically seductive form of an ornament or an effective image. (b) With the aid of the radio, the living room is transformed into a public place. (c) All the mythical powers which the masses are capable of developing are exploited for the purpose of underscoring the significance of the masses as a mass. To many it then appears as though they were elevated in the masses above themselves (Witte 1975: 61–62).

Chapter 7. The Tension of Absurdity

1. Benjamin uses the term "dream" in many ways, always trying to convey that state of liminality that is veiled in illusion, which is at once alienated from reality and, according to Buck-Morss (1983: 214), "the false consciousness of a collective subjectivity." In post-Enlightenment Europe, dreaming was the literary device used to convey altered states of existence, other planes of being that Burmese Buddhists have no trouble describing. To dream in Buddhism is to seek or gain prophecy, knowledge, prescience, or other advantages. Psychiatric patients' dreams are nightmares where they descend to lower planes of exis-

tence or when the barriers between the human sphere and the lower regions are broken down. In urban Burma there is a collective experience, but it is not held in a domain of dreams, as dreams are not veiled illusions. Rather, the modern urban experience is the veiled illusion of reality that Burmese people seek to escape from.

2. In one of the most famous Surrealist texts, Aragon's "Paris Peasant," "Aragon presented the modern city of Paris as the most surrealistic object of all . . . where, because of the uneven development of the different strata that make up modern society, the modern and the pre-modern co-exist" (Abbas 1989: 62). Told properly, this fairy tale would use enchantment to disenchant the world: "We here construct an alarm clock which rouses the kitsch of the last century to 'assembly'—and this operates totally with cunning [K 1,3]. It would dissolve the dream, empowering the collective politically by providing the historical knowledge required to realize that dream" (Buck Morss 1983: 213).

3. The "secret" peace talks between the SPDC and the NLD began in October 2001. One of the first concessions on the part of the regime was to stop the vilification of Aung San Suu Kyi while the negotiations were occurring. They ended with the arrest of Aung San Suu Kyi in May 2003, but limp onward with the promise of a new constitution committee and the eventual implementation of a "roadmap to democracy."

4. The *chetyars* are a prominent merchant class from Tamil Nadu. Among the twice-born castes, these traders are nevertheless relatively low in the Indian caste hierarchy.

5. Members of the development committee can be seen in the lake behind Aung San Suu Kyi's residence, clearing weeds and algae. They also work as street cleaners and rubbish collectors.

6. This is also seen in the ruling council's references to Aung San Suu Kyi as their "younger sister."

7. *Dat* has become an all encompassing logic that ties together astrology, numerology, luck, karma, the properties of both black and white magic, the capricious nature of the animist *Nat* spirits, and the form of Buddhist knowledge-through-practice known as *samatha. Dat* also fuses together in one order of causality various knowledge and divination systems that permeated Burma from Hindu, Ayurvedic, European, Tantric, Mahayan Buddhist, and animist Southeast Asian traditions at different times in Burma's history.

Dat can most simply be defined as the basic essence or properties of matter, and it is the alignment and combination of objects, words, and events containing particular kinds of *dat* that allow Burmese people to take actions in the present to change their future circumstances. Within such an encompassing rubric, there is nothing that can escape the logic of *dat* causality. The naming of children and the divining of lottery numbers, the reasons for illness and misfortune and the restoration of health, are all covered by the logic of *dat. Dat saya* (practitioners) come in a multitude of varieties, each with his or her own specializations. Terms such as "auspiciousness" link weather patterns, planet positions, and the waxing and waning of the moon with daily events and are essential for most Burmese when planning important activities. Supernatural entities are controlled, and black witchcraft is performed, using numerological practices as well as magical tattoos and amulets.

8. Maung Htin Aung argues that the cult dissociated itself from magic and witchcraft practices in the fifteenth century and became imbued with aspects of alchemic and Buddhist practice (Maung Htin Aung 1959: 54–55). Many Bur-

mese people credit the successful use of *in:* as a primary factor in the withdrawal of the British from Burma since *in:* can be used to "overcome opposing forces" (Maung Htin Aung 1959: 79 n. 28). *In:* have multiple uses. A 1951 official review of indigenous medicine chronicles several uses including (1) charms used for treatment against evil spirits; (2) the administration of the ashes of burned *in:* orally as disease treatment; (3) tattooing of *in:* for spirit protection, snakebite protection and other wounds; and (4) as love potions or to win the esteem of superiors (Government of Burma 1951: 18–19).

Spiro also reports an older practice of inscribing *in:* on metal for insertion underneath the skin, and that in are also used in China (Spiro 1967: 36,176). He gives two examples of *in:*, a symbol of a bull made from letters of the Burmese alphabet, and a magical Buddha drawn with nine strokes using Burmese letters. He describes in some depth both the therapeutic use of the *in:* and the symbolism and significance of the magical Buddha (36). Tin Nyunt Pu (1980) demonstrates the importance of *in:* as a vehicle for the expression of emotional distress. He describes how patients diagnosed with paranoid schizophrenia at the State Mental Hospital (now the Yangon Psychiatric Hospital) conceptualize their illness as friends, neighbors, and other lay people burning *in* to cause them harm.

9. Many magical and medico-religious practitioners use *in:* as part of their healing or magical repertoires. It is unusual in lower Burma to find such a practitioner creating new *in:* . A majority of the *in:* known throughout Burma have been lost, in part because of the military council's banning of monks practicing magic and healing. Most contemporary practitioners copy *in:* from *gain* texts and other occult works.

10. Crawford notes that in the nineteenth century almost all Burmese males were tattooed from the navel to the knee. Bird and animal figures, *Nats*, demons, and *in:* were tattooed in a painful, expensive procedure (quoted in Spiro 1967: 37). In 1928, Shenoi (1928: 127) reported that tattooing of birds and animals remained a very common practice, especially for protection against sword and gunshot wounds. By the 1960s, extensive tattooing was becoming very unusual in men under forty years of age, although tattooing regularly occurred on a smaller scale as supernatural protection (Spiro 1967: 37).

11. Another old and tested way of finding truth is by reading Buddhist doctrine; the Dhamma (the Word of the Buddha) is given as much reverence as Buddha images and pagodas. That is why the building of "Ne Win's pagoda" has aroused such anger in Rangoon. Because of the extremely strong belief in reincarnation, Burmese Buddhists are incensed with Ne Win's attempt to circumvent the evil he has committed earlier in his life by making a large amount of merit before he dies. Building pagodas is considered the primary means in Southeast Asia of making a large store of merit (Tambiah 1976).

12. The paper is also known among expatriates as "the Nightmare of Myanmar."

13. Children's resistance to the regime is beautifully depicted in a children's story based upon an incident in a Rangoon school in 1990. The story by Allan Baillie (1994), entitled "Rebel," involves a general arriving at the school and pronouncing his control over all the students and staff members. A child's *hpana*, or sandal, sails over the heads of the soldiers and knocks the hat of the general onto the ground. The general orders all the staff and children to be brought before him to find the child with a missing sandal. The school assemble before the general, but they are all barefoot, with a large pile of sandals left inside the classroom.

14. See Foucault (1965) for a discussion of Pinel's concept of moral treatment.

Chapter 8. Fragments of Misery: The People of the New Fields

1. Forced labor is defined by the International Labor Organization (ILO) as follows: "Under the Convention Against Forced Labor (ILO No. 29) which Burma has signed and ratified, forced labor means 'all workers or service which is exacted from any person under the menace of any penalty and for which that said person has not offered himself [or herself] voluntarily'" (ERI and SAIN 1996). Previous forms of corvée and "community" labor utilized in Southeast Asia are very different from the forced labor being imposed upon Burmese in their townships. For example, working on a road consecutively for seven days without payment or compensation is clearly not an act of community maintenance, but the expansion of the junta's infrastructure. In previous years, villagers who did not keep their portion of the communal boundary fence in good order were simply warned that they would not be able to live within its bounds. In contrast, the threat of violence and retaliation (that makes resistance difficult or impossible) hangs over township dwellers who refuse to participate in forced labor. In addition, a system of corruption and patronage exists which makes the notion of "community" labor absurd. Within Burma forced labor has reached epidemic proportions as the State readily sacrifices the lives of its population in order to immortalize itself in the landscape.

Human rights activists have seized upon the Yadana pipeline as an example of the solidification of the military regime through forced labor. The Yadana gas fields project is a joint venture operation between the regime and Unocal that ships gas from the site of its recovery offshore in Burma, across a huge pipeline into Thailand. Activist groups that have interviewed forced laborers involved in the construction of the pipeline conclude that their "research indicates that gross human rights violations, including summary executions, torture, forced labor and forced relocations, have occurred as a result of natural gas developments funded by European and North American corporations" (ERI and SAIN 1996: i). The forced labor that has ensued as a result of the regime's need for the hard currency represented by gas revenues has caused Yozo Yokata, Special UN Reporteur to Myanmar, to comment that "The pipeline is simply a new landscape in which . . . control is now exerted" (Yokata 1995: 26).

2. At the time of the household surveys, the unofficial exchange rate was U.S. $1 = 164 kyat.

3. I include here data about these issues, but I refrain from publishing interview segments from children and did not formally interview them. Their testimonies were certainly voluntary, but I am uncomfortable treating the torment of children on the same level as that of adults and mindful of the ethical issues attendant on such data gathering.

Bibliography

Abbas, Ackbar. 1989. "On Fascination: Walter Benjamin's Images." *New German Critique* 48 (Fall): 43–62.

Adams, Vincanne. 1996. "Karaoke as Modern Lhasa, Tibet: Western Encounters with Cultural Politics." *Cultural Anthropology* 11 (4): 510–46.

Adorno, Theodor W. 1973 [1962]. *Negative Dialectics.* New York: Seabury Press.

Albright, Madeleine K. 1995. "Burmese Daze." *Burma Debate* 2 (6): 18–19.

All Burma Federation of Student Unions (ABFSU). n.d. "Brief History of All Burma Federation of Student Unions (ABFSU)." www.fmccb.tripod.com/abfsu.htm.

All Burma Students' Democratic Front (ABSDF). 2001. "Statement of the Sixth General Conference of the ABSDF." April 10. www.geocities.com/absdg_au/media/ab69.html.

All Burma Young Monks' Union (ABYMU). 1997. "Statement of the ABYMU Regarding Current Action Against the Buddhist Monks by the SLORC Military Regime, July 16." *BurmaNet News,* July 17.

Allot, Anna J. 1994. *Inked Over, Ripped Out: Burmese Storytellers and the Censors.* Chiang Mai: Silkworm Books.

Alternative ASEAN Network on Burma (ALTSEAN-Burma). 1998. *Voices of Women in the Struggle.* Bangkok: Altsean-Burma.

Amnesty International (AI).1997. *Myanmar: 1996 Worst Year for Human Rights This Decade.* London: AI Index ASA, 12 February.

Anagnost, Ann. 1994. "The Politicized Body." In Angela Zito and Tani E. Barlow, eds., *Body, Subject, and Power in China*, 103–30. Chicago: University of Chicago Press.

Anderson, Benedict. 1991. *Imagined Communities: Reflections on the Origin and Spread of Nationalism.* London: Verso.

Anonymous. 1997. "Independent Essay, September 3." *BurmaNet News,* September 5. 1997

Appadurai, Arjun. 1990. "Topographies of the Self: Praise and Emotion in Hindu India." In Catherine A. Lutz and Lila Abu-Lughod, eds., *Language and the Politics of Emotion*, 92–112. Cambridge: Cambridge University Press.

Ardeth Maung Thawnhmung. 2001. "Paddy Farmers and the State: Agricultural Policies and Legitimacy in Rural Thailand." Dissertation, University of Wisconsin, Madison.

Arendt, Hannah. 1958. *The Origins of Totalitarianism.* New York: Meridian Books.

Aung Kin. 1999. "Power and Burmese Society." *Democratic Voice of Burma,* January–February:1–6. www.communique.no/dvb/archive/1999/special/talks/read.html.

Aung San Suu Kyi. 1998. "The Game Rules in Burma: There Are No Rules." *Asahi Evening News,* June 25.

———. 1997a. "Letter from Burma (No. 9)." *Manichi Daily News,* Monday, October 20.

———. 1997b. "Foreword." In Peter Carey, ed., *Burma: The Challenge of a Divided Society,* ix–x. Hampshire: Macmillan.

———. 1996. Letter from Burma (No. 23)." *Manishi Daily News,* Monday, April 29.

———. 1993. Towards a True Refuge" Eighth Joyce Pearce Memorial Lecture, delivered by Michael Aris, May 19. University of Oxford. www.danenet.wicip .org/fbc/refuge.html

———. 1990. *Freedom from Fear and Other Writings.* Harmondsworth: Penguin.

Aye Aye Thein, K. Ba Thike, and Myint Maung Maung. 1995. *A Study on Teenage Pregnancy in North Okkalapa.* Yangon: Myanmar Research Congress.

Ba Han. 1968. "Spiritism in Burma." *Journal of the Burma Research Society* 47: 3–9.

Ba Thike, K. 1997. "Abortion: A Public Health Problem in Myanmar." *Reproductive Health Matters* 9: 94–100.

Ba Thike, K, Khin Thet Wai, Le Le Win, Saw Kler Khu, Myint Maung Maung, et al. 1992. "Socioeconomic Differentials of Women with Severe Septic Abortions." *Myanmar Medical Journal* 37: 1–4.

Ba Thike, K, Khin Thet Wai, Nan Oo, and Khin Htar Yi. 1993. "Contraceptive Practice Before Female Sterilization." *Asia-Oceania Journal of Obstetrics and Gynaecology* 19: 241–48.

Baillie, Allan. 1994. *Rebel.* Illustrated by Di Wu. New York: Ticknor and Fields Books for Young Readers (Houghton Mifflin).

Ball, Desmond. 1998. *Burma's Military Secrets: Signals Intelligence (SIGINT) from the Second World War to Civil War and Cyber Warfare.* Bangkok: White Lotus Press.

Bataille, Georges. 1979. "The Psychological Structure of Fascism." *New German Critique* 16 (Winter): 64–87.

Baudelaire, Charles. 1962 [1857]. *The Flowers of Evil.* New York: New Directions.

Baudrillard, Jean. 1993. *Symbolic Exchange and Death.* London: Sage Publications.

Bekker, Sarah M. 1989. "Changes and Continuities in Burmese Buddhism." In Josef Silverstein, ed., *Independent Burma at Forty Years: Six Assessments,* 58–59. Ithaca, N.Y.: Cornell University Southeast Asia Program.

Benjamin, Walter. 1985. "Central Park I." Trans. L. Spencer. *New German Critique* 34 (Winter): 1–27.

———. 1983. *Das Passagen Werk,* Frankfurt au Main: Suhrkamp.

Bennett, Linda Rae, and Lenore Manderson, eds. 2003. *Violence Against Women in Asian Societies.* New York: Routledge.

Bernstein, Dennis, and Leslie Kean. 1997. "Hanging Drug Couriers but Investing with Their Suppliers." *The Nation,* October 20.

———. 1996. People of the Opiate: Burma's Dictatorship of Drugs." *The Nation,* December 16.

Blonsky, Marshall, ed. 1995. *On Signs.* Baltimore: Johns Hopkins University Press.

Bo Kywe and Maung Maung Lin. 1993. "Birth Spacing Practices in Twenty Townships in Six Divisions." Yangon: Community Health Care Project, Department of Health. Unpublished.

Brac de la Perrière, Bénédicte. 2002. "Transmission, Change and Reproduction in the Burmese Cult of the 37 Lords." Paper presented at Burma Studies Conference, Burma-Myanma(r) Research and its Future, Gothenberg, Sweden, September 21–25.

————. 1998. Le Roulis de la Dame aux Flancs d'Or: Une fête de *naq* atypique en Birmanie centrale." *L'Homme* 146: 47–85.

————. 1995. Urbanisation et légendes d'introduction du Bouddhisme au Myanmar (Birmanie)." *Journal de Anthropologies* 61–62: 41–63.

————. 1992a. Sambya': Un quartier a la périphérie de Rangoun." In Jacqueline Matras-Guin and Christian Taillard, eds., *Habitations et habitat d'Asie du sud-est continentale: Pratiques et representations de l'espace.* 231–54. Paris: L'Harmattan.

————. 1992b. La fête de Taunbyon: Le grand rituel du culte des *naq* de Birmanie (Myanmar)." *Bulletin de l'École française d'extrême-orient* 79 (2): 201–31.

————. 1989. *Rites et possessions en Birmanie.* Paris: CNRS.

Brückner, Peter, Wilfried Gottschalch, Eberhard Knödler-Bunte, Olav Münzberg, and Oskar Negt. 1977. "Perspectives on the Fascist Public Sphere." *New German Critique* 11 (Spring): 94–132.

Buchheim, Hans. 1968. *Totalitarian Rule: Its Nature and Characteristics.* Middletown, Conn.: Wesleyan University Press.

Buck-Morss, Susan. 1989. *Dialectics of Seeing: Walter Benjamin and the Arcades Project.* Cambridge: MIT Press.

————. 1983. "Benjamin's Passagenwerk: Redeeming Mass Culture for the Revolution." *New German Critique* 29 (Spring/Summer): 211–40.

Cahn, Michael. 1984. "Subversive Mimesis: T. W. Adorno and the Modern Impasse of Critique." In Mihai Spariosu, ed., *Mimesis in Contemporary Theory: An Interdisciplinary Approach,* vol. 1, *The Literary and Philosophical Debate.* Philadelphia: John Benjamins.

Callahan, Mary P. 2003. *Making Enemies: War and State Building in Burma.* Ithaca, N.Y.: Cornell University Press.

————. 1998. The Sinking Schooner: Murder and the State in 'Democratic' Burma." In Carl Trocki, ed., *Gangsters, the State, and Democracy in Southeast Asia.* Ithaca, N.Y.: Cornell University Southeast Asia Program.

Cangi, Ellen Corwin. 1997. *Faded Splendour, Golden Past: Urban Images of Burma.* New York: Oxford University Press.

Caouette, Therese, Kritaya Archavanitkul, and Hnin Hnin Pyne. 2000. *Sexuality, Reproductive Health, and Violence: Experiences of Migrants from Burma in Thailand.* Bangkok: Institute for Population and Social Research, Mahidol University.

Carey, Peter, ed. 1997. *Burma: The Challenge of a Divided Society.* Hampshire: Macmillan.

Catley, Bob. 1996. "Myanmar: The Next Frontier." *Quadrant* 40 (April): 48–51.

Central Intelligence Agency (CIA). 2002. *The World Factbook: Burma 2002.* www .cia/gov/cia/publications/factbook/geos/bm.html

Chaturawong, Chotima. 2002. "The Architecture of Burmese Buddhist Monasteries in Upper Burma: The Biography of Trees." Paper presented at Burma Studies Conference, Gothenburg, Sweden, September 21–25.

Cohen, Lawrence. 1998. *No Aging in India: Alzheimer's, the Bad Family, and Other Modern Things.* Berkeley: University of California Press.

Comaroff, Jean, and John Comaroff. 1991. *Of Revelation and Revolution: Christianity, Colonialism, and Consciousness in South Africa.* Chicago: University of Chicago Press.

Covington, Richard. 2002. "Sacred and Profaned: Misguided Restorations of the Exquisite Buddhist Shrines of Pagan in Burma May Do More Harm Than Good." *Smithsonian* (December): 1–4.

Daniel, Valentine. 1996. *Charred Lullabies: Chapters in an Anthropography of Violence.* Princeton, N. J.: Princeton University Press.

Das, Veena. 2000. "The Act of Witnessing: Violence, Poisonous Knowledge and Subjectivity." In Veena Das, Arthur Kleinman, Mamphela Ramphele, and Pamela Reynolds, eds., *Violence and Subjectivity*, 205–25. Berkeley: University of California Press.

———, ed. 1990. *Mirrors of Violence: Communities, Riots, and Survivors in South Asia.* Delhi: Oxford University Press.

Das, Veena, Arthur Kleinman, Mamphela Ramphele, and Pamela Reynolds, eds. 2000. *Violence and Subjectivity.* Berkeley: University of California Press.

Davis, Anthony, and Bruce Hawke. 1998. "Burma: The Country That Won't Kick the Habit." *Jane's Intelligence Review* 10 (3): 26.

de Certeau, Michel. 1985. "Practices of Space." In Marshall Blonsky, ed., *On Signs*, 122–45. Baltimore: Johns Hopkins University Press.

Delvecchio Good, Mary-Jo, and Byron Good. 1988. "Ritual, the State, and the Transformation of Emotional Discourse in Iranian Society." *Culture, Medicine and Psychiatry* 12 (1): 46–63.

Democratic Voice of Burma (DVB). 2003. "Burma Purchases 50 Tanks from Ukraine." Press Release. July 29. www.burmaproject.org/072903ukraine_50_tanks_purchased.html.

Desjarlais, Robert R. 2003. *Sensory Biographies: Lives and Deaths Among Nepal's Yolmo Buddhists.* Berkeley: University of California Press.

———. 1992. *Body and Emotion: The Aesthetics of Illness and Healing in the Nepal Himalayas.* Philadelphia: University of Pennsylvania Press.

Diller, Janelle M. 1997. "The National Convention: An Impediment to the Restoration of Democracy." In Peter Carey, ed., *Burma: The Challenge of Change in a Divided Society*, 27–54. Hampshire: Macmillan.

Dixon, Gale. 1993. "Ethnicity and Infant Mortality in Malaysia." *Asia-Pacific Population Journal* 8 (2): 23–54.

Earth Rights International (ERI) and Southeast Asian Information Network (SAIN). 1996. "Total Denial: A Report on the Yadana Pipeline Project in Burma." *Earth Rights International and Southeast Asian Information Network*, July 10.

Ebihara, May M., Carol A. Morton, and Judy Ledgerwood, eds. 1994. *Cambodian Culture Since 1975: Homeland and Exile.* Ithaca, N.Y.: Cornell University Press.

Economist Intelligence Unit (EIU). 1996. *Country Report: Myanmar, Second Quarter.* Kent: Redhouse Press.

Economist. 1995. "Drugs: The Golden Triangle's New King." February 4: 31–32.

Eggar, Arthur. 1957. "Collectanea 'Win-Laik-Pya: or the Soul Butterfly'." *Folklore* 67. London: Folk-Lore Society.

Escobar, Arturo. 1994. *Encountering Development: The Making and Unmaking of the Third World.* Princeton, N.J.: Princeton University Press.

Farmer, Paul. 1996. "On Suffering and Structural Violence: A View from Below." *Daedalus* 125 (1): 261–83.

———. 1992. *AIDS and Accusation: Haiti and the Geography of Blame.* Berkeley: University of California Press.

Feldman, Allen. 1991. *Formations of Violence: The Narrative of the Body and Political Terror in Northern Ireland.* Chicago: University of Chicago Press.

Ferguson, John P., and E. Michael Mendelson. 1981. "Masters of the Buddhist Occult: The Burmese Weikzas." In *Essays on Burma*, 62–80. Contributions to Asian Studies 16. Leiden: E.J. Brill.

Figa-Talamanca, Irene. 1986. "Illegal Abortion: An Attempt to Assess Its Cost to Health Services and Its Incidence in the Community." Unpublished manuscript.

Financial Times. 1998. "Six Face Death Penalty in Burma." *Financial Times.* April 30.

Fink, Christina. 2001. *Living Silence: Burma Under Military Rule.* Bangkok: White Lotus.

Foucault, Michel. 1995 [1979]. *Discipline and Punish: The Birth of the Prison.* 2nd ed. New York: Vintage Books.

———. 1965. *Madness and Civilization.* New York: Pantheon Books.

Franco, Jean. 1985. "Killing Priests, Nuns, Women, Children." In Marshall Blonsky, ed., *On Signs,* 414–20. Baltimore: Johns Hopkins University Press.

Geertz, Clifford. 1973. *The Interpretation of Culture: Selected Essays.* New York: Basic Books.

Good, Byron J., Mary-Jo Delvecchio Good, et al. 1994. "In the Subjunctive Mode: Epilepsy Narratives in Turkey." *Social Science and Medicine* 38 (6) (March 15): 855–92.

Government of Burma (RCE). 1951. Report of the Committee of Enquiry into the Indigenous System of Medicine, Rangoon, Superintendent, Government Printing and Stationery.

Green, Linda. 1999. *Fear as a Way of Life: Mayan Widows in Rural Guatemala.* New York: Columbia University Press.

———. 1998. "Lived Lives and Social Suffering: Problems and Concerns in Medical Anthropology." *Medical Anthropology Quarterly* 12 (1): 3–7.

———. 1995. "Living in a State of Fear." In Carolyn Nordstrom and Antonius C. G. M. Robben, eds., *Fieldwork Under Fire: Contemporary Studies of Violence and Survival,* 105–27. Berkeley: University of California Press.

Greenwood, Nicholas. 1994. *Alternative Guide to Burma.* London: Burman Action Group.

Guardian. 1989. "Democrats Under House Arrest." July 22.

Hall, D. G. E. 1955. *A History of South-East Asia.* New York: St. Martin's Press.

Hartmann, Betsy, and James K. Boyce. 1983. *A Quiet Violence: View from a Bangladesh Village.* New Jersey: Zed Books.

Head, Jonathan. 2001. "Senior Burmese Official Killed." BBC News, February 23: 1.

Hiegel, Jean-Pierre, and Colette Landrac. 1993. "Les Khmers rouges et les autres." *Nouvelle Revue d'Ethnopsychiatrie* 22–23: 41–68.

Hla Pe, Khin Khin Aye, Malar Myint, May Thet Khine, Thein Thein Htay, et al. 1992. "Birth Spacing Practices Among the Rural Populations of Kyo-Kone and Sarbu-Daung Rural Health Centers in Hlegu Township." *Myanmar Medical Journal* 37: 1–11.

Houtman, Gustaaf. 1999. *Mental Culture in Burmese Crisis Politics: Aung San Suu Kyi and the National League for Democracy.* Tokyo: Institute for the Study of Languages and Cultures of Asia and Africa, Tokyo University of Foreign Studies.

Human Rights Watch. 1999. "Human Rights Watch Burma: Overview of Human Rights Developments 1998." www.hrw.org/wr2k.Asia-01.htm#TopOfPage

Jenkins, Janis. 1991. "The State Construction of Affect: Political Ethos and Mental Health Among Salvadoran Refugees." *Culture, Medicine, and Psychiatry* 15: 139–65.

Jordt, Ingrid. 2002. "Patron-Client Ties and the Process of Political Legitimation in Burmese State-Society Relations." Paper presented at Burma Studies Conference, Burma-Myanma(r) Research and Its Future, Gothenberg, Sweden, September 21–25.

———. 2001. "The Mass Lay Meditation Movement and State-Society Relations in Post-Independence Burma." Ph.D. dissertation. Harvard University.

K (U Khin Zaw). 1981. *Burmese Culture: General and Particular.* Rangoon: Sarpay Beikman.

Kafka, Franz. 1948. *The Penal Colony: Stories and Short Pieces.* New York: Schocken Books.

Kalweit, Holger. 1992. *Shamans, Healers, and Medicine Men.* Boston: Shambhala.

Kapferer, Bruce. 1988. *Legends of People, Myths of State: Violence, Intolerance, and Political Culture in Sri Lanka and Australia.* Washington, D.C.,: Smithsonian Institution Press.

Kawanami, Hiroko. 2002. "Religious Ideology, Representation, and Social Realities: The Case of Burmese Buddhist Womanhood." Paper presented at Burma Studies Conference, Burma-Myanma(r) Research and Its Future, Gothenberg, Sweden, September 21–25.

———. 1994. *Keepers of the Faith: The Buddhist Nuns of the Sagaing Hills.* (film).

Kean, Leslie, and Dennis Bernstein. 1997. "Aung San Suu Kyi. The Progressive Interview, Free Burma Coalition." March. www.danenet.wicip.org/fbc/interview.htm.

Kennedy, Charles H., and David J. Louscher. 1991. "Civil-Military Interaction: Data in Search of a Theory." In Charles H. Kennedy and David J. Louscher, eds., *Civil Military Interaction in Asia and Africa,* 1–10. Leiden: E.J. Brill.

———, eds. 1991. *Civil Military Interaction in Asia and Africa.* Leiden: E.J. Brill.

Khin Than Tin and Khin Saw Hla. 1990. "Causes of Maternal Deaths in Affiliated Teaching Hospitals." Yangon: Myanmar Medical Association.

Kirmayer, Laurence J. 1994. "Pacing the Void: Social and Cultural Dimensions of Dissociation." In David Spiegel, ed., *Dissociation: Culture, Mind, and Body,* 91–122. Washington, D.C.: American Psychiatric Press.

Kleinman, Arthur, and Byron Good, eds. 1985. *Culture and Depression: Studies in Anthropology and Cross-Cultural Psychiatry of Affect and Disorder.* Berkeley: University of California Press.

Kleinman, Arthur, and Joan Kleinman.1994. "How Bodies Remember: Social Memory and Bodily Experience of Criticism, Resistance, and Delegitimation Following China's Cultural Revolution." *New Literary History* 25 (3) (Summer): 707–36.

Klima, Alan. 2002. *The Funeral Casino: Meditation, Massacre, and Exchange with the Dead in Thailand.* Princeton, N.J.: Princeton University Press.

Knödler-Bunte, Eberhard. 1977. "Fascism as Depoliticized Mass Movement." *New German Critique* 11 (Spring): 39–48.

Kracauer, Siegfried. 1975. "The Mass Ornament." *New German Critique* 5 (Spring): 67–76.

Krasu, Mary. 1992. "An Overview of Maternal Morbidity in Myanmar. Proceedings of a Seminar on Maternal Morbidity Obstetric and Gynecological Section." Yangon: Myanmar Medical Association.

Kumada, Naoko. 2002. "Dagò, Cosmogony and Politics: Religion and Power in Burmese Society." Paper presented at Burma Studies Conference, Burma-Myanma(r) Research and its Future, Gothenberg, Sweden, September 21–25.

Leehey, Jennifer. 2000. "Censorship and Burmese Political Imagination." Paper presented at Northern Illinois University, October.

———. 1997. "Message in a Bottle: A Gallery of Social/Political Cartoons from Burma." *Southeast Asian Journal of Social Science* 25 (1): 151–66.

———. 1995. "Allusions to the Mood in Burma." *SEASPAN: The Northwest Regional Consortium for Southeast Asian Studies* 9 (1): 7–11.

Lehman, Frederick K. 1987. "Monasteries, Palaces, and Ambiguities: Burmese Sacred and Secular Space." *Contributions to Indian Sociology* 21 (1): 169–86.

Levy, Adrian, and Cathy Scott-Clarke. 1998. "Junta Forces Farmers to Grow Opium." *Sunday Times* (London), May 10.

Levy, Robert I. 1973. *Tahitians: Mind and Experience in the Society Islands.* Chicago: University of Chicago Press.

Lintner, Bertil. 1998. "Velvet Glove." *Far Eastern Economic Review,* May 7.

―――. 1996a. "Drug Buddies: The Heroin Trade Fights Back—with Official Help." *Far Eastern Economic Review* 159, November 14: 37–38.

―――. 1996b. "A Blind Eye to Drugs." *Far Eastern Economic Review* 159, November 6: 8.

―――. 1994a. *Burma in Revolt: Opium and Insurgency Since 1948.* Boulder, Colo.: Westview Press.

―――. 1994b. "A Piece of the Action: Burma-China Drug Trade Thrives with Official Complicity." *Far Eastern Economic Review* 157, December 22: 27.

―――. 1993a. "Hooked on the Junta: US Drug Agency Assailed for Links to Burmese Generals." *Far Eastern Economic Review* 156, November 18.

―――. 1993b. "The Politics of the Drug Trade in Burma." Indian Ocean Centre for Peace Studies Occasional Paper 33. University of Western Australia.

―――. 1991. "Review Article: Poisons and Politics." *Far Eastern Economic Review* 154, November 14: 52–54.

―――. 1990a. *Outrage: Burma's Struggle for Democracy.* London: White Lotus.

―――. 1990b. "The New Dealer." *Far Eastern Economic Review,* June 28: 22–23.

Lock, Margaret. 1993. *Encounters with Aging: Mythologies of Menopause in Japan and North America.* Berkeley: University of California Press.

Lottermoser, Friedgard. 1991. "Buddhist Nuns in Burma." *Sakyadhita Newsletter* 2 (2) (Summer). www.sakyadhita.org/NewsLetters/newsindx.htm#22.

Lubeight, Guy. 1995. "Données stratégiques d'un aménagement uyrbain en Birmanie. De Rangoun à Yangon." In *Cités d'Asie: Les cahiers de la recherche architecturale,* 35–36. Marseilles: Parenthèses.

Lum, Casey Man Kong. 1998. "The Karaoke Dilemma: On the Interaction Between Collectivism and Individualism in the Karaoke Space." In Toru Mitsui, and Shuhei Hosokawa, eds., *Karaoke Around the World: Global Technology, Local Singing,* 166–77. New York: Routledge.

Lutz, Catherine A. 1988. *Unnatural Emotions: Everyday Sentiments on a Micronesian Atoll and Their Challenge to Western Theory.* Chicago: University of Chicago Press.

Lutz, Catherine A., and Lila Abu-Lughod, eds. 1990. *Language and the Politics of Emotion.* Cambridge: Cambridge University Press.

Mansfield, Stephen. 1998. "Road to Mandalay Lined with Capitalists." *Manichi Daily News,* Japan, February 5.

Marshall, Andrew. 2002. *The Trouser People: The Quest for the Victorian Footballer Who Made Burma Play the Empire's Game.* London: Penguin Books.

Maung Htin Aung. 1967. *A History of Burma.* New York: Columbia University Press.

―――. 1959. *Folk Elements in Burmese Buddhism.* London: Oxford University Press.

McCrae, Alistair. 1990. *Scots in Burma.* Paseley: James Paton.

Merleau Ponty, Maurice. 1962. *Phenomenology of Perception.* New York: Routledge.

Mi Mi Khaing. 1962. *Burmese Family.* Bloomington: Indiana University Press.

Ministry of Health and United Nations Population Fund. 1999. *A Reproductive Health Needs Assessment in Myanmar.* Yangon: Ministry of Health and UNFPA.

Mitsui, Toru, and Shuhei Hosokawa, eds. 1998. *Karaoke Around the World: Global Technology, Local Singing.* New York: Routledge.

Mockenhaupt, Brian. 2001. "Wordsmithery: Control over Writers and the Media." *Far Eastern Economic Review* 164, September 20: 37.

Moe Aye. 1998. "The Last Days of Mr. Leo Nichols." In All Burma Students' Democratic Front, eds., *Tortured Voices: Personal Accounts of Burma's Interrogation Centers*, 131–39. Bangkok: ABSDF.

Moreau, Ron. 1996. "Ghosts in the Street: The Junta Cracks Down on New Student Protests." *Newsweek*, December 23.

Myo Myint. 1987. "The Politics of Survival in Burma: Diplomacy and Statecraft in the Reign of King Mindon, 1853–1878." Ph.D. dissertation, Cornell University.

Nadeau, Maurice, ed. 1965. *The History of Surrealism.* New York: Macmillan.

Nash, June C. 1966. "Living with Nats: An Analysis of Animism in Burman Village Social Relations." In Manning Nash, ed., *Anthropological Studies in Theravada Buddhism,* 117–36. Cultural Report Series 13. New Haven, Conn.: Yale University Southeast Asian Studies.

Nash, Manning, ed. 1966. *Anthropological Studies in Theravada Buddhism.* Cultural Report Series 13. New Haven, Conn.: Yale University Southeast Asian Studies.

National Coalition Government of Union of Burma (NCGUB). 1999. "Statement on the 54th Anniversary of Resistance Day." March 28. Washington, D.C.: NCGUB.

National League for Democracy (NLD) Central Executive Committee. 1999. "National League for Democracy Statement 50(3/99): A Discourse on the Fifty-Fourth Anniversary of Resistance Day." NLD Statements and Letters. www.angelfire.com/ok/NLD/s5099.html

Negt, Oskar. 1976. "The Non-Synchronous Heritage and the Problem of Propaganda." *New German Critique* 9 (Fall): 46–70.

Nemoto, Kei. "Aung San Suu Kyi: What does she aim at?" *Genbunken* 73: 21–32. Tokyo: Institute of Modern Culture Studies, Senshu University.

New Light of Myanmar. 2001. "Fully Active with Plans for Development of Women's Sector: Mass of Myanmar Women Urged to be More Serious in Safeguarding Cultural Traits." January 25: 1.

———. 1996a. *New Light of Myanmar* IV (78) (June 29).

———. 1996b. *New Light of Myanmar* IV (79) (June 30): 5.

———. 1996c. *New Light of Myanmar* IV (82) (July 6): 3.

———. 1996d. *New Light of Myanmar* IV (109) (August 3): 12.

———. 1996e. *New Light of Myanmar* IV (131) (August 25): 2, 6.

———. 1996f. *New Light of Myanmar* IV (133) (August 27): 6.

———. 1996g. *New Light of Myanmar* IV (134) (August 28): 7, 12.

———. 1996h. *New Light of Myanmar* IV (152) (September 16): 2, 5.

———. 1996i. *New Light of Myanmar* IV (162) (September 26): 5.

———. 1996j. *New Light of Myanmar* IV (166) (September 30): 3.

———. 1996k. *New Light of Myanmar* IV (166) (September 30): 5.

———. 1996l. *New Light of Myanmar* IV (169) (October 3): 5.

———. 1996m. *New Light of Myanmar* IV (171) (October 5): 5.

———. 1996n. *New Light of Myanmar* IV (180) (October 14): 5.

———. 1996o. *New Light of Myanmar* IV (185) (October 19): 3, 5.

———. 1996p. *New Light of Myanmar* IV (192) (October 26): 3, 5.

———. 1996q. *New Light of Myanmar* IV (197) (October 31): 3.

Nordstrom, Carolyn. 1997. *A Different Kind of War Story.* Philadelphia: University of Pennsylvania Press.

Nordstrom, Carolyn, and JoAnn Martin, eds. 1992. *The Paths to Domination, Resistance, and Terror.* Berkeley: University of California Press.

Nordstrom, Carolyn, and Antonius C. G. M. Robben, eds. 1995. *Fieldwork Under Fire: Contemporary Studies of Violence and Survival*. Berkeley: University of California Press.

Nwe Nwe Yin. 2002. "Karaoke Craze Sends Local Video Industry Soaring." *Myanmar Times and Business Review* 6: 102.

Obeyesekere, Gannanath. 1985. "Depression, Buddhism, and the Work of Culture in Sri Lanka." In Arthur Kleinman and Byron Good, eds., *Culture and Depression*, 134–52. Berkeley: University of California Press.

Orwell, George. 1949 [1934]. *Burmese Days: A Novel*. London: Secker and Warburg.

People's Tribunal on Food Scarcity and Militarization in Burma. 1999. *Voice of the Hungry Nation*. Hong Kong: Asian Human Rights Commission, October.

Peterson, Edwards. 1969. *The Limits of Hitler's Power*. Princeton, N.J.: Princeton University Press.

Philp, Janette, and David Mercer. 2002. "Politicised Pagodas and Veiled Resistance: Contested Urban Space in Burma." *Urban Studies* 39 (9): 1587–610.

———. 1999. "Commodification of Buddhism in Contemporary Burma." *Annals of Tourism Research* 1: 21–54.

Phra Ajaan Lee Dhammadharo. 1956. "Namo tasso bhagavato arahato sammasambuddhass [Veneration to the Exalted One, the Homage Worthy, the Perfectly Self-Enlightened]." *Inner Wealth: Part One, The Last Sermon*. www.buddhistinformation.com/inner_wealth.htm.

Pye, Lucian W. 1963. *Politics, Personality, and Nation Building: Burma's Search for Identity*. New Haven, Conn.: Yale University Press.

Rabinach, Anson. 1977. "Ernst Bloch's *Heritage of Our Times* and Fascism." *New German Critique* 11 (Spring): 5–21.

Reuters. 1996. "Activists' Sentences Confirmed: Suu Kyi's Secretary and Bodyguard Jailed." *Bangkok Post*, August 29.

Robben, Antonius C. G. M. 2000. "State Terror in the Netherworld: Disappearance and Reburial in Argentina." In Jeffrey A. Sluka, ed., *Death Squad: The Anthropology of State Terror*, 91–113. Philadelphia: University of Pennyslvania Press.

Robben, Antonius C. G. M., and Carolyn Nordstrom. 1995. "The Anthropology and Ethnography of Violence and Sociopolitical Conflict." In Carolyn Nordstrom and A. C. G. M. Robben, eds., *Fieldwork Under Fire: Contemporary Studies of Violence and Survival*, 1–23. Berkeley: University of California Press.

Robinne, François. 2002. "Sending Back the Soul Amongst the Christian Kachin in Burma." Paper presented at Burma Studies Conference: Burma-Myanma(r) Research and Its Future, Gothenburg, Sweden, September 21–25.

Rosaldo, Michelle Z. 1980. *Knowledge and Passion: Ilongot Notions of Self and Social Life*. Cambridge: Cambridge University Press.

Rozenberg, Guillaume. 2002. "Reciprocity and Redistribution in the Quest for Sainthood in Burma: Thamanya Sayadaw's Birthday." Paper presented at Burma Studies Conference: Burma-Myanma(r) Research and Its Future, Gothenburg, Sweden, September 21–25.

Russell, James A., ed. 1995. *Everyday Conceptions of Emotion: An Introduction to the Psychology, Anthropology, and Linguistics of Emotion*. Dordrecht: Kluwer Academic.

Ryle, John. 1999. "Disneyland for Dictators." *New York Review of Books*, January 14: 8.

Sao Yin Aung. 1965. *The Village of the Generals*. Bangkok: Saengjuen Sarawin.

Sartre, Jean-Paul. 1972. *The Psychology of Imagination.* London: Methuen.

Scarry, Elaine. 1985. *The Body in Pain: The Making and Unmaking of the World.* Oxford: Oxford University Press.

Schechner, Richard, and Willa Appel, eds. 1990. *By Means of Performance: Intercultural Studies of Theatre and Ritual.* Cambridge: Cambridge University Press.

Scheper-Hughes, Nancy. 1992. *Death Without Weeping: The Violence of Everyday Life in Brazil.* Berkeley: University of California Press.

Schober, Juliane. 1995. "The Politics of Contested Meanings: State Patronage of the Chinese Tooth Relic and the Construction of Burmese National Culture." Paper prepared for AAR Seminar on Relics, Philadelphia, November 19.

———. 1988. "The Path to Buddhahood: The Spiritual Mission and Social Organization of Mysticism in Contemporary Burma." *Crossroads: An Interdisciplinary Journal of Southeast Asian Studies* (Fall).

Schwartz, Theodore, Geoffrey M. White, and Catherine A. Lutz, eds. 1992. *New Directions in Psychological Anthropology.* Cambridge: Cambridge University Press.

Schwarz, Adam. 1994. *A Nation in Waiting: Indonesia in the 1990s.* Boulder, Colo.: Westview Press.

Scott, James C. 1992. "Domination, Acting, and Fantasy." In Carolyn Nordstrom and JoAnn Martin, eds., *The Paths to Domination, Resistance, and Terror,* 55–83. Berkeley: University of California Press.

———. 1985. *Weapons of the Weak: Everyday Forms of Peasant Resistance.* New Haven, Conn.: Yale University Press.

Selth, Andrew. 1997. *Burma's Intelligence Apparatus.* Working Paper No. 308. Canberra, Australia: Strategic and Defence Studies Centre, Australian National University.

Seremetakis, Nadia. 1991. *The Last Word: Women, Death, and Divination in Inner Mani.* Chicago: University of Chicago Press.

Shattuck, Roger. 1965. "Introduction: Love and Laughter: Surrealism Reappraised." In M. Nadeau, ed., *The History of Surrealism,* 11–34. New York: Macmillan.

Sheldon, Michael. 1991. *Orwell: The Authorized Biography.* London: Heinemann.

Shenoi, B. R. 1928. "A Folklore Charm Against Bodily Injuries, Hypodermic Insertion of Gold Needles." *Indian Medical Gazette,* March.

Shweder, Richard A., and Robert A. LeVine, eds. 1984. *Culture Theory: Essays on Mind, Self and Emotion.* Cambridge: Cambridge University Press.

Silverstein, Josef, ed. *Independent Burma at Forty Years: Six Assessments.* Ithaca, N. Y.: Cornell University Southeast Asia Program.

Singer, Noel F. 1995. *Old Rangoon: City of the Shwedagon.* Oxford: Kiscadale Publications.

Skidmore, Monique. 2003a. "Darker Than Midnight: Fear, Vulnerability, and Terror Making in Urban Burma (Myanmar)." *American Ethnologist* 30 (1) (February): 1–17.

———. 2003b. "Behind Bamboo Fences: Forms of Violence Against Women in Myanmar." In Lenore Manderson and Linda Rae Bennett, eds., *Violence Against Women in Asian Societies,* 76–92. New York: RoutledgeCurzon.

———. 2002. "Menstrual Madness: Women's Health and Wellbeing in Urban Burma (Myanmar)." In Andrea Whittaker, ed., *Women's Health in Mainland South Asia, Women and Health,* Special Issue, 35 (4): 81–99.

———. 1996. "In the Shade of the Bodhi Tree: Dhammayietra and the Re-Awakening of Community in Cambodia." *Crossroads: An Interdisciplinary Journal of Southeast Asian Studies* 10 (1):1–32.

———. 1994. "The Politics of Space and Form: Cultural Idioms of Resistance and Re-Membering in Cambodia." *Santé, Culture: Culture, Health* 10 (1–2): 35–60.

Sluka, Jeffrey A., ed. 2000. *Death Squad: The Anthropology of State Terror.* Philadelphia: University of Pennsylvania Press.

Smith, Martin. 1999. *Burma: Insurgency and the Politics of Ethnicity.* 2nd ed. London: Zed Books.

———. 1996. *Fatal Silence: Freedom of Expression and the Right to Health in Burma.* London: Article 19.

———. 1991. *Burma: Insurgency and the Politics of Ethnicity.* London: Zed Books.

Spariosu, Mihai, ed. 1984. *Mimesis in Contemporary Theory: An Interdisciplinary Approach.* Vol. 1: *The Literary and the Philosophical Debate.* Philadelphia: John Benjamins.

Spiegel, David, ed. 1994. *Dissociation: Culture, Mind, and Body.* Washington, D.C.: American Psychiatric Press.

Spiro, Melford E. 1977. *Kinship and Marriage in Burma: A Cultural and Psychodynamic Analysis.* Berkeley: University of California Press.

———. 1967. *Burmese Supernaturalism.* Englewood Cliffs, N.J.: Prentice Hall.

Stackhouse, John. 1995. "The Golden Smile of the SLORC." *Toronto Globe and Mail,* April 8, 10.

Steinberg, David. 2001. *Burma: The State of Myanmar.* Washington, D.C.: Georgetown University Press.

Stewart, Susan. 1984. *Narratives of the Miniature, the Gigantic, the Souvenir, the Collection.* Baltimore: Johns Hopkins University Press.

Stollman, Rainer. 1978. "Fascist Politics as a Total Work of Art: Tendencies of the Aestheticization of Political Life in National Socialism." *New German Critique* 14 (Spring): 41–60.

Suárez-Orozco, Marcelo M. 1990. "Speaking of the Unspeakable: Toward a Psycho-Social Understanding of Responses to Terror." *Ethos* 18 (3): 353–83.

Tambiah, Stanley J. 1992. *Buddhism Betrayed? Religion, Politics, and Violence in Sri Lanka.* Chicago: University of Chicago Press.

———. 1984. *The Buddhist Saints of the Forest and the Cult of Amulets: A Study in Charisma, Hagiography, Sectarianism, and Millennial Buddhism.* Cambridge: Cambridge University Press.

———. 1976. *World Conqueror and World Renouncer: A Study of Buddhism and Polity in Thailand Against an Historical Background.* Cambridge: Cambridge University Press.

Taussig, Michael P. 1997. *The Magic of the State.* New York: Routledge.

———. 1992. *The Nervous System.* London: Routledge.

———. 1987. *Shamanism, Colonialism, and the Wild Man: A Study in Terror and Healing.* Chicago: University of Chicago Press.

Tin Nyunt Pu. 1980. "Cultural Influence on Symptomatology of Schizophrenic Patients in State Mental Hospital, Rangoon." Burma Research Congress Abstracts, Medical Science Research Division, 13–14.

Tosa, Keiko. 2002. "Weikza: The Case of Thamanya Taung Hsayadaw." Paper presented at Burma Studies Conference: Burma-Myanma(r) Research and Its Future, Gothenburg, Sweden, September 21–25.

Trocki, Carl, ed. 1998. *Gangsters, the State, and Democracy in Southeast Asia.* Ithaca, N.Y.: Cornell University Southeast Asia Program.

Turner, Victor. 1990. "Are There Universals of Performance in Myth, Ritual, and Drama?" In Richard Schechner and Willa Appel, eds., *By Means of Performance:*

Intercultural Studies of Theatre and Ritual, 8–18. Cambridge: Cambridge University Press.

U Nu. 1988. "Nats." *Crossroads: An Interdisciplinary Journal of Southeast Asian Studies* (Fall).

U Tin U (Myaung). 2002. *The Buddha's Teaching: The Doctrine and the Practice.* Yangon: Hninn Oo Lwin Publishing House.

United Nations Children's Fund (UNICEF). 1995. *Children and Women in Myanmar: A Situational Analysis.* Yangon: UNICEF.

Warren, Kay, ed. 1993. *The Violence Within: Cultural and Political Opposition in Divided Nations.* Boulder, Colo.: Westview Press.

White, Geoffrey M., and John Kirkpatrick, eds. 1985. *Person, Self, and Experience: Exploring Pacific Ethnopsychologies.* Berkeley: University of California Press.

Wikan, Unni. 1990. *Managing Turbulent Hearts: A Balinese Formula for Living.* Chicago: University of Chicago Press.

Witte, Karsten. 1975. "Introduction to Siegfried Kracauer's 'The Mass Ornament.'" *New German Critique* 4 (Winter): 59–66.

Women's Organizations from Burma and Women's Affairs Department, NCGUB. 2000. "Burma: The Current State of Women—Conflict Area Specific: A Shadow Report to the 22nd Session of CEDAW." Unpublished Report.

Woolf, Stuart Joseph. 1968. *The Nature of Fascism.* New York: Random House.

World Health Organization (WHO). 1997. *An Assessment of the Contraceptive Mix in Myanmar.* Geneva: World Health Organization.

Wyatt, David K., ed. 1994. *The Nan Chronicle.* Ithaca, N.Y.: Cornell University Southeast Asia Program.

Yokata, Yozo. 1995. Human Rights Questions: Human Rights Situation and Reports of Special Rapporteurs and Representatives. Situation of Human Rights in Myanmar, United Nations, February.

Young, Serinity. 1999. *Dreaming in the Lotus: Buddhist Dream Narrative, Imagery and Practice.* Boston: Wisdom Publications.

Zito, Angela, and Tani E. Barlow, eds. 1994. *Body, Subject and Power in China.* Chicago: University of Chicago Press.

Index

Acknowledgments

This book has been long in the making. It started life as surreptitious glimpses over the Thai-Burma border with my partner, Colin Rieger, in the early 1990s, and then as an extended field trip to Burma with my friend, Lesley Dunstone, in 1994. It grew into a Ph.D. topic, expertly guided by my mentors: Margaret Lock, and Ellen Corin. Margaret has taught me the mechanics of continually making one's work better, a great skill to teach a young anthropologist. Ellen Corin taught me how to write and how to write powerfully and perhaps even occasionally with a degree of elegance, and I am indebted to her for her patience. Allan Young taught me almost all I know of medical anthropology. I cannot think of a more privileged place than McGill University in the 1990s to have been a student of medical anthropology.

In Australia, thanks to Monica Minnegal, Peter Dwyer, Martha Macintyre, and Mandy Thomas who read drafts and made supportive and helpful comments. I acknowledge the support of the Faculty of Arts at the University of Melbourne including the provision of fieldwork funding and travel allowances and wish to thank the Burmese community in Melbourne for insight and enthusiasm, especially Angelay (Toe Zaw Latt).

In America, I am indebted to the staff and administrators of the Joan B. Kroc Institute for International Peace Studies at the University of Notre Dame, and to fellow Rockefeller Visiting Fellows for their companionship, support and intellectual stimulation. I am especially grateful for the personal and intellectual support of Carolyn Nordstrom, Shannon Speed, Victoria Sanford, Cynthia Mahmood, and Patricia Lawrence. The generous support of the Rockefeller Foundation and the Kroc Institute enabled me a quiet space of reflection and writing. A Wenner-Gren Fund for Anthropological Fieldwork doctoral dissertation grant enabled the fieldwork upon which much of this book is based. My editors, Cynthia Mahmood and Peter Agree have been unfailingly supportive and enthusiastic of the project and it has been a delight to join the merry band at the University of Pennsylvania Press.

I acknowledge permission to reprint previously published work as follows. Earlier versions of portions of Chapter 3 appeared in "Darker Than Midnight: Fear, Vulnerability, and Terror Making in Urban Burma (Myanmar)," *American Ethnologist* 30 (1) (February 2003): 1–17, reprinted by permission of the American Ethnological Society. Earlier versions of portions of Chapter 8 appeared in "Behind Bamboo Fences: Violence Against Women in Myanmar," in Lenore Manderson and Linda Rae Bennett, eds., *Violence Against Women in Asian Societies*, 76–92 (New York: RoutledgeCurzon, 2003), reprinted by permission of RoutledgeCurzon; and "Menstrual Madness: Women's Health and Well-being in Urban Burma (Myanmar)," in Andrea Whittaker, ed., *Women's Health in Mainland South Asia, Women and Health*, Special Issue, 35 (4) (2002): 81–99 (New York: Haworth, 2002), reprinted by permission of Haworth Medical Press. I am indebted to the author of "Ko Ma," who has given permission for his work to be freely disseminated but who cannot, at this time, be named. My thanks also to SEASPAN: The Northwest Regional Consortium for Southeast Asian Studies and Jennifer Leehey for permission to reprint "Over the Mountain Ranges" and to Dominic Faulder, Ron Gluckman, and Colin Rieger for permission to reproduce their photographic images.

It is impossible to repay the debt I owe to hundreds of people who have entrusted me with aspects of their personal lives and inner landscapes. Within Rangoon and Mandalay my circle of women friends have doggedly remained with me despite my best efforts to detach myself from them for fear of possible consequences that being associated with me may bring. They have taught me about how one can be wonderfully happy living in Rangoon, if one just tries continually to ignore "the situation." In Burmese homes, in those private lives only occasionally touched by the regime, Burmese social life is interesting, robust, and filled with love, hope, irony, and a wickedly dark sense of humor. I thank my Burmese friends for deliberately and unconditionally leading me to these understandings.

Finally, a number of aid workers, journalists, and diplomats fed me, sheltered me, plied me with gin and tonic, and were steady friends during the fieldwork period and beyond. Some have become dear friends, and together we share a love of Burma and of adventure, and I value these friendships immensely. Although there were times when we all lost perspective or succumbed to the misery of military occupation and restricted freedoms, I have special memories of the times when we shared our secrets and resolutely turned our back on the "situation" and made merry havoc around Rangoon in the early hours of the morning.